Wagner to "The Waste Land"

Wagner to "The Waste Land"

A Study of the Relationship of Wagner to English Literature

Stoddard Martin

BARNES & NOBLE BOOKS
TOTOWA, NEW JERSEY

First published in the U.S.A. 1982 by
BARNES & NOBLE BOOKS
81, Adams Drive, Totowa,
New Jersey, 07512
ISBN 0–389–20250–9

Printed in Hong Kong

Library of Congress Cataloging in Publication Data

Martin, Stoddard, 1948–
  Wagner to the Waste land.

  Includes index.
    1. English literature—19th century—History and
criticism. 2. Wagner, Richard, 1813–1883. 3. English
literature—20th century—History and criticism.
4. Romanticism. I. Title.
PR468.W34M37 1982   820′.9′008   81–17634
ISBN 0–389–20250–9   AACR2

Contents

Preface

The purpose of this book is to outline the relationship of the art, thought, life and "myth" of Richard Wagner to late Romantic and early Modernist literature in English. Definition of a Wagnerian tradition, while implicit, is not necessarily intended. If it were, the approach might properly be to explore the polarity between the "heroic vitalist" Wagnerism of Shaw and Lawrence and the more predominant "art for art's sake" Wagnerism evident from Swinburne through the men of the 1890s to Joyce and Eliot. As it is, considering that Wagnerism was a product of that strain of Romanticism in which the cult of the individual artist reached a zenith, emphasis is given to the important individual writers themselves. The result is a succession of chapters on each. Exceptions to this are the first chapter and the last. The first deals with the French of the *fin-de-siècle* as a group, the intent being to collect from them Wagnerian motifs that became pertinent to the English, whom their Wagnerism and aesthetics in general influenced. The last deals with *The Waste Land* on its own, the intent being to emphasize the unique relevance of Wagner to it among Eliot's works; also its particular status as an endpoint, graveyard perhaps even, of an epoch of Wagnerism in literature.

Taking on such a vast subject involves obvious risks. The mere student can hardly claim competence in all relevant areas. While an ideal of completeness and balance has been kept in mind, more attention has sometimes been devoted to areas where greater competence or interest has been felt. Considerations of space and competence have also led to neglect of some important matters and all-too-brief treatment of others. In this category fall the influence of English Romanticism on Wagner, Byron and Bulwer-Lytton in particular;[1] the importance of Grail legends to Tennyson and the Pre-Raphaelites in general, and of Nordic sagas to William Morris in particular. The influence of German Romantic philosophy in England from the time of Coleridge and Carlyle is a vital issue which is insufficiently explored in this primarily aesthetic study, as is the later development of indigenous fascist thought. In general the reader must be warned that, since the bounds of the subject as a whole have not been previously charted, and since many of the possibilities raised can only be falsified or proved by the appearance of information either at present (as in the case of *The Waste Land*) or forever unavailable, unanswered questions have been raised and the method on occasion has become frankly speculative.

The only full-length studies on Wagner and literature to date are Max Moser's *Richard Wagner in der englishchen Literatur des XIX Jahrhunderts* and Grange Woolley's *Richard Wagner et le symbolisme français*. In English the only volume on the subject is Elliott Zuckerman's *The First Hundred Years of Wagner's "Tristan"*, which provides the *Zeitgeist* and touches on much of what we shall discuss, but does not focus primarily on literature. A book entitled *Richard Wagner and the Modern British Novel* by Bernard di Gaetani is, I understand, under preparation at the time of writing. But the best existing work on Wagner and English literature has been done by William Blisset in his articles on Moore, Joyce and Lawrence; also Herbert Knust in his *Wagner, the King, and "The Waste Land"*, which is as detailed a study on Wagner's relationship to a single work as one could hope to find. Although these works have been helpful, most attention has been devoted to the works of the writers themselves, in conjunction with the germane criticism on them. Some effort has been made to give attention to works not frequently discussed – Symons's creative works, for instance, and the plays of Lawrence; also to aesthetic theory, where it coincided with Wagner's, as is the case with that of most of the men of the 1890s.

In general background much has been gained from Joseph Campbell's *The Masks of God: Creative Mythologies*, a massive work which defines the type of the Western literary myth by close scrutiny of the mediaeval Tristan and Parzival epics, the related works of Wagner, and major novels of Joyce and Mann. Mann, whose novels provide the best examples in any language of how Wagner might be successfully adapted to literature, is referred to throughout. So too is Nietzsche, whose reaction against Wagner provides an essential link in any discussion of Wagner's relationship to subsequent art and thought. On the relationship of German Romantic philosophy to literature, Ronald Gray's *The German Tradition in Literature* has been useful; for an aesthetic overview of the entire period, Richard Ellmann's and Charles Fiedelson's *The Modern Tradition* and Frank Kermode's *Romantic Image*; for Modernism more particularly, two classics on the subject, Edmund Wilson's *Axel's Castle* and Hugh Kenner's *The Pound Era*. Other works that have been helpful on more specific matters are cited in the opening paragraphs to the relevant chapters.

On the relationship of Wagner and Romanticism to the rise of fascism, Houston Stewart Chamberlain's works, Eric Bentley's *The Cult of the Superman*, and Peter Viereck's *Metapolitics* have proved provocative. As to Wagner himself, a broad general knowledge of the music dramas and aesthetic theories has been assumed; also wide reading in the vast secondary literature, including such studies as Robert Gutman's *Richard Wagner: The Man, his Mind, and his Music*, Bryan Magee's *Aspects of Wagner* and Faber's recently published *Wagner Companion*. But the most useful works for determining the aspects of Wagner that inspired the literary imagination are undoubtedly the unique studies of literary artists themselves: Baudelaire's *Richard Wagner et "Tannhäuser" à Paris*, Nietzsche's *The Case of Wagner*, Shaw's *The Perfect Wagnerite*, Symons's Wagner essay in *Studies in Seven Arts* and Mann's "The Sufferings and Greatness of Richard Wagner". As to knowledge of music beyond that of Wagner, this study proceeds from the position first enunciated by Baudelaire: that perception of the importance of Wagner to literature does not require a musicologist's expertise.[2]

Titles of foreign works are generally retained – *Götterdämmerung* instead of *The Twilight of the Gods* (or *Dusk Falls on the Gods*, as Shaw would have it), *La Revue wagnérienne* instead of *The Wagnerian Review*. Exceptions to this occur where usage has favoured the English – *The Flying Dutchman* instead of *Der fliegende Höllander*, *Beyond Good and Evil* instead of *Jenseits von Gut und Böse*. Translations are avoided except where the figures under discussion would naturally have read English versions, as in the case of the Ellis translation of Wagner's *Prose Works* and the Levy edition of the *Complete Works* of Nietzsche. Standard collections of each writer's works are used when available. Exceptions to this occur where new critical editions are preferable, as in the case of *The Picture of Dorian Gray*; or where original texts provide pertinent passages amended in posthumous editions, as in the case of some of Lawrence's works. In references a short form is used after the first occurrence of the cited work, but full details of each work are provided in the notes following the text.

Finally, before starting our Parsifalian journey towards *The Waste Land*, it should be emphasized that this is a study of Wagner's *relationship* to some outstanding writers in English, not a strict

chronicle of his *influence* on them. Were it the latter, discussion would
have to be confined to specific instances of Wagner-experience,
reactions as recorded in letters and elsewhere, stated sympathies
with Wagnerian aesthetics, and overt instances of *allusion* (direct
reference) to Wagner's works. As it is not, discussion will move
beyond conscious influences and allusions to more general *echoes* and
similarities of subject, theme, configuration, myth, style, philosophy
and metaphysics. Much of what we shall consider falls properly
under the heading of *Zeitgeist* and is a matter of general sympathies
between Wagner and other artists of the late Romantic epoch. It
might be observed further that, though claims of direct and constant
influence are not the point, influence in any case can only be felt
when there is a receptive spirit in the individual artist and his native
culture. From this perspective, the risks of overstepping the bounds
of intelligent inquiry may turn out to be considerably less grave than
they appear at the outset.

Acknowledgements

I would like to thank the following people for encouragement and advice: Professor Katharine Worth, Dr Keith Walker and Dr Richard Cave of the University of London; Professors James Wilson, John Alcorn and Richard Wiseman of California State University, San Francisco.

Fond thanks are also due to those who assisted financially and personally in the period of writing this book: Edin Beard, Jane Corbett, Arnold Dvorkin, James Jameson, Anne Forestier-Walker and Kenneth Michael Williams.

S. M.

1 Wagner and the French

In 1850 Franz Liszt, having recently moved from Paris to Weimar to become court music director, produced the premiere of *Lohengrin*. Wagner's operas had been banned throughout most of Germany owing to his revolutionary activities in Dresden in 1849, and it was hoped that Liszt's production would lead to their quick acceptance elsewhere. This did not happen. Nevertheless, the premiere produced two articles that may have influenced the eventual acceptance of the idea of producing Wagner in Paris. The first, by Liszt himself, is notable for its citation in subsequent French writings on Wagner, including Baudelaire's *Richard Wagner et "Tannhäuser" à Paris* and Dujardin's *La Revue wagnérienne*. The second, by a poet sometimes described as the "grandfather" of the Symbolist movement, Gérard du Nerval, is notable as the first in a long series of admiring reactions to Wagner by this type of French man-of-letters.[1]

Over the next decades the French came increasingly to recognize Wagner's significance to literature. In this introductory chapter we shall discuss this French background, making particular mention of figures such as Mallarmé and Laforgue who were most to influence the English. There are no studies in English of Wagner and the French, although Zuckerman in his *First Hundred Years of Wagner's "Tristan"* offers a chapter on the subject. Of French studies I have found Grange Woolley's *Richard Wagner et le symbolisme français* most helpful.

LES PREMIERS AMIS

The French were initially as reluctant to produce Wagner as the Germans. In the midst of a reaction to their own upheavals of 1848, they were wary of work by a revolutionary, especially work rumoured to be erotic and immoral. The conservative cultural climate of Second Empire Paris can be measured by the suppressions in 1857 of *Madame Bovary* and *Les Fleurs du mal*. In the same year however, Théophile Gautier, considered by some as the "father" of the Symbolist movement, wrote an article on the controversial German composer which was no less sympathetic than Nerval's.[2] Gautier's words were noticed in influential artistic circles and may have helped pave the way for the Wagner productions in Paris in 1861. These productions were as much a *cause célèbre* for a young generation of artists as the premiere of *Le Sacre du printemps* was to be for their Modernist counterparts in 1913. For Paris at large, however, the productions were anything but a success. A typical comment from the Press was that *Le Vaisseau fantôme* (*The Flying Dutchman*) caused "le mal de mer".[3] And the performances of *Tannhäuser* at the Opéra were subverted by the late-coming "gentlemen" of the Jockey Club, who were irate at Wagner's refusal to move the Venusberg ballet to the second act, so that they might have their customary show of legs.

It was in this atmosphere that Charles Baudelaire, first of the Symbolists in all but name, wrote the study which was to become the manifesto for literary Wagnerians of the following decades, and "to provide them with their favourite quotations about the interdependence of the arts".[4] Stylistically, Baudelaire devoted his greatest attention to the prelude to *Lohengrin*, which moved him to an impressionistic prose reverie and to quotation of his own sonnet "Correspondances" (from *Fleurs du mal*) in which, he implied, he had been attempting a similar effect. Metaphysically, Baudelaire was most profoundly interested in the struggle of Tannhäuser between the erotic allures of Venus (which moved him to another prose reverie) and the redemptive love of the chaste Elisabeth; for in this the French poet saw a mirror-image of the erotic anguish and suspension between damnation and salvation which were the dominant motifs of his own life and work. *Wagner et "Tannhäuser" à Paris* was thus in effect as much a study of Baudelaire and his aesthetic as of Wagner and his. And in its final pages Baudelaire blended many of Wagner's theories from *Oper und Drama* with his own visions of a poetry-of-the-future to conclude,

> Dans un avenir très-rapproché on pourrait bien voir non pas seulement des auteurs nouveaux, mais même des hommes anciennement accrédités, profiter, dans une mésure quelconque, des idées émises par Wagner, et passer heureusement à travers la brèche ouverte par Lui.[5]

Had Baudelaire lived, he might have proved the first "accredited" French poet to profit from the ideas of Wagner. As it was, his own creative gift was spent by the time he wrote his study, and he died a miserable death within a few years of its publication. Wagner was not again produced in Paris, nor his artistic influence generally felt, until the 1880s. Meanwhile Wagner himself, disillusioned by his reception in the French capital, departed suddenly, leaving others who had befriended him against the tide of popular opinion bemused. Léon Leroy, a critic prominent among *les premiers amis français*, saw the composer's flight as a demonstration of behaviour "nerveux et violent", but chose to interpret it as a sign of genius rather than mere rudeness.[6] Like Baudelaire, Leroy was moved to write a study on Wagner; and he and a handful of minor artists took it upon themselves to keep the reputation of the German composer alive in the French capital through the 1860s. Increasingly this reputation came to be based on Wagner's personality and philosophy as well as his art. What attracted the French in these secondary areas is expressed by this recollection of the Master's countenance from the poet and composer Auguste de Gaspérini:

> Au fond de ces expressions diverses de la physionomie, je démêlais le Tristan découragé par de trop lourdes épreuves et aspirant déjà, sans s'en douter peut-être, au *grand anéantissement*, le disciple convaincu de Bouddha et de Schopenhauer . . . .[7]

LES DÉCADENTS

After a period of nomadic wandering, the "convinced disciple" attracted the patronage of King Ludwig II of Bavaria. Ludwig intervened to have Wagner pardoned for his old revolutionary activities; and, back in his homeland at last, the composer began to produce new works. *Tristan und Isolde* was premiered in 1865, *Die Meistersinger* in 1868, and the first two dramas of *Der Ring des Nibelungen* shortly after. Wagner's reception in Bavaria was, for the time at least, as grand as he had dreamed of; and there was no longer any question of his first trying to establish himself in a non-German city such as Paris. Paris, if it wished Wagner, would henceforth have to come to him. And so it did. In the summer of 1869 three young Parisian *pèlerins* made their way to the Wagnerian retreat at Treibschen, to which another celebrated young pilgrim, Friedrich

Nietzsche, was also proceeding for the first time. The three – Catulle Mendès, his wife Judith Gautier and the Count Villiers de l'Isle-Adam – were of that generation that had just been coming of age during the *Tannhäuser* furore of 1861. Each was to play an important role in the development of Wagnerism in France in the following decades.

Mendès wrote an article about the pilgrimage, "Notes du Voyage", in which he took pains to flatter the Parisians with the information that Wagner "comptait la mort de Baudelaire et celle de Gaspérini parmi les plus grand chagrins de sa vie".[8] Such partisanship was characteristic of this Franco-Jewish poet. During the following years, while war was bringing German unification at French expense and Wagner was publishing his most chauvinist and anti-Semitic pronouncements, Mendès continued to serve as his chief apologist to a hostile French public. In 1885 he contributed two articles to *La Revue wagnérienne*; in 1886 he published a book of essays entitled *Richard Wagner*; in 1899 he published a study of the influence of Wagner on French literature entitled *L'Oeuvre wagnérienne en France*. In every way Mendès encouraged the enthusiasm for Wagner among French poets until, by the 1890s, it had spilled over into such general affectation that one young Decadent actually assumed the *nom de plume* of Tristan Klingsor. On the other hand, Mendès was ever concerned to point out that Wagner's art was distinctly German, i.e. long-winded, lacking vivacity, laboured in development of character and idea; and that the French, while adapting Wagnerian forms and methods, should take care to make their art equally distinctive of their nation and race, i.e. "clair, précis, rapide au but . . . puissant, hautain, sublime et net".[9]

Besides being Mendès' wife, Judith Gautier was the daughter of Théophile Gautier and the "charmer" of Baudelaire. She became Wagner's amorous correspondent in 1877, just at the time he was beginning to compose *Parsifal*. Arguments have been raised against the widespread assumption that Gautier was Wagner's inspiration for Kundry; but much suggests it. Her father had described her adolescent personality as partaking of "épilepsie-catalepsie", and that is an apt description of the mysterious disposition to be found in Wagner's *femme fatale*.[10] Moreover, Gautier's marriage to a Parisian Jew who had a professional curiosity in the creator of *Parsifal* suggests an intriguing parallel to the configuration of Kundry/Klingsor/Grail Knight. The Decadent Paris of the period has long been regarded as one inspiration for Wagner's Magic Garden, and

Gautier's position as a central female among the Decadents is the probable explanation for Wagner's sudden initiation of the correspondence. As the letters passed, Wagner's prime motive became to solicit lush fabrics and synthetic perfumes with which to decorate the music-room at Wahnfried where he was composing. The extent of the sixty-five-year-old's actual "amorous" intentions might be inferred from the fact that, when he fatigued with writing the letters himself, his wife Cosima took up the pen.

Count Villiers de l'Isle-Adam was, like Mendès, to remain a devout Wagnerian through the heyday of *La Revue wagnérienne*, to which he contributed a piece entitled "La Légende de Bayreuth". Of the three *pèlerins* of 1869 he was to be the most influential among subsequent writers, owing to his mystical drama *Axël* (1890). In English his appreciators would include W. B. Yeats and Arthur Symons. To the latter the Decadent *prince des poètes*, Paul Verlaine, was to comment, "I am far from sure that the philosophy of Villiers de L'Isle-Adam will not one day become the formula for our century."[11] What was this philosophy?

Fundamentally [Symons wrote], the belief . . . common to all Eastern mystics. And there is in everything he wrote a strangeness, certainly both instinctive and deliberate, which seems to me to be the natural consequence of his intellectual pride. It is part of his curiosity in souls – as in the equally sinister curiosity of Baudelaire – to prefer the complex to the simple, the perverse to the straightforward, the ambiguous to either. His heroes are incarnations of spiritual pride, and their tragedies are the shock of spirit against matter, the temptation of spirit by spiritual evil. They are on the margins of a wisdom too great for their capacity; they are haunted by dark powers, instincts of ambiguous passions. And in the women his genius created there is the immortal weariness of beauty; they are enigmas to themselves; they desire, and know not why they refrain, they do good and evil with the lifting of an eyelid, and are guilty and innocent of all the sins of the earth.[12]

This philosophy of Villiers, we see, echoed the attraction of Gaspérini to the Buddhistic and self-annihilating impulses in Wagner; also the attraction of Baudelaire to the sinful Venus, the struggles of Tannhäuser, and the strange sublime mist of the *Lohengrin* prelude. Among its major motifs were: the struggle against erotic temptation; the quest for spiritual purity and transcendence; and the nature of woman as guilty and innocent, frenetically energized and immortally weary at the same time.

THE CASE OF *PARSIFAL*

Symons's description of Villiers's heroes as "incarnations of spiritual pride" might well be a description of Amfortas, and of his characters as "haunted by dark powers" and "on the margins of a wisdom too great for their capacity" a description of Kundry and Klingsor as well as several previous Wagnerian personae. Clearly the philosophy in which Verlaine perceived "the formula for our century" had much in common with the spirit of Wagner's last work. As Woolley has pointed out,

> Trois de ses oeuvres les plus aimées, *Lohengrin, Tannhäuser,* et surtout *Parsifal,* en juxtaposant les deux modes de la vie et de l'amour, l'érotique et le mystique, témoignent de la bataille spirituelle qui se livrait incessamment dans l'esprit du Maître et à laquelle il devait, sans aucun doute, une grande partie de son inspiration tonale. L'atmosphère mystique qui se répand autour de ses oeuvres relève surtout d'un vague panthéisme schopenhauerien, fataliste et bouddhique. Mais comme prétendrait Nietzsche, le mysticisme renonciateur du catholicisme chrétien n'est qu'une autre expression de ce pessimisme oriental néfaste. Ainsi *Parsifal,* l'oeuvre qui réconciliera le monde catholique avec Wagner, si elle marque le retour au catholicisme du Maître vieillissant, reste néanmoins, en parfaite harmonie avec le romantisme mystique et fataliste de ses oeuvres antérieures.[13]

Parsifal merged the ritualism of Christianity, on which the Catholic French had been brought up, with Eastern mysticism, which had been attracting the Parisian elite since the Parnassian 1850s and had by the 1880s become an essential in "the formula for our century". This metaphysical position could hardly help but make *Parsifal,* of all Wagner's *oeuvre,* a particular cult-work for a generation to whom the ultimate choice after a career of sensual indulgence was typically either "the pistol or the foot of the cross".[14]

The fact was nowhere more caustically analysed than in *The Case of Wagner,* a diatribe published in 1886 by that other "pilgrim" of

1869, Friedrich Nietzsche. In the years since Triebschen Nietzsche had become disgusted with his youthful idol; and *The Case of Wagner* branded *Parsifal* as the ultimate "decadent" artwork, and its creator as "the artist of decadence".[15] Nietzsche pitied the youths being "lured" to their "destruction" at Bayreuth in the manner in which he had observed first with the French in 1869. He railed against the deification of the artist which Wagner had encouraged, and which the French were imitating in their increasing cult-worship of poet-heroes such as Verlaine and Mallarmé. He criticized the "fog" and "unending melody" of the Wagnerian ideal, while that ideal was simultaneously being preached as aesthetic gospel from the pages of *La Revue wagneriénne.* Nietzsche charged Wagner, Bayreuth and *Parsifal* with the growth of Decadence in France, and for importation of the "disease" into Germany. At the same time he pointed out that the creator of *Parsifal* had himself absorbed much from the French, not only from Judith Gautier and pilgrim-aesthetes of various summers, but also from those like Flaubert who "loathed life" and sought to turn Art into a new religion. The characters of *Parsifal* were those of Flaubert writ large, Nietzsche contended; and the reason why the French were so quick to embrace Wagner's last drama was that it gave back in pseudo-heroic drapery the very types to be found in their own art.

The French influenced *Parsifal* and *Parsifal* the French, but just exactly how much? One answer might be found in the case of the Decadent *prince des poètes.* Early in his career, Verlaine, probably thinking as much of Baudelaire as of Wagner, alluded to Tann-häuser in a poem, "Nuit de Walpurgis classique". This allusion moves Woolley to remark, "C'est justement l'érotisme de décadent que . . . Nietzsche attaque dans la musique de Wagner que Verlaine semble traduire par ses vers".[16] Such eroticism was *like* that of Wagner, but its origin was undoubtedly personal. This was even more clearly the case with the famous sonnet "Parsifal", one of three vaguely Wagner-inspired poems Verlaine wrote at the height of the Wagnerian vogue of the 1880s.[17] Like Wagner's hero, Verlaine's Parsifal had to resist the sexual allurement of "les filles" and "la femme belle" before he could realize his true spiritual destiny. But, unlike Wagner's hero, Verlaine's was also called upon to resist the temptation of "la Chair de garçon". This signal difference, which Verlaine confessed to have been autobiographi-cally inspired,[18] demonstrates how the typical Decadent would

appropriate a Wagnerian framework to explore a situation fascinating to the "sinful" Paris of the time, but, more likely than not,
foreign to Wagner's taste.

LA REVUE WAGNÉRIENNE

Verlaine found in Wagner an erotic suggestiveness on which he
could expand, artistic models for the struggle between sin and
salvation which he like Baudelaire regarded as the dominant theme
in his life and art, and a metaphysic which had much in common
with what he saw to be "the formula for our century". But Verlaine
was no devout Wagnerian either in interest or in aesthetics. Widely
recognized as the most musical of poets long before the Wagnerian
1880s, Verlaine hardly needed to imitate the methods of the *Meister*
in the manner of some of his more fawning contemporaries. Though
he published "Parsifal" in *La Revue wagnérienne*, he found the
theoretical pronouncements of that journal tiresome, and had little
time either for the growing enthusiasm for things German in general
among younger poets.[19] In sum, beyond what Woolley describes as
"une certaine correspondance entre les dissonances de la musique
de Wagner et du vers de Verlaine",[20] the sympathy between the
work of the German "artist of decadence" and the premier French
Decadent was not great.

But Verlaine's was not the only case. At the same time as his
influence was at its peak, the Symbolist movement, as yet unnamed,
was developing along self-consciously Wagnerian lines. Central to
this was the above-mentioned *Revue wagnérienne*. This journal
brought together the energies of many of the great French writers of
the day, Mendès, Villiers and Verlaine, as we have seen. It also
published some non-French Wagnerians, most notable among
whom was Houston Stewart Chamberlain, the English philosopher
and historian who was later to marry Wagner's daughter, become
high-priest of the Wagner establishment at Bayreuth, and influence
the growth of National Socialism through his metapolitical tract
The Foundations of the Nineteenth Century. The man primarily
responsible for the *Revue* was Edouard Dujardin, an ubiquitous
enthusiast whose efforts were to help not only French poets of the
1880s, but also such English prose stylists of a latter day as George
Moore and James Joyce. Though a poet and novelist of note in his
own right, Dujardin was first and always an appreciator of other
masters. The extent of his reverence for the old German *Meister* and

a new French exemplar, the spirit of his *Revue*, and the musical texture of his criticism is summed up by this passage:

> Pendant qu'avec Hugo, les poètes en France, les romantiques, Baudelaire, le Parnasse . . . , cherchaient une forme d'art qui dirait la vie totale de l'être en le langage de la langage de la littérature, voilà qu'un étranger, un musicien, avait, de sa part, cherché une forme aussi, mais en le langage de la musique, apte à un tel but; et de la musique, par Wagner, donc serait né cet art (oeuvre de notre siècle), que, de la littérature attendaient trois générations de poètes. Alors, le poète esthéticien . . . qui, de la subtile moelle de soixante années d'efforts à l'idéale, éclosait à la fin de ce siècle, fleur essentielle de notre âme, M. Stéphane Mallarmé, commença instituer, en face du poème synthétique "des délicatesses et des magnificences immortelles, innées, qui sont à l'insu de tous dans le concours d'une muette assistance".[21]

The *Revue* was committed to the furthering of a Symbolist ideal through discussion of the *Gesamtkunst* theories of Wagner ánd the poetic ideal of Stéphane Mallarmé. Mallarmé himself was, at least at first, something less of a Wagner-fanatic than his mentor, Dujardin. According to Woolley, Mallarmé only discovered the essential sympathy between Wagner's aesthetic and his own after Dujardin took him to a concert in 1885: "Mallarmé, très ému, lui avait dit qu'il sentait que cette musique exprimait ce que, lui, tâchait d'exprimer par la poésie".[22] A year later Mallarmé published in the *Revue* the article, "Rêverie d'une poète contemporaine", that was regarded as spelling out the goal of the Symbolist movement – indeed, of much of French literature for the next half-century. Wagner's music, Mallarmé wrote, had evoked the inner music of the Unconscious and shown the way towards expression of the Ideal. In this it had usurped the true task of poetry. Henceforth the poet must reclaim this task. The musical potential of words must be explored with scientific exactitude. The poetry of the future must be made in such a way as to evoke the inner music more completely and complexly than ever before.[23]

SYMBOLISM AND THEATRE

Mallarmé's poetry was characterized less by the sort of vague imitation of Wagnerian myth and borrowing of bric-à-brac typical of Decadent verse than by a systematic adaptation of the musical methods of Wagner in accordance with the principles set down in "Rêverie". The most notable manifestations of this are in the later poems, such as "Un Coup de dès n'abolira jamais le hasard". In "Un Coup" Mallarmé was seeking to make "the infallible symbolic statement" by "conquering chance".[24] This he proposed to accomplish by patterning his words so that all the reciprocal correspondences between them would be worked out, the factual could give way to the suggestive, and an atmosphere of obscurity might be obtained. In this atmosphere newly forged all-inclusive words would find the "elbow room" to induce a sort of narcotic spell in which the Ideal would be perceived. The goal was that "the general and universal will be discovered at the very roots of subjectivity". The obvious risk, one that Mallarméans of another generation were also to run (Gertrude Stein and James Joyce to name two[25]), was that such subjectivity and obscurity would render any discovery, at least for the common reader, virtually impossible.

Besides his efforts as a poet, Mallarmé was also the leading theorist of those who wished to adapt the methods of Wagner for Symbolist theatre. His other contribution to *La Revue wagnérienne*, the sonnet "Hômmage", outlined his vision of such a theatre. Wagner, he wrote, had rescued drama from Naturalism by the suggestive power of music and the revival of myth. Once again, it was the Symbolist's task to return the suggestive power from music to the word; also, as we have seen Mendès contending, to replace Wagner's vulgar German Romantic mythology with the more typically French Classical and sublime. The Symbolist dramatist must seek aesthetic beauty in every aspect of production. In the end, the effect should be like that of the High Mass, only more abstract, recondite and narcotic. Mallarmé spent the last decade of his life talking of his intention to attempt such a drama; but, like Baudelaire before him, he died before he had fully profited from the example he had perceived in Wagner. The enduring image for following generations was of Mallarmé dreaming of his Symbolist drama while the Wagnerian orchestra "dictated".

Suggestions of the form this drama might have taken were present in poems such as "Hérodias", which Mallarmé had conceived as a dramatic monologue. Realization of the ideal in a full-length play, however, was left to Maurice Maeterlinck, one of those who had drunk in the poet's theories during the famous "Tuesday evenings".

Maeterlinck was Flemish and his dramas would put less emphasis on the power of the word alone than on a leitmotival patterning of symbols, silences, pauses and movements along with spare poetic speech. Of Maeterlinck's achievement Symons says,

> No dramatist has ever been so careful that his scenes should be in themselves beautiful, or has made the actual space of forest, tower, or seashore so emotionally significant. He has realized, after Wagner, that the art of the stage is the art of pictorial beauty, of the correspondence in rhythm between the speakers, their words and their surroundings.[26]

Maeterlinck's extreme care for the beautiful and "emotionally significant" in his plays was no less than that of Mallarmé in his poems. His *Pélleas* ranks with Villiers' *Axël* as the most memorable of French attempts at Symbolist drama (though not in the least because it was made by Debussy into the "anti-*Parsifal*" opera which has been called the French *Tristan*). Like the author of *Axël*, Maeterlinck was to become a seminal figure to "a handful of English playwrights weary of poetic rhetoric but desirous of poetic effect".[27] He would provide them the most theatrically viable models of how, short of employing the Wagnerian orchestra, one might create dramas suggestive of the Infinite.

LAFORGUE AND IRONY

Public notice of the Decadents and Symbolists quickened after the appearance of *À rebours* in 1884. The author of this unusual novel was another of the select number that Dujardin asked to contribute to *La Revue wagnérienne*. Joris-Karl Huysmans's piece was entitled "L'Ouverture de Tannhäuser", and this work of Wagner's held special significance for the hero of *À rebours*. Like Baudelaire and Verlaine, Des Esseintes suffered from suspension between sensual indulgence and Catholic salvation. In other respects Des Esseintes suggested the Symbolist aesthete like Mallarmé "qui a poussé jusqu'à la dernière absurdité l'application de la doctrine de la correspondance entre les arts".[28] *À rebours* was as typical of the 1880s in Paris as Verlaine's poetry and Mallarmé's theorizing. Several books with similar world-weary dandiacal heroes with Wagnerian pretensions appeared in its wake. In one of these, *Les Déliquescences d'Adorè Floupette*, could be discerned traits not only of the prominent Parisian aesthetes of the day, but also of a younger poet whose works were hardly known in Paris until Dujardin published them posthumously in the 1890s.[29]

Jules Laforgue lived his entire brief adult life in Berlin in the capacity of tutor to the Empress Augusta. The Empress, like Nietzsche, detested Wagner and doted on *Carmen*;[30] this however did not prevent swan motifs, cries of Valkyries in the wind, and borrowed titles ("Vaisseau fantôme") from appearing in her tutor's poetry. In Paris that poetry would be classified as neither Decadent precisely, nor Symbolist, but as *vers-libre*. This distinction qualified it as no less Wagnerian. As Dujardin would point out (Dujardin being, along with everything else, the inventor of the vers-libre movement), *vers-libre* had its origins in the music of Wagner as well:

> Je m'étais dit qu'à la forme *musique libre* de Wagner devait correspondre une forme *poésie libre*. . . . Et c'est précisément ce que j'exposais à Laforgue, lors de notre première rencontre, fin Mars 1886, à Berlin.[31]

Dujardin was introduced to Laforgue through a mutual Wagnerian friend. This would suggest that Laforgue was quite familiar with Wagner before their 1886 meeting. Nevertheless, it was probably the enthusiastic *literary* Wagnerism espoused by Dujardin (and by Chamberlain, who was with them in Berlin) that encouraged the Empress's delicate young tutor to bring Wagner more evidently into his work.

The year and a half between this meeting and Laforgue's untimely death was, as in the case of Baudelaire's last years, the period of the great Wagner-interest. From it came the Wagnerian bric-à-brac of the poems, the aesthetic principle that poetry should follow the music of Wagner in synthesizing "la voix de la fôret", and the *Moralités légendaires*. This last work was a Symbolist retelling of six literary myths. Of the six, "Hamlet" drew on motifs from Wagner's *Siegfried*, and "Lohengrin, fils de Parsifal" constituted the most extensive prose adaptation from Wagner in any language to that date.[32] Laforgue's "Lohengrin" deserves special attention by anyone concerned with the subsequent relationship of Wagner to literature. The common ground between it and Wagner's opera is obvious enough. The substantial differences grow out of the contrast between the grandeur of the characters in Wagner's ideal realm and the effeteness of their counterparts in the more real, however fictionalized, world in which the pre-Modernist artist felt compelled to place them.

Laforgue's hero is a meagre waif in comparison to Wagner's robust knight, and his Elsa distinctly less attractive than Wagner's pure but mortally weak heroine. In Laforgue's tale Elsa with "infernal" sincerity begs Lohengrin to make love to her; but only moments before she has refused his overture, "Seriez-vous libidineuse?", with the coy rejoinder, "J'ignore le sens de ce mot." Lohengrin in turn thereupon refuses her, mentioning among other reasons that he detests her "maigres haunches". Besides "maigres haunches", Elsa has a prominent "pomme a Adam", which Lohengrin strokes as he refuses to make love with her. This may be meant to suggest that the true nature of the overture is a homosexual act; alternatively, that we are to see in this Elsa the eternal temptress and destroyer, Eve, whom Baudelaire and others saw in Wagner's.[33] In any case, Laforgue's young hero recoils in faint horror. And, operating on an impulse reminiscent of the one that motivated Parsifal to turn from Kundry and set off back towards Montsalvat, he seeks a melancholy transcendence in "les altitudes de la Métaphysique de l'Amour".

The extent to which Laforgue himself subscribed to this Parsifalian principle of renunciation, or to which his *moralité* might have been intended as a parody of the "moral" of Wagner's last work, is shrouded by a pervasive irony. Attention is continually being shifted from action (which, denuded of Ortrud's plottings and much of the rest of Wagner's paraphernalia, is rather bare) towards the texture of costume or of youthful flesh, the movements of the sea and the wind and the moon, or such bourgeois trivialities as whether the hero should address the heroine as *tu* or *vous*. The manner anticipates that of Thomas Mann in a Wagnerian novella such as *The Blood of the Wälsungs*, in which a mock-heroic Siegmund devotes his most serious attention to sartorial matters and bookbindings; or in a novel such as *The Magic Mountain*, in which a climactic love-scene pivots on whether the hero should address his beloved as *du* or *Sie*.[34] Such deflation of the heroic may seem to make an absurdity of Wagner. On the other hand, it was motivated by a desire shared with Wagner and all the French we have been discussing, that is *épater le bourgeois*: to challenge contemporary *haute bourgeois* civilization for its conservatism, complacency and philistinism.

LAFORGUE AND GERMAN ROMANTICISM

What was acceptable in "all-too-human" real life was increasingly unacceptable to that type of artist who sought to glimpse the Ideal. To protect himself and his ideal, this type of artist had several avenues open to him. He could either escape into myth, as Wagner in *Lohengrin*, or turn and attack, as Wagner in the prose tracts that followed his expulsion from Germany. He could strip unacceptable "real" life down to its sordid underclothes, as Flaubert and Baudelaire in the works for which they were prosecuted in 1857; undertake to shock society directly, as Rimbaud and Verlaine in the irreverent vagaries of the 1870s; or couch every utterance in a subtle and corrosive irony, as Laforgue in the 1880s and Mann two decades later. What separates Laforgue and Mann from many of their precursors was that their impulse to shock turned inward as well as outward, in apparent recognition that their type of artist was himself no less bourgeois – and no less absurd – than the "real" world he so yearned to transcend. This position would be typical of the last Romantics. And in Laforgue's case it may have derived from the same origin as in Mann's, for Laforgue was the outstanding example of that generation of French poets who took an active interest in the German Romantic tradition.

French attraction to German Romanticism had begun to grow in the 1840s, when the first phase of indigenous French Romanticism was losing impetus. The attraction was initially to German music, Beethoven and Weber.[35] But by the 1860s, when the second or "Parnassian" phase of French Romanticism was in full progress, it began to move to German philosophy also. As we have seen in the case of Gaspérini, a handful of French artists were becoming conversant with the theories of Arnold Schopenhauer. This was in part through their admiration for Wagner, to whom the discovery of Schopenhauer's *The World as Will and Idea* had been "the most important event in his whole life".[36] As Wagner's reputation grew, the influence of Schopenhauer spread. And the generation coming of age in the 1870s found another deeply sympathetic expression of "the formula for our century" in this body of thought which focused on ancient Aryan religions, the philosophy of India, essential Christianity, and Western art from the Greeks to Beethoven; and which encouraged subjective idealism, existential pessimism, re-nunciation of the external world, and retreat to the contemplation of High Art. The twenty-year-old Laforgue, for example, was so moved on discovering Schopenhauer that he set down in his notebook this harsh ascetic rule: "Il faut souffrir au moins deux ans: jeûner, souffrir de la continence, saigner de pitié et d'amour universel."[37] Such resolutions would appear throughout the writings of Laforgue's generation with the regularity of similar motifs in the last and most Schopenhauerian of Wagner's dramas. So too would such paradoxical Schopenhauerian principles as that "One must fight down Will in order to contemplate that which is outgrowth of Will", and that woman is archetypally unobjective and perverse. But, as one might expect considering the years he spent in Berlin, Laforgue's own knowledge of German philosophy went considerably further than the Schopenhauerianism fashionable in Paris by the 1880s.[38] His preoccupation with the Unconscious, for instance, was probably derived from reading Hartmann's *Philosophy of the Unconscious* when it had appeared in the late 1870s. He was no doubt also familiar with Hartmann's eighteenth-century precursor, Schelling, who had proposed that man must penetrate the unconscious meanings of Nature and search the "hieroglyphs of the soul" before he could understand himself. Of course, many of these ideas had been present in indigenous French thought from the time of Rousseau, and were apparent in French literature of the mid-nineteenth century, which Laforgue had studied with equal assiduity. Thus it should not come as a surprise that Laforgue's most important theoretical statement should echo both the image, "fôret des symboles", around which Baudelaire had built his sonnet "Correspondances", and the last passions of that poet's life, Impressionist art and Wagner's music:

> Le tout est une symphonie qui est la vie vivante et variante comme "les voix de la fôret" des théories de Wagner en concurrence vitale pour la grande voix de la fôret, comme l'Inconsient, loi du monde, est la grande voix mélodique, résultante de la symphonie des consciences de race et d'individus.[39]

"*LA FÔRET DES SYMBOLES*"

In his study of Wagner Mann was to write that Wagner's music had the power to "open a perspective that leads back to the earliest and most primitive of our picture dreamings".[40] Such a perspective was exactly what Laforgue wanted art to accomplish; and the above passage should make it clear that it was from the example of Wagner, along with study of German Romantic philosophy and Baudelairean aesthetics, that he developed this position. The position was one of many he held in common with Mallarmé, whose concept of the Unconscious he also dwelt on in his notebooks: "L'Inconscient; le principe, après l'effort, l'apothéose de la conscience artistique parnassienne se consolant dans des protestations bouddhiques, le principe en poésie du bégaiement, de l'en allé."[41] Laforgue's own concept of the Unconscious was not so precise; in fact, it appears to have been too vast for definition. Where Mallarmé conceived the Unconscious to be something which the artist might ultimately capture and master in the ideal work of art, Laforgue seems to have seen it as an "unending" sea in which the artist could only lose his footing and be mastered.[42] Here we might find an explanation for the almost senile diffidence in Laforgue's writings as opposed to the theoretical assurance in Mallarmé's; Laforgue's frail, poignant, almost accidental style as opposed to Mallarmé's cold, systematic, hardly human ideal. But, having pointed out such differences between Laforgue and his most influential contemporary, we should emphasize that their intentions were similar; and that Laforgue's *oeuvre* was highly Mallarméan in its other-worldly atmospheres.

Though it was with the word "fôret" that Laforgue characterized his idea of the Unconscious, this "fôret" was no more a naturalistic forest of normal lime trees and woodbirds than it had been for Baudelaire. It was, in Wagnerian terms, a forest where woodbirds suddenly acquired the power of speech, and breezes whispered of deepest origins; a *Parsifal*-like sacred wood by a sacred lake over which a sacred swan was flying to its mate, or a magic garden where flowers blossomed into maidens who wove fatally seductive charms around wandering young "guileless fools". For it was always with the shimmering magically illuminated inklings of fantasy and dream-scape that this type of Symbolist filled his external world. The wind, the sea, the moon – the elements Laforgue evokes in "Lohengrin, fils de Parsifal" are, like the spirits of ancient gods that Yeats's peasants would perceive in such elements, living presences: aspects of human consciousness itself, not just manifestations of dumb Nature.[43] They appear and reappear in deliberate patterns that invest them with leitmotival significance. At the end of the second paragraph of "Lohengrin, fils de Parsifal" we are told that the action is taking place "en vue de la mer éternelle des beaux soirs". At the end of the next paragraph we are told that it is taking place "en vue de la mer surhumaine des beaux soirs".

The repetition creates an incantatory rhythm, a magical ritualistic spell. The word that transforms, "éternelle" to "surhumaine", signifies that the setting is more than just a normal seaside under the stars. The images and technique recall Baudelaire and the supernaturalism of Baudelaire's favourite, Poe; also elements from early German Romantic poetry and opera, Goethe and Weber and Marschner, for instance. They reveal, moreover, an aspiration to the suggestiveness of certain Wagnerian moments: the third act of *Tristan*, in which the hero lies by the sea awaiting deliverance into death and eternity; or, perhaps more appropriate in this case, the second act of that drama, with which they share night as setting. This choice of night, we should note, is typical for Symbolist romance of this kind. The purple hues of darkness, the evanescent brilliance of the moon – all the sensual shadows which cloak Lohengrin and Elsa as they hover on the verge of making love serve to increase the suggestion of the eternal and supernatural. They create that type of atmosphere, charged with strange and potentially destructive eroticism, that can also be seen in the central love-in-the-garden scene of *Pélleas*; an atmosphere imprinted on the imagination of the age by, more than any other single tableau, Wagner's hyperpassionate *Liebesnacht*.

CONCLUSION

Tristan was produced in Paris in the late 1880s, *Pélleas* in the early 1890s. Wagner had died in 1883, Laforgue in 1887. In 1896 Verlaine died. The following year the Parisian literati chose Mallarmé, long Verlaine's rival, for the title *prince des poètes*. This event must have seemed to some degree hollow, for by the mid-1890s the revolt against the movements of the 1880s had begun. The young Proust attacked Mallarmé in an article entitled "Contre l'obscurité"; and one of the many successors to *La Revue wagnérienne* published a chapter from Tolstoi's *What Is Art?* which declared that Baudelaire was too much effort, Verlaine too obscure, and Mallarmé and Maeterlinck too dogmatic and unclear.[44] In 1898 Mallarmé died. By the turn of the century the Symbolist movement in France had receded into history, and the Wagnerism that had grown up with it was beginning to fade, if somewhat more gradually. The significance of Wagner for literature which the Symbolists had discovered, however, was by no means forgotten. Indeed, what Baudelaire and his successors had begun others were now taking up in new and different ways – not only a younger generation of Parisian aesthetes such as Proust, but Naturalists such as Zola, who had joined a Wagner society in Marseilles.[45]

In England and Ireland such artistic ambassadors as Symons, Moore and Yeats were spreading the word. In Germany writers such as Stefan Zweig and the young Thomas Mann, though already steeped in indigenous Wagnerism, were eager to find out how the "decadent" French against whom Nietzsche had railed had adapted the ideas of the *Meister* of Bayreuth to literature. And what of particular significance for literature had the French discovered in Wagner? (1) A sublime and suggestive music on which to pattern their words. (2) An articulation of the particular struggle between sin and salvation which haunted the age. (3) A sympathetic overarching philosophy in which Catholicism and Eastern mysticism were merged. (4) A shared desire to turn away from the bougeois preoccupations of the age towards the contemplation of High Art. (5) A demonstration, complementing Poe's, of how to use the supernatural to provide symbols for the inner and outer unknown. (6) An ability, exceeding that of any previous art, to "open a perspective" – through incantatory rhythms, leitmotival techniques, and strange new harmonies and dissonances – to the unconscious memories of the race.

2 Swinburne

In 1857 Swinburne was a twenty-year-old undergraduate at Oxford. He had recently met Dante Gabriel Rossetti, Edward Burne-Jones and William Morris. These three Pre-Raphaelites were to have considerable effect on his development over the following decades. Morris in particular was to have an immediate influence. He had just completed a volume of "more or less Arthurian romances and lyrics" which he now showed to Swinburne. From this the aspiring poet drew ideas for a project on which he was at work. That project was a long poem of ten cantos. Of the ten only seven were ever written. Of the seven Swinburne regarded the last six as "too feeble" to publish. The one he did publish in 1858 in an Oxford undergraduate magazine was entitled *Queen Yseult*. Critics have debated the sources for this poem. Edmund Gosse says it was taken, like Morris's work, primarily from Malory.[1] Jean Overton Fuller points back further to the *Sir Tristrem* of Thomas of Ercildoune.[2] For our purposes however, the source is less important than the coincidence that Swinburne had set out to write, at exactly the same time as Wagner was composing *Tristan*, a major work on the same subject.

Wagner was largely unknown in England at this time. Orchestral excerpts from his operas had been given in London in 1855, but no complete work was produced until the mid 1870s. Full productions in German had to wait until 1892, when Gustav Mahler conducted a Wagner season at Covent Garden, including the first complete *Ring* in England. Earlier productions were given in Italian, in which form *Tannhäuser* was premiered in 1876 and *Tristan* in 1882.[3] Considering this slow and incomplete arrival of Wagner to England, it is clear that none of Swinburne's works on Wagnerian subjects could have been inspired by direct experience of the corresponding dramas. Considering the wide attraction of Arthurian legends to English poets of the mid-century, it is perhaps not surprising that the twenty-year-old should have attempted his *Queen Yseult*; but Swinburne's later compositions of "Laus Veneris" and

Tristram of Lyonesse are a different matter. These poems demonstrate
that, direct Wagner-experience or not, the English poet shared a
remarkable sympathy of interests with the German composer. The
nature of this sympathy, which Swinburne himself was to note in a
roundel on the occasion of Wagner's death, is what we shall try to
determine in this chapter. Previous studies on the subject have been
done by F. J. Sypher in his article "Swinburne and Wagner" and by
Zuckerman in his appendix to *The First Hundred Years of Wagner's
"Tristan"*.

"LAUS VENERIS" AND THE FRENCH FASCINATION

In the spring of 1863 James Whistler took the young Swinburne on
an aesthetic journey to Paris. During this journey the American
painter took his companion to the studio of Fantin-Latour, where
the major work-in-progress was a painting entitled "Tannhäuser in
the Venusberg". Fantin-Latour, like much of artistic Paris of the
time, was still talking about the furore of the 1861 production of
Tannhäuser, and his painting partook of the Baudelairean fascination for the "evil" Venus. Swinburne was introduced to the work
of the author of *Richard Wagner et "Tannhäuser" à Paris* and took the
occasion, allegedly while in a Turkish bath, to write the first English
review of *Les Fleurs du mal*. This review was in turn acknowledged by
Baudelaire in a letter which likened Swinburne's praise to the praise
he had accorded Wagner in his study.[4] Through a series of mishaps
Swinburne never knew he had received Baudelaire's letter. In
apology for what he assumed to be an error on his part, Baudelaire
then sent the *littérateur anglais* an autographed copy of his Wagner
study.[5] This copy probably did not reach Swinburne soon enough to
influence the composition of "Laus Veneris". Just when that poem
was written, however, has been a matter of considerable debate.
Consensus is that it was conceived even before the journey to Paris –
Fuller, arguing just that, proposes that Whistler took Swinburne to
Fantin-Latour's studio precisely because he knew that his young
friend was writing a poem on the very subject that the artist was
painting.[6]

This argument would ask us to believe that with no exposure to
the contemporary Parisian vogue for *Tannhäuser* the young English
poet, across the channel, should have undertaken a major poem on
that very subject. This seems improbable; still, many critics have

agreed to it and gone in search of sources elsewhere. Unlike the legends of Arthurian romance, the *Tannhäuser* legend had not been a common subject in English poetry. The legend itself was German. But, since "it is doubtful that Swinburne had a knowledge of German or any acquaintance with any German literature in the original", he could only have come upon it in a translation. Two translations would have been available him at the time: Carlyle's rendering of Tieck's *Der getreue Eckart*, and a contemporary version of an old German ballad published in an August 1861 edition of *Once a Week*. Swinburne himself contributed to *Once a Week*; and the fact that this German ballad appeared in it only a few months before Swinburne is said to have first conceived "Laus Veneris" leads C. K. Hyder for one to name it as the probable source.[7]

The matter is more complicated however. As Hyder himself points out, other versions of the tale were beginning to appear in England around this time, and most of them would have become known to Swinburne. Morris wrote a version entitled "Hill of Venus" sometime in the 1860s. Swinburne's friend Lord Houghton wrote a version entitled "Venus and the Christian Knight". At about the same time as the translation appeared in *Once a Week*, Julian Fane and Robert Lytton, under pseudonyms, published "a redaction of Wagner's opera in the form of a Tennysonian idyll called *Tannhauser, or the Battle of the Bards*". Perhaps Swinburne began his poem after reading one or all of these English versions, as Hyder supposes. Even so, this does not discount the likelihood that a major inspiration must have been the rumour of Wagner's opera and its stormy reception. In the first place it seems improbable that the sudden surge of English interest in the legend could have been unrelated to these things. In the second, the suggestion that Swinburne began "Laus Veneris" before Whistler took him to Paris does not establish that he wrote it all at one sitting, or how much he may have revised it after the trip. Thus there remains significant question as to how much the French fascination may have inspired the final version first published in *Poems and Ballads* in 1866.

"LAUS VENERIS" AND DECADENCE

The answer must be construed from certain speculations. First, the compulsive creative habits of the young Swinburne make it likely that he would have written the entire poem in one or two feverish spasms at the time of original inspiration.[8] Second, the rumour of the *Tannhäuser* furore in the city of arts which the young poet wished to visit seems a far more likely inspiration for a poem of the flame-like intensity of "Laus Veneris" than some translation in a magazine. Third, such a rumour may well have reached Swinburne's ears – through visitors and correspondents to Whistler, for instance – months before he went to Fantin-Latour's studio or reviewed *Les Fleurs du mal*. Fourth, if the history of his writings on Baudelaire is indicative of how the young Swinburne often worked (he wrote his review without ever having seen a complete copy of Baudelaire's book, and wrote "Ave atque Vale" on the strength of a rumour of Baudelaire's death that was half a year premature),[9] then we might readily believe that he could have written the whole of "Laus Veneris" on the basis of rumours of the enthusiasm of Baudelaire and other artists for Wagner's work and for the character of his Venus, and nothing more – no translation, no English text at all.

In defence of this argument it should be said that "Laus Veneris" does not read like a poem carefully researched.[10] It is the feverish monologue of an insomaniac who is both horrified and delighted by the prospect of his damnation. Details of plot are few and vague, and what details there are match those of Wagner's version better than many others. Swinburne's knight recollects such Wagnerian experiences as: riding along the Rhine, singing in defence of passionate love at a songfest, joining a group of piligrims to Rome to seek forgiveness, and being rejected by the Pope with the statement that no forgiveness will be granted "until this dry shred staff . . . bear blossom and smell sweet" (*P*, i, 24). True, much of Wagner's plot is ignored, and all of his characters save Venus and the knight. But this is no more an argument against Wagner as a source than the absence of Ortrud and Telramund from Laforgue's "Lohengrin". Indeed, as in the case of Laforgue's tale, the absence of much of Wagner's paraphernalia serves to concentrate attention on the psychological struggle caused by temptation to a "sinful" love, which particularly fascinated the French after Baudelaire.

The decadence of "Laus Veneris" is of the very sort for which Baudelaire was attacked in *Les Fleurs du mal*.[11] A typical reaction was that it was "the work of either a misdirected and most disagreeable youth or of a very silly man".[12] Venus herself is "a vengeful goddess" who combines "eroticism and cruelty". Her love-grotto is strewn with corpses, blood, and the bones of "discarded lovers"; and next to her bed stands a figure of Love wearing "gilt thorns for a crown" and weaving fabrics out of the dead lovers' hair. At the same time this Venus has a curious passivity, a kind of gentleness even. While the knight is giving his feverish monolgue, she is sleeping peacefully by her side, moving him to describe her eyelids as "flower on flower" (his by contrast feel like "fire on fire"). This mixture of qualities – eroticism and cruelty, passivity and flower-like gentleness –is typical of the sort of female who was beginning to haunt the age. Swinburne's Venus has much in common with the women of *Les Fleurs du mal*. And, besides recalling Wagner's Venus, she anticipates the German composer's most decadent creature, Kundry, with whom she seems to share the distinction of having been present at the Crucifixion of Christ.[13]

If Swinburne's Venus is a *décadente*, his "Tannhäuser" distinguishes himself as equally (he suggests more) decadent by choosing to remain with her. His reaction to the Pope's rejection of forgiveness anticipates the defiant embracings of damnation of, for instance, Rimbaud. He spurns the idea of salvation. He declares that repentance no longer exists in his "wan body and shaken soul". He has rushed back from Rome towards the reappearing vision of his Venus; and, where such a vision for Wagner's knight is finally eclipsed by a reminder of the pure love of Saint Elisabeth, for Swinburne's it shines forth as radiant and enduring as the Botticelli painting:

> As when she came out of the naked sea
> Making the foam as fire whereon she trod.
>
> (*P*, 1,25)

Where Wagner's knight sinks to a penitent death by the side of the martyred Elisabeth, Swinburne's glories in the fire of Venereal lust anew:

> As after death I know that such-like flame
> Shall cleave to me for ever; yea, what care.
>
> (*P*, 1,26)

Reunited with his pagan goddess at last, Swinburne's knight – in the face of his eternal damnation – proclaims, "Ah love, there is no better life than this" (*P*, 1, 26). Thus sin is embraced. And "Laus Veneris", in the manner we have seen Verlaine doing in his

"Parsifal", adjusts the resolution of the Wagner work to achieve a more shocking effect.

This being said, it should be pointed out that the metaphysical framework of Wagner's model remains essentially intact. Part of this framework is the association of desire and sin with love and death. This is a theme which appears in Swinburne's work with as much regularity as it does in Wagner's. In "Laus Veneris" it is first suggested by the image of Love weaving the dead lovers' hair; then it is stated directly; it is repeated in various permutations with leitmotival regularity; and at the end it is restated with new force in the comparison of the "flame" of death and damnation to the body of the love-goddess to whom the knight "cleaves". Another part of the Wagnerian framework is the conflict arising from the split of Love into carnal and Christian halves. Nietzsche railed at Wagner for dramatizing such a split;[14] and James Joyce was to comment on the conflict ironically, "What sort of fellow is this Tannhäuser who, when he is with Saint Elisabeth, longs for the bordello of Venusberg, and when he is at the bordello longs to be with Saint Elisabeth?"[15] But for Swinburne, as for Baudelaire and the French Decadents, such a conflict seemed both artistically and personally appropriate.[16] And in adopting it he, like many of his French contemporaries, tipped the balance in favour of erotic indulgence where Wagner always opted in the end for Christlike renunciation.

MUSIC AND THE SHELLEYAN AESTHETIC

Swinburne could not have read Wagner's prose works until too late to have influenced his important theoretical statements, for the English translations of these works did not start to appear until 1892. That he was ignorant of the German Romantic tradition in general was pointed out by Franz Hueffer, Wagnerian critic and translator, in a review of his 1871 collection, *Songs before Sunrise*:

> The unsympathetic exclusion of Germany, "by whose forest-hidden fountains freedom slept armed" (whatever that means), from partaking in the emancipation of man is a proof that our poet knows but little of the country of Heine and Schopenhauer, and but little of the infinite depth in the conception of human freedom which has been sounded by its greatest thinkers.[17]

One might imagine that Swinburne would have made up for his ignorance by an appreciation of German music at least, as was the case with many of the French. The critics tell us, however, that Swinburne was also deficient when it came to listening to music:

> There is hardly any evidence that he was a competent judge of musical techniques and forms. Nor does the fact that he composed parts of *Atalanta in Calydon* while listening to Mary Gordon practice Handel on the organ, and parts of *Tristram of Lyonesse* while "stimulated" by Wagner reveal any genuine technical comprehension.[18]

That Swinburne was not knowledgeable about German art and music seems conclusive. This does not, however, preclude the possibility that this aesthetic had much in common with Wagner's. The same was true of Baudelaire, after all; and it did not prevent him from imitating the prelude to *Lohengrin* in a prose reverie, nor from finding Wagner's musical methods applicable to poetry.

As regards music, the important point is neither the fineness of "ear" nor the degree of technical comprehension, but the intensity of the poet's appreciation for that art and of his desire to reproduce its effects in the written word. Swinburne did have an intense appreciation of music; much of his poetry sounds like an impressionistic transcription of music; and his aesthetic was entirely music-orientated. His ideal has been described as a "music" of art created by a "harmony" of "internal" and "external" music (internal coming from the individual subconscious, external from the "voice" of Nature) and creating sublime "suprasensual" states of "pure aesthetic intuition".[19] According to Edmund Gosse, Swinburne "occupied himself not much, or at all, with the development of Symbolism".[20] Nevertheless, his ideal obviously has much in common with the Wagnerian ideals of Mallarmé and the contemporary French. In English the similar ideal – that all art aspires to the condition of music – is commonly associated with the name of Walter Pater. But, as R. L. Peters says, Swinburne "undoubtedly saw in Pater's statements principles which he himself had felt keenly and had helped to frame".[21]

It is generally agreed that Swinburne derived his aesthetic from Shelley, who "outsang all poets on record but some two or three".[22] In Hueffer's view this influence was probably what led Swinburne to that "lengthy exuberance" which was his greatest flaw: "The lyric of Shelley, it must be remembered, is not, like the German, a development of the popular song, but is the poetical expression of the prolonged and passionate contemplation of a speculative idea."[23] "Prolonged", "passionate" and "speculative" are words which recur regularly in criticisms not only of Shelley, but also of Swinburne and of an artist out of that very German tradition which Hueffer proposes as the antipode. As Zuckerman says, "Swinburne's verbal excesses were like Wagner's musical excesses; and the criticism of Swinburne sounds like the criticism of Wagner."[24] Thus indirectly Heuffer's criticism of Shelley points towards a similarity between the poetry of Swinburne's favourite English predecessor and the music of Wagner. It is but one step further for us to ask what similarity might be found between the aesthetic of Shelley and that of the German composer.

The answer is a great similarity indeed. As one of Swinburne's favourite passages from the *Defence of Poetry* demonstrates, Shelley found music to provide the perfect metaphors for the inner psychology of man:

> Man is an instrument over which a series of external and internal impressions are driven like the alternations of an ever-changing wind over an Aeolian lyre, which move it by their motion to ever-changing melody. But there is a principle within the human being, and perhaps within all sentient beings, which acts otherwise than in the lyre, and produces not melody alone, but harmony, by an internal adjustment of the sounds or motions thus excited to the impressions which excite them.[25]

Like Wagner's, Shelley's ideal was the synaesthetic art which existed in "the youth of the world". Like Wagner, Shelley lavished special praise on the Greeks; for the Greeks had been the first to employ "language, action, music, painting, the dance, and religious institutions to produce a common effect".[26] Many passages in the *Defence of Poetry* sound remarkably like the arguments for a *Gesamtkunst* which Wagner was to advance in *Oper und Drama*, or which the Wagnerphile young Nietzsche was to celebrate in *The Birth of Tragedy*. And Shelley's vision clearly looks forward to the synaesthetic ideal that Wagner attempted at Bayreuth and that Mallarmé, following Wagner, outlined for his Symbolist theatre of the Classical sublime.

Of course, Shelley did not create synaesthetic art himself, nor did Swinburne. But, like Baudelaire and Mallarmé, these English Romantics were appreciators of the many arts and believers in their correspondence; and, like these French, their synaesthetic impulse is apparent in imitations of the effects of other arts, music in particular, in their poetry. In Swinburne's case this is most apparent in works of the middle years. The French sestina "Nocturne" for example, written in 1876 and sent to Mallarmé for publication in *La République des lettres*, is a direct attempt at verbal music.[27] Another fine example is "The Lute and the Lyre", which follows the Wagner roundels in *A Century of Roundels*, published in 1883.[28] As with "Nocturne", the title itself suggests music; also as with "Nocturne", the word "music" enters the poem early, and the metaphor of music is the dominant motif. In "The Lute and the Lyre" Swinburne actually goes so far as to contrast the "reluctant voice" of verse with the "exultant voice" of music. Of this we should take note, as it suggests a distinction between the Swinburnian ideal and that of the Mallarméan French, with which it might otherwise appear identical. Where Mallarmé would say that music had usurped the proper task of verse and temporarily assumed a higher place in the hierarchy of the arts, Swinburne eagerly declares that music is the superior art – at least in the evocation of "deep desire". And "deep desire", as we have seen in "Laus Veneris", was ever the transcendent emotion that Swinburne wished to evoke.

TRISTRAM OF LYONESSE

A Century of Roundels appeared the year after Swinburne published *Tristram of Lyonesse*. This poem was perhaps Swinburne's most ambitious. Certainly it was his grandest on a subject shared with Wagner. When first projecting it in 1869, Swinburne admitted to being affected by Wagner – "The thought of Wagner's music ought to abash but does stimulate me".[29] But, as it developed over the next decade, the poem departed from Wagner's version to treat in detail the whole of the legend which the German *Meister* had so drastically reduced to fulfil the needs of his drama. During composition Swinburne no doubt consulted as many poetic versions of the legend as were available in English. These would have included Matthew Arnold's "Tristram and Iseult", which (other than a brief treatment by Sir Walter Scott) was the first in the language; also Tennyson's Tristram idyll in *Idylls of the King*, the inaccuracies of which so annoyed Swinburne that he devoted much of his first canto to correcting them.[30] Another source undoubtedly was his own juvenile effort, *Queen Yseult*.

As in these versions, Swinburne's *Tristram* ends by having two Iseults: Iseult of Ireland, whom the hero takes to marry his uncle but falls in love with on the way, and Iseult of Brittany ("Iseult of the White Hands"), whom he marries much later himself. Also as in these versions much attention is paid to the lineage of Tristram, the deeds of valour performed in his youth, and such peripheral matters as the beauty of Guinevere, the bravery of Arthur, and the activities of Lancelot and Merlin. Indeed, so much of Swinburne's finished poem echoes the English versions of the tale (and ultimately Malory) that some question arises as to just how much and in what way he was actually "stimulated" by Wagner. Of this we can say little. He no doubt heard a great deal about Wagner before and during the period of composition; but, beyond hearing excerpts on piano and perusing the libretto, he could not have had any direct experience of the drama. Still, the fact that his next published book was to contain tributes to the composer and drama suggests that the original "stimulation" retained force throughout the period of composition. Furthermore, there is the fundamental aesthetic sympathy between his work and Wagner's, the significance of which goes beyond superficial considerations of plot. It can be summed up in one word – music.

Tristram of Lyonesse is musical throughout: musical in a rich, profuse and passionate way that suggests that it was composed out of a quite different inspiration from that which moved the twenty-year-old Oxonian to write the methodical short lines and factual curt verses of *Queen Yseult*.[31] The music begins to swell, like Wagner's *Sehnsuchtsmotiv*, from the first line of the "Prelude": "Love, that is first and last of all things made" (*P*, II, 5). It builds single-mindedly on that motif of Love. Music then becomes the central image of the startling line which begins the first section of the poem proper: "About the middle music of the spring" (*P*, II, 13). Thereafter music is referred to and used metaphorically on countless occasions. The most memorable of these comes in what might be called the *Liebesnacht* of the second section. This scene is directly preceded by Tristram's rescue of Iseult (of Ireland) from Palamede in a battle described thus:

The jarring *notes* of that tempestuous *tune*
Fell, and its mighty *music* made of hands
Contending, *clamorous* through the loud waste lands.

(P, II, 47)

I have added italics to indicate the extent to which Swinburne
wished to suggest music here. As the love-scene unfolds, he
continued to do so, building towards a climax in which the lovers,
clinging to one another, pass into a "suprasensual swoon" described
thus:

and all the woodland soul was stirred,
And depth and·height were one great *song* unheard,
As though the world caught *music* and took fire
From the instant heart alone of their desire

(P, II, 52)

LOVE-DEATH

Perhaps no other poet we shall discuss, and probably only Shelley of
the English Romantics, was more at one with Wagner's sentiment
that he "could not conceive of the spirit of music otherwise than as
love".[32] This deep metaphysical association of music and love is the
major motif of both Swinburne's and Wagner's Tristans; and woven
into it are two other elements as well – the sea, and death.
Zuckerman is so struck by the common affinity of Swinburne and
Wagner for the sea that he titles his appendix "A note on Swinburne
and the Sea":

Just as there were Wagnerian waters for the . . . drowning of
music lovers, there was a Swinburnian sea of words. The sea was,
in fact, an all-purpose image for Swinburne . . . His *Tristram*,
like Wagner's, begins aboard ship.[33]

Swinburne's *Tristram*, also like Wagner's, ends with a tableau of the
lovers lying embraced in death at the edge of the eternal sea:

And over them, while death and life shall be,
The light and sound and darkness of the sea.

(P, II, 151)

Here and throughout *Tristram of Lyonesse*, expanding on the theme we noted in relation to "Laus Veneris", Swinburne emphasizes the association between love and death with a musical onrush of words clearly intended to produce the kind of dramatic effect which Wagner had produced by the wavelike convulsions of Tristan's delirium and Isolde's *Liebestod* in the finale of his drama.

Of this longing for love-death which *Tristram of Lyonesse* so celebrates, Oliver Elton says in comment on an earlier Swinburne work: "It is a feeling much derided, and wholly unaffected. . . . To youth in its dark hour the end is a treasure lusted for, it is the desire of no consciousness, it is the release from irritation, it is the crown of the garland of sleep".[34] This "feeling of youth" is the very Schopenhauerian desire for transcendence which moved Wagner's lovers; which attracts Laforgue's Lohengrin to "les altitudes de la Métaphysique de l'Amour", which Nietzsche feared would lead the German "youthlet" to his destruction at Bayreuth, and which was to lead a number of Mann's early protagonists to their destruction. But some of Mann's characters who give way to such yearnings (Thomas Buddenbrook and Gustav Aschenbach, for instance) are not so young. And Wagner and Swinburne, both forty-five when they produced in their Tristans their most extreme expressions of such a desire, must (if Elton's perception is considered accurate) have been either aiming for a considerably younger audience or experiencing a sudden blazing revival of youthful longings.

Something of the sort may have been true in the case of Wagner, whose drama had greater appeal to the youth of a new generation than to his contemporaries. *Tristram of Lyonesse*, however, did not enjoy great success with any audience, and about the time of its publication Swinburne began to be regarded by younger poets as a precursor whose inspiration was drying up. Cited in evidence of this were the facts that, as he grew older, Swinburne ceased to admire Baudelaire and Whitman and others for whom he had held passionate enthusiasm in his youth. Whether in this process he came to admire Wagner less is uncertain; but clearly his enthusiasm for the German composer had reached a zenith by the time of Wagner's death, which moved him to write the three roundels.[35] The first two of these are poetic impressions of Wagnerian preludes which had particularly moved Swinburne. In them he succeeds with un-characteristic succinctness in capturing in words the precise curve of the prelude in question. Intentionally or not, he also echoes previous written impressions of the same music. In "Tristan" it is his own

Tristram whose last section, "The Sailing of the Swan", is governed by a similar brooding Fate. In "Lohengrin" it is Baudelaire's reverie, after Liszt, on that prelude, which also concentrates on the descent and ascent of the spirit of pure Love.

CONCLUSION

The third roundel, "The Death of Richard Wagner", is less succinct and more meditative than the two "preludes". It anticipates the grand and misty textures of the tributes to the *Meister* that were to appear three years later in *La Revue wagnérienne*. The first stanza opens with a gloom in which music and life are paradoxically present; a pun is then made: "Mourning on earth, as when dark hours descend" (*P*, II, 549). Wagner is identified with a soul which harbours "songs of death and birth"; an image of dying speech is sounded; then the opening pun is repeated. The second stanza opens with an image of "the world's great heart"; this breaks up into various elements of Nature, which

> found in [Wagner's] mastering art
> Speech as of powers whose uttered words laid bare
> The world's great heart.
>
> (*P*, II, 550)

Thus the elements are reintegrated into the original image again. The final stanza describes in somewhat longer and freer lines "the spell of the mage of music" flying up "from the depths of the sea", up and up further – as if one of Shelley's spirits, West Wind or skylark or cloud – into the heavens. There it commingles with God; creates "dark delight"; then finally realizes a "doom divine as sundawn risen to sight". The closing pun, "sundawn", recalls the opening one, "mourning on earth"; and, like a leitmotiv modulating from minor to major key, it reinforces the paradoxical message of the poem – that Wagner's death contains life: the passionate, Dionysian life of his transcendental, musical art.

Like many of those French Decadent tributes to Wagner, this roundel seems more a reaction to two decades of rumour and reputation of the composer than an expression of personal debt to an artist who, after all, seems to have remained a somewhat hazy and distant figure. Vagueness and paradox are the notes the roundel so musically strikes. They are the notes we should likewise strike in summing up Swinburne's relationship to Wagner. He was "stimulated" by the German composer, but hardly in a concrete or measurable way. His aesthetic, with its impulse to synaesthesia and its conviction that music is the highest of the arts was Wagnerian; but it was derived mostly from Shelley and the general Romantic tradition. His poetry has moments of clear contact with Wagner – in favoured images such as the sea, themes such as the association of love with death, style which was equally passionate and prolonged, and subjects from the rediscovered body of partially pagan north European myths. But these are as much matters of coincidence as of influence; and of the wide unspecific sympathy of interest among a large number of European artists in the waning years of the nineteenth century.

3 Wilde

In "The Garden of Eros" in his first book, *Poems* (1881), Wilde identified the tradition in English to which he wished to belong. Like Swinburne, he admired Shelley and the Shelleyan quality of "singing":

> when Keats died the Muses still had left
> One silver voice to sing his threnody. . . .[1]

Also he admired the author of "Laus Veneris" himself:

> his honied lute
> Hath pierced the cavern of the hollow hill,
> And Venus laughs to know one knee will bow before her still.

This allusion was the first of Wilde's many to the Tannhäuser legend. In it we can see that he was fascinated by the "sinful" Venus. At the same time, we might detect some scepticism about that defiant lack of penitence by which Swinburne's knight ultimately returns to decadence and destruction. The other ending of the tale, the Wagnerian one in which Tannhäuser seeks Christian salvation and dies a penitent, also attracted Wilde. This too we can see in one of the early poems, "Rome Unvisited", in which the persona is a sorrowful solitary "pilgrim from northern seas" who journeys to Rome to see the Pope:

> O joy to see before I die
> The only God-anointed King.
>
> (*W*, 729)

In these lines Wilde anticipated the desire to "see" Christ which he was to experience in Reading Gaol, and the journey to Rome he was

was to make a few months before his death. By that time he was to have identified his heroes and himself with Tannhäuser so repeatedly that he was able to view the matter as a sort of sacred joke:

> I have seen nothing like the extraordinary grace of his [the Pope's] gesture, as he rose, from moment to moment, to bless – possibly the pilgrims, but certainly me. . . .
>
> I was deeply impressed, and my walking-stick showed signs of budding; would have budded indeed, only at the door of the chapel it was taken from me by the Knave of Spades. This strange prohibition is, of course, in honour of Tannhäuser.[2]

The image of the flowering staff was one of Wilde's favourites; but, as we can see here, he was not always overly concerned with accuracy when alluding to it. In standard versions of the tale, including Wagner's and Swinburne's and Morris's (which Wilde probably also knew),[3] the question is whether the *Pope*'s staff will flower. Wilde's cavalier substitution of the pilgrim's staff in the form of his own walking-stick points up that side of Wilde which was less concerned with the accuracy of mythic detail than with the moment's opportunity to amuse.

Wilde's relationship to Wagner is full of ambiguity. He was not an ardent partisan like his compatriots Shaw and Moore. This is not to say that his appreciation of Wagner was shallow; but it certainly was not that type of passion that led to the painstaking study of scores or the annual pilgrimages to Bayreuth. In comparison to some contemporaries Wilde must seem merely a social Wagnerian: a Wagnerian inasmuch as the Society of the day was discovering the German composer and finding his music fashionable. But Wilde was more than this. As the premier "tragic" figure of the English Decadence, Wilde was, like Baudelaire and the French, a philosophic Wagnerian: one who discerned in Wagner's work a symbolic representation of the struggles of his own career. Moreover, like Swinburne in the indigenous tradition, Wilde was an aesthetic Wagnerian: one who believed that music was the ideal towards which all other arts should aspire. For these reasons I have chosen to begin discussion of Wagner and literature in England in the 1890s with Wilde rather than with the more obvious candidates, Shaw and Moore. No critical work of consequence has been offered on Wilde and Wagner to date. In this chapter we shall depend on a close look at the texts themselves.

MUSICAL ANTIPODES

Besides identifying their author with the "musical" tradition in English poetry and the Tannhäuser legend, the early poems make reference to two different types of music which we should note. In "In the Gold Room: A Harmony" a woman plays piano music which conjures natural images of a strongly Impressionist flavour:

> Her ivory hands on the ivory keys
>   Strayed in a fitful fantasy,
> Like the silver gleam when the poplar trees
>   Rustle their pale leaves listlessly,
> Or the drifting foam of a restless sea
> When the waves show their teeth in the flying breeze.
>
> (*W*, 772)

This "fitful fantasy" is not passionate and Dionysian, but psychological and delicate. It suggests the poplars of a Monet landscape, or the sea-surge against the coast of Majorca which Lord Henry Wotton would imagine in relation to a piece of Chopin. The piano music Wilde had in mind here was undoubtedly Chopin's or something very like it. This type of music was to figure as importantly in Wilde's later works as the Wagnerian. Indeed, at times, it was to provide an exquisite and gentle opposite to a Wagnerian music much grander and more evocative still.

Wagnerian music was to become for Wilde like that type described in a moment of brooding self-contemplation in "Humanitad":

> The minor chord which ends the harmony,
>   And for its answering brother waits in vain
> Sobbing for incompleted melody,
>   Dies a Swan's death; but I the heir of pain,
> A silent Memnon with blank lidless eyes,
> Wait for the light and music of those suns which never rise.
>
> (*W*, 793)

Perhaps Wilde actually had some piece of Wagner's in mind here. In any case, one can easily imagine *Lohengrin* behind the images of the brother who does not appear and of the swan; also a number of Wagnerian passages, the *Sehnsuchtsmotiv* notably, behind the description of a "minor chord which ends the harmony" and then waits in vain for a major resolution. This poem demonstrates that, where Wilde related impressionistic piano music to natural landscapes, he related a music of brooding and unresolved minor chords to the supernatural: a dream-scape in which a swan dies while "Memnon with blank lidless eyes" waits for "suns which never rise". In this he was making a connection like the one the French were making between a Wagnerian type of music and the super-natural "fôret des symboles".

It would be wrong to give the impression that Wilde preferred one type of music to another, Wagner say to Chopin, any more than that he preferred Symbolist to Impressionist art. Both attracted him a different moments in his career. Nevertheless, one of the things we might notice about *The Picture of Dorian Gray* (1891) is that it sets the development of its hero against a subtle and symmetrical pattern of musical references, and changing preferences. When introduced, Gray is "seated at the piano . . . turning over the pages of a volume of Schumann's 'Forest Scenes'".[4] Schumann is German like Wagner, and the title of the work Wilde has chosen to mention might call to mind the Wagnerian forest of *Siegfried*, perhaps even the "fôret des symboles" as well. On the other hand, the work is impressionistic, for piano, and in texture has more in common with Chopin than with Wagner. Thus, if the piece is taken to be an index of Gray's musical taste at the outset of his development, he has the potential to move either direction: towards the Wagner or Chopin.

DORIAN THE DECADENT

In which direction does he move? After several weeks of being "awakened" to his inner passions by Lord Henry, Gray reveals his partisanship for Wagner by defending that composer against the silly philistinism of Lady Wotton, who "simply worships" pianists (*D*, 45). *Lohengrin* is the opera in question during this exchange, and it is an apt choice from Wagner's *opus* to appear at this juncture in the novel. Being a tale of ill-fated marriage, it both reflects on Lord and Lady Wotton's relationship (one of estrangement) and serves as a foreshadowing of Gray's imminent ill-fated affair with Sybil Vane. There are superficial indications here that Wilde may have int-ended some deeper parallels to Wagner's opera; but the novel does not develop in a style of systematic paralleling to Wagner's work that was to characterize Moore's *Evelyn Innes*. Wilde required something different. His "Lohengrin" could not remain pure; his "Elsa" could not be a figure of such psychological complexity as to be culpable for her ultimate desertion. Sybil thus does not ask "forbidden questions", she merely becomes a bad actress. Gray deserts her nevertheless. She commits suicide. He embarks on his progress as a Decadent.

At the centre of this progress, Lord Henry sends Gray a book much like the ideal book he once expressed a desire to write himself.[5] Wilde's description of Lord Henry's gift sounds many of the motifs sounded in Huysmans's *À rebours* and typical of the *Zeitgeist* of artistic Paris of the day:[6]

> The style in which it was written was that curious jewelled style . . . that characterizes the work of some of the finest artists of the French school of *Symbolistes*. . . . The life of the senses was described in the terms of mystical philosophy. One hardly knew at times whether one was reading the spiritual ecstasies of some mediaeval saint or the morbid confessions of a modern sinner. It was a poisonous book. The heavy odour of incense seemed to cling about its pages and to trouble the brain. The mere cadence of the sentences, the subtle monotony of their music, so full as it was of complex refrains and movements elaborately repeated, produced in the mind of the lad, as he passed from chapter to chapter, a form of reverie, a malady of dreaming, that made him unconscious of the falling day and creeping shadows.
>
> Cloudless, and pierced by one solitary star, a copper-green sky gleamed through the windows. (*D*, 125–6)

In the phrase "morbid confessions of the modern sinner" Wilde may have been thinking of the author of *Les Fleurs du mal* and *Journaux intimes*. In "the spiritual ecstasies of the mediaeval saint" with which these morbid confessions link we might perceive a further connection to Baudelaire; also to his cherished *Tannhäuser*, which is any case suggested by the allusion to the "one solitary" evening star, Venus. In the "subtle monotony of their music" of the sentences described, as well as of the sentences describing, we recognize ourselves amidst the sort of over-ripe Wagnerian prose that the Symbolists were cultivating. And indeed, the net effect of the entire passage is to suggest the Wagnerian mood of mysticism and incense-scents and "malady of dreaming" which the book itself creates.

The effect of this literary experience on Gray is so profound that "for years [he can] not free himself" (*D*, 126). Like Baudelaire and the Decadents and Mann's Wagnerians, he becomes a dandy, "an hedonist", a "worshipper of the senses". At the same time, like the Wagner of *Parsifal* or Verlaine or Mann's Thomas Buddenbrook after his marriage to a Wagnerian, he grows fascinated with Roman Catholicism and the Mass. For a time he studies mysticism; then "at another time he devote[s] himself entirely to music" (*D*, 134). His musical tastes now move from the European and Romantic to the gypsy and Arabian. While under the spell of such exotica, "Schubert's grace, and Chopin's beautiful sorrows, and the mighty harmonies of Beethoven himself, [fall] unheeded on his ear". Subsequently he becomes attracted to various forms of Latin American music, then primitive music of other more obscure origins.

> Yet, after some time, he wearied of them, and would sit in his box at the Opera, either alone or with Lord Henry, listening in rapt pleasure to "Tannhäuser", and seeing in the prelude to that great work of art a presentation of the tragedy of his own soul.
>
> (*D*, 135)

With Gray's particular "tragedy" thus identified with Tannhäuser's, the novel can hasten towards its inevitable conclusions. Gray progresses deeper into sin, then recoils. First this is to wish for some *Götterdämmerung* or *anéantissement*:

> "*Fin de siècle*", murmured Lord Henry.
> "*Fin du globe*", answered his hostess.
> "I wish it were *fin du globe*," said Dorian with a sigh.
> "Life is such a great disappointment."
>
> (*D*, 179)

Then it is to seek oblivion in opium. Finally, like Tannhäuser, it is to renounce sinfulness and try to be "good".

Gray fittingly makes his final turn towards "the good" while back at the piano. Lord Henry has asked him to play a piece of Chopin. As Gray obliges, Lord Henry is moved to the reverie which recalls a stanza of "In the Gold Room: A Harmony": "How lovely that thing you are playing is! I wonder did Chopin write it at Majorca, with the sea sweeping round the villa, and the salt spray dashing against the panes? It is marvellously romantic" (*D*, 216). This return to Chopin might seem to resolve the musical oppositions of the novel in favour of the more delicate Impressionist type of music. On the other hand, Lord Henry's sudden desire to hear this music must be taken in an ironic light; for it is precisely the type of piece that the man who "ran away with" Lady Wotton played so "exquisitely". There is no evidence that this type of music has won some sudden victory in Gray's preferences. He has, after all, not chosen it himself. Nor has Wilde informed us of any renascent taste for Chopin and Schubert and Beethoven since the days of his more exotic musical interests; nor of any slackening of his special love for *Tannhäuser*. Considering as much, we might conclude that the fact that Gray's first and (nearly) last appearances in the novel are connected with this more delicate type of music only provides the frame in which to view his more characteristic Dionysian musical passions.

Wilde's intentions may have been to conclude with an affirm-ation of "the good". The net effect of the novel however is more ambiguous. Lord Henry remains the figure who took Gray to his nights at the opera and gave him the book through which he realized his intimate attachment to the struggle of Tannhäuser. The fact that he ends up plaintively asking to be played a Chopin-like delicacy cannot erase the fact that the resounding moment of the novel was when he, in "low musical" tones, "awakened" Gray. This awakening was to the "evil" to which Baudelaire had awakened a generation of Decadents; to the "Dionysian" that Nietzsche portrayed Wagner as having reawakened European art through his music; most of all, to the deeper stirrings of young Dorian's own subconscious. And, like the evocations of the Unconscious sought by Mallarmé and Laforgue, this awakening was brought about by a type of music: a music at least as passionate as Wagner's, but created in the Wildean manner out of "mere words":

> Music had stirred him like that. Music had troubled him many times. But music was not articulate. It was not a new world, but rather another chaos, that it created in us. Words! Mere words! How terrible they were! How clear, and vivid, and cruel! One could not escape from them. And yet what a subtle magic there was in them! They seemed to be able to give a plastic form to formless things, and to have a music of their own as sweet as that of voil or of lute. Mere words! Was there anything so real as words? (*D*, 19)

WILDE THE WIT

Perhaps the most "unreal" words spoken in *The Picture of Dorian Gray* are those of Lady Wotton about Wagner and music:

> "I like Wagner's music better than anybody's. It is so loud that one can talk the whole time without other people hearing what one says. That is a great advantage: don't you think so, Mr Gray?" . . .
>
> Dorian smiled, and shook his head: "I'm afraid I don't think so, Lady Henry. I never talk during music – at least, during good music. If one hears bad music, it is one's duty to drown it in conversation."
>
> "Ah! . . . but you must not think I don't like good music. I adore it, but I am afraid of it. It makes me too romantic. I have simply worshipped pianists – two at a time, sometimes, Harry tells me. I don't know what it is about them. Perhaps it is that they are foreigners. They all are, ain't they? Even those born in England become foreigners after a time, don't they? It is so clever of them, and such a compliment to art."   (*D*, 45)

Lady Wotton's position as the conventional bourgeoise stands in opposition to the type of aesthete represented by her husband and Gray. Wilde puts reservations about Wagner into her mouth which he simultaneously undercuts by exposing the philistinism that hovers right behind them. Lady Wotton's reservations come less from a dislike of Wagner than for a vague feeling of danger which his music brings on. For this conventional timidity of Dionysian art we are tempted to forgive her (she does love music in general after all, doesn't she?) when, suddenly, she makes a mockery of her position by revealing her "love" to be a shallow fancy for the affected and "unreal" foreignness of piano-players. *Épater le bourgeois* is Wilde's intention in such seductively witty passages. He brings it off with an irony that links him to Laforgue and Mann as well as to the directly combative authors of "Laus Veneris" and *Les Fleurs du mal*. It was a talent he was soon to exploit with success in the comedies.

In *The Importance of Being Earnest* (1895) another Wildean bourgeoise is made to utter a similar philistinism about music. Wilde apparently regarded it as normal to the type:

> French songs I cannot possibly allow. People always seem to

think that they are improper, and either look shocked, which is vulgar, or laugh, which is worse. But German sounds a thoroughly respectable language, and, indeed, I believe it is so. (*W*, 329)

It is not only the fact that Lady Bracknell is only interested in the socially utilitarian aspects of music which makes her statement ludicrous, but also the fact that her swipe at the German language is entirely beside the point. As Wilde had pointed out through Ernest in "The Critic as Artist" (*Intentions*, 1891), the German language has nothing directly to do with music:

> I took the Baroness Bernstein down to dinner last night, and, though absolutely charming in every other respect, she insisted on discussing music as if it were actually written in the German language. Now, whatever music sounds like, I am glad to say that it does not sound in the smallest degree like German. (*W*, 1011)

Ernest dismisses the Baroness's foolishness as facilely as Dorian Gray dismisses Lady Wotton's, and as the comic hyperbole allows Lady Bracknell's opinions to dismiss themselves. But, in dismissing the Baroness, Ernest shows a propensity to oversimplify and overstate which makes his opinion seem shallow as well. The comic success of the remark depends on a slap at the German language just as much as Lady Bracknell's. This seems in conflict with the philosophy of a higher "cosmopolitanism" which Wilde propounds further on in "The Critic as Artist". Moreover, the proposition that music does not sound like the German language seems in any case empty and supercilious.

Such utterances from Wilde's mouthpieces, even from Wilde himself, frequently display, at least on this subject of music, a type of shallowness that makes them equally ludicrous to the utterances of his obvious philistines. While in most cases the effect is that of a sort of jocular self-parody, at times the utterances do actual violence to Wilde's stated aesthetic convictions. A case in point comes when Moncrieff responds to the bell in *The Importance of Being Earnest*: "Ah! that must be Aunt Augusta. Only relatives, or creditors, ever ring in that Wagnerian manner" (*W*, 327). Here Moncrieff implies not only that Wagnerian music is loud, a common enough anti-Wagnerian cliché; but also that Wagner in general is as offensive and nagging as creditors or Lady Bracknell, an opinion which he probably does not hold and which Wilde himself certainly did not. The blitheness with which this inference is allowed to pass is of a kind with Wilde's carelessness with mythic detail. In both cases the superficial need of the moment is the ruling consideration. If the Pope's staff must metamorphose into a walking-stick in order to turn a phrase, so be it; if a clichéd idea is needed to bring a laugh at a juncture in a comedy, so be it. To Wilde the wit nothing could remain sacred. All opinions, including his own, were to be mocked as readily as to be stated. In life as well as art Wilde himself was fond of the Wagnerian-loudness cliché: he used it in a letter to describe the healthy wailings of his infant son Cyril (*L*, 177).

WILDE THE AESTHETE

Thus Wilde the "social" Wagnerian, the Wilde of the comedy of manners, the Wilde always deflating all-too-human "real" life. The other Wilde, the philosophic and aesthetic, remained thoroughly reverent about Wagner and his art. This is apparent in the extensive statement in "The Critic as Artist" about the appeal of the music of *Tannhäuser* to him:

> Sometimes, when I listen to the overture to *Tannhäuser*, I seem indeed to see that comely knight treading delicately on the flower-strewn grass, and to hear the voice of Venus calling to him from the caverned hill. But at other times it speaks to me of a thousand different things, of myself, it may be, and my own life, or of the lives of others whom one has loved and grown weary of loving, or of the passions that man has known, or of the passions that man has not known, and so has sought for. Tonight it may fill one with that $EP\Omega\Sigma$ $T\Omega N$ $A\Lambda Y N AT\Omega N$, that *Amour de l'Impossible*, which falls like a madness on many who think they live securely and out of reach of harm, so that they sicken suddenly with the poison of unlimited desire, and, in the infinite pursuit of what they may not obtain, grow faint and swoon or stumble. To-morrow, like the music of . . . the Greek, it may perform the office of a physician, and give us an anodyne against pain, and heal the spirit that is wounded, and "bring the soul into harmony with all right things". And what is true about music is true about all the arts. Beauty has as many meanings as man has moods. Beauty is the symbol of symbols. Beauty reveals

everything, because it expresses nothing. When it shows us itself, it shows the whole fiery-coloured world. (*W*, 1029–30)

This celebration of the Wagnerian magic sounds notes typical of the best of such reveries. The music can carry one back to what Mann would call "our earliest picture dreamings": either the hellish beauty of a "fiery-coloured" world, a Venusberg magnificently lit by "fires that are not those of the sun" as Baudelaire described it;[7] or the heavenly beauty of a Classical Greek tableau – something like Hans Castorp's dream vision while frozen in the snow in the central chapter of *The Magic Mountain*, a scene of Classical perfection which suddenly transforms into one of diabolical ugliness and cannibalism. The music can awaken erotic impulses which make one "faint and swoon and stumble" towards the sort of destruction which Aschenbach would experience in *Death in Venice* (and which in a different form shadows Dorian Gray throughout his progress). Or it can "give us an anodyne against pain, and heal the spirit that is wounded"; that is, take on the Christlike sympathy that Parsifal takes on in performing the ritual healing of Amfortas.

Wilde put this appreciation in the mouth of Gilbert, a musician who, like Dorian Gray, is introduced at the piano. From the first Gilbert is more eager to play "some mad scarlet thing" than to talk. Yet, in spite of his inordinate love of music, he maintains that the "supreme highest arts" are Life and Literature. And, like Mallarmé, he calls on writers of the future to make their art more methodically – even scientifically – musical. The writer must study "the metrical movements of a prose as scientifically as a modern musician studies harmony and counterpoint, and, I need hardly say, with much keener aesthetic instinct" (*W*, 1016). The writer must be even more diligent at his task than the contemporary master of musical prose in English:

> Even the work of Mr Pater, who is, on the whole, the most perfect master of English prose now creating amongst us, is often far more like a piece of mosaic than a passage in music, and seems, here and there, to lack the true rhythmical life of words and the fine freedom and richness of effect that such rhythmical life produces. (*W*, 1016)

Gilbert goes on to pursue a number of other ideas current in the two traditions Wilde knew best, the French Symbolist and the English from Shelley to Swinburne. Much of what he states might equally have been found in the critical pronouncements of Wagner. In all, he proposes little that is new. But his expression is charged with the very musical charms he so admires. And we might go so far as to call "The Critic as Artist" *musical* criticism; and the prose in which it is written, like that of Mallarmé or Dujardin, musical – even Wagnerian – prose.

Wilde himself never described his prose as Wagnérian. Nevertheless, the style of "The Critic as Artist" shares with Wagner's music the capacity to open out towards "unending melody" and to the further reaches of metaphysical speculation; and the aspiration to a musical texture is clear. One of the techniques Wilde uses to achieve such a texture is that characteristic punctuation in which we find an extensive, careful, and sometimes surprising use of the comma. At the same time, Wilde seems to have sought to avoid use of dashes, colons, semi-colons – those technical indices of the relative value of phrases typical of more painstaking cerebrists such as Henry James. The marks avoided tend to halt and shift the flow of a thought, while the marks favoured tend to encourage flow and simplify the relationships between subsidiary ideas. As a result, the argument of "The Critic as Artist" appears to proceed with single-minded directness. The analogy would be to the way Wagner developed a single musical theme, the *Sehnsuchtsmotiv* for instance, along a chromatic scale. One foot is put forwards, the new step is tested; the new level is contemplated with care, then the first foot stretches forwards again towards the inevitable next step; and so forth. This is a linear, almost processional, style of development. It disallows the intrusion of any secondary motif which cannot be woven harmonically into the dominant. It seems the prime characteristic that Wilde's self-consciously "musical" prose shares with Wagner's music.

SALOMÉ

Avowedly the most "musical" of Wilde's finished works, *Salomé* (1891) employs an overtly chromatic and leitmotival development of word, phrase and idea. As in "The Critic as Artist", we experience the sensation of proceeding in the half-steps of the chromatic scale. All focus is on the single dominant idea, in this case not the all-embracing value of Criticism but the inevitable destructiveness of Absolute Passion. All action proceeds towards its consequence with the directness of the *Sehnsuchtsmotiv* proceeding towards its musical and metaphysical resolution in the *Liebestod*. As in *Tristan*, the process is sensual, sure-footed and characterized by a refusal to rush amid strange dissonant beauties of sound. The form is incantatory. The purpose is to induce the sort of reverie that Mallarmé would fall into while listening to Wagner's orchestral *longueurs*. Wilde uses words here as Wagner used notes. Motif follows motif: the strangeness of the moon, the noise of the Jews debating, the strange allure of the princess, Hérodias and her luxury, Iokanaan and his prophecies, the strange allure of Salomé and the moon, and so forth. The first few speeches form a sort of prelude. Then Salomé appears, the drama proceeds, and these original motifs interweave ánd build upon one another until their inevitable resolutions are achieved.

We are certainly in the realm of *Tristan* here. We are also in the realm of those Baudelairean French who wished to catch the soul quivering on the verge of self-destruction, and to draw out the act for as long as possible in order to study its pathological motive in every luminous detail. *Salomé*'s language is Wilde's attempt at the French of the Symbolists, its style their style, its concern their concerns. Wilde himself noted the relationship of the play to the plays of Maeterlinck, and he justified his use of French by the argument that the "essential foreignness" of the language to that "Flamand" was a source of its "suggestive power".[8] Aubrey Beardsley emphasized Wilde's debt to Flaubert by placing a volume of *Trois contes*, which included the seminal "Hérodias", on a table in one of the drawings he did for the English edition of the play. The additional influences of Mallarmé, Huysmans, and the general Decadent fascination for the biblical story were equally public knowledge.[9] The pervasive influence of Wagner on this strain of French culture on which Wilde was drawing suggests the overall relationship of Wagner to *Salomé*. The influence of that same strain on Wagner while he was composing *Parsifal* may help explain the similarity in style, concerns, and appeal of that work to Wilde's.[10]

Not the least similarity is the overarching motif of male chastity.[11] The attempt at seduction of Parsifal by Kundry and that of Iokanaan by Salomé are both cases of the holy man being lured by the decadent *femme fatale*. In both cases the holy man resists. Parsifal's resistance leads to the redemption and grateful death of the *femme fatale*, Iokanaan's to his own death and indirectly to the sudden end of an ostensibly unredeemed Salomé. This difference in resolution might suggest that the aging Wagner's is the more puritan of the two works; but in fact *Salomé* goes to far greater dramatic length to drive home the moral that sexual passion is self-annihilating. As a work specifically focused on this theme, *Salomé* has more in common with *Tristan* than with *Parsifal*; for in the latter the primary focus is on the struggle between Good and Evil, and the sexual theme is degraded to the status of an illustration. But, as a work of atmospheres, in which Christian lore and sexual politics intermingle and the Decadent fascination for the East is exploited, *Salomé* is very close to *Parsifal* indeed. One could even go so far as to speculate on the metaphysical similarities between Salomé/ Herodias and the two sides of the schizophrenic Kundry; between Herod with his paranoias, perverse passions and resentments, and the vicious Klingsor; between Iokanaan, who is the doomed old prophet and agonized lamenter as well as the joyful awaiter of Christ, and Titurel, Amfortas and even Gurnemanz – as well as Parsifal.

THE ARTIST AS HERO

Near the end of the second part of "The Critic as Artist", Gilbert reveals that many of his opinions find their origins in the early German Romantics – "that Aufklärung, that enlightening which dawned on Germany in the last century" (*W*, 1046). He goes on to suggest that the noblest posture for the individual artist to take in relation to the world is the one of critical cosmopolitanism exemplified by Goethe:

> The emotions will not make us cosmopolitan, any more than the greed for gain could do so. It is only by the cultivation of the habit of intellectual criticism that we shall be able to rise superior to race-prejudices. Goethe – you will not misunderstand what I say – was a German of the Germans. He loved his country – no man more so. . . . Yet when the iron hoof of Napoleon trampled upon vineyard and cornfield, his lips were silent. "How can one write songs of hatred without hating?" he said to Eckermann, "and how could I, to whom culture and barbarism are alone of importance, hate a nation which is among the most cultivated of

the earth, to which I owe so great a part of my own cultivation?" This note, sounded in the modern world by Goethe first, will become, I think, the starting point for the cosmopolitanism of the future. Criticism will annihilate race-prejudices by insisting upon the unity of the human mind in the variety of its forms. (*W*, 1057)

The reader may be arrested by the phrase "race-prejudices" here; and, having in mind Wagner's anti-Semitism and nationalism of the later years, and his subsequent deification by the Nazis, he might find Gilbert's utopian idea to have little to do with Wagner. But what Wilde appears to be driving at here is based on a particular view of the artist that grew out of that German *Aufklärung*, found its way to England first through Coleridge and Carlyle, to France through the musical and philosophical interests of some mid-century poets, and to the twentieth-century Modernists through the pan-European Decadent Romanticism of the *fin-de-siècle*. In this view of the artist, behaviour is determined by the belief that the primary responsibilities are to "culture and barbarism", and to the tradition of which the artist is a part. Thus he and his heroic exemplars must refuse to become yea-sayers to bourgeois morality, or apologists for uncongenial political imperatives. In this sense we can see that what Wilde is talking about here is not only Goethe, who refused to oppose Napoleon, but also Thomas Mann, who would be forced to leave Germany by his antipathy for the Nazi ascendancy; likewise Richard Wagner, who was forced into exile for opposing an *ancien régime* which seemed to him to perpetuate the philistine attitudes towards creative art in his day.

The ideal Wilde hoped man might achieve involved learning to live by an "artistic" critical dialogue rather than by mere prejudices. But events had shown and would show again that, in the "real" world where Wilde, like Mann and Wagner, had to live, the placing of such a high value on the discernment of the individual "artist-nature" held a danger of placing him at odds with his state and society-at-large. The results were, in short, not always so happy as in the case of Goethe. And, indeed, the tradition which placed such a high value on the individual artist ultimately encouraged its artists to regard the society around them as philistine and potentially hostile, and to retreat to elitist citadels of the craft. Thus Wagner at Bayreuth, Mallarmé in Paris, Wilde in London, Yeats in Ireland – surrounded by cults of disciples, this type of artist was encouraged to create sublime works of self-aggrandizement; beautiful illusions in which the ideal artist-nature would merge with the ideal man-of-action to give birth, with all the artifices and allures of calculated stylizations, to its apotheoses: Siegfried the Liberator, crucified by the machinations of the *haute bourgeoisie*; Parsifal the Saviour, triumphant over the enemies of sacred *Kultur*; the perfectly beautiful and isolated paragons – the artist become hero, become saviour, become martyr, become Christ.

The temptation of such an apotheosis was too seductive for an artist like Wilde to resist; and, like the repentant Tannhäuser, we see him turning towards a "higher purity". The turning becomes most apparent in the celebrated letter to Alfred Douglas, *De profundis* (1897): but, as Wilde himself was to point out in that letter, it is foreshadowed in *Dorian Gray* and *Salomé* and, most remarkably perhaps, in the fairy-tale "The Young King" (*A House of Pomegranates*, 1891). The progress of the Young King is from the temptations of material riches to the realization of spiritual perfection. Like Siegfried, he has grown up unparented in the forest, his mother having passed away in childbirth. Eventually he is brought to the court, where he finds himself surrounded by *objets* and jewels and works of art. The splendour and novelty of these things stun him, and he proceeds to worship them. As he does, the first of many strong hints of Wagner appears:

> It was said that a stout Burgomaster, who had come to deliver a florid oratorical address on behalf of the citizens of the town, had caught sight of him kneeling in real adoration before a great picture that had just been brought from Venice, and that seemed to herald the worship of some new gods.   (*W*, 225)

This curious in-joke reflects ironically, and perhaps unintentionally, on the exalted position of the artist which Wagner espoused and Wilde shared. On one hand, we might see Wagner in his *Meistersinger* garb come to deliver Hans Sachs's ponderous pronouncements on Germanic art; alternatively, Wagner of the *Ring* come to declare the dawning of the worship of the pagan Nordic pantheon. On another, we might see Wagner as the garrulous Gurnemanz lingering to watch as a young Parsifal gazes in wonder at the Grail ritual; in which case the Young King corresponds for the moment not only to the hero of Wagner's last drama, but also to the artist-disciple type of the age (even perhaps to King Ludwig II himself) kneeling in reverence before the icon of the *heilige Kunst* of the Master Artist, who had died a decade earlier in a sumptuous palazzo in Venice.

THE PARSIFALIAN TURNING

What Wilde intended by this allusion is unclear. Probably it is another instance of the blithe aside, stimulated in this case by a current fancy for Wagnerian resonances (which is demonstrated elsewhere in *A House of Pomegranates*, notably in the "ring" motif of "The Fisherman and his Soul"). But "The Young King" partakes of Wagner on a more thoroughgoing level as well, in the sustained parallels to *Parsifal*. We are alerted to these by the "cup of dark-veined onyx", which metamorphoses in one of the Young King's dreams into the cup containing Ague which Death pours on his toilers, and finally appears as "the chalice of yellow wine" which stands Grail-like before the image of Christ on the altar when the Young King is being crowned. The Parsifal motif is most evident in the figure of the Young King himself. Like Wagner's hero, he is converted by wanderings into a pure and Christlike individual. Carrying a simple shepherd's staff as his sceptre, he goes through the city towards the Cathedral and the ignorant people mock his poor dress. "It is the King's fool who is riding by," they call out. "Nay, but I am the king", he replies (*W*, 231). The fact is that, like Parsifal, he is both: king and divine fool.

The soldiers and knights can hardly understand the Young King's conversion. Even the priest fails to recognize the spirit of the Saviour in him. But, then, as he stands before the altar praying "in real adoration", divinity comes shining and hovering around him:

Through the painted windows came the sunlight streaming upon him, and the sunbeams wove round him a tissued robe that was fairer than the robe that had been fashioned for his pleasure. The dead staff blossomed, and bore lilies that were whiter than pearls. The dry thorn blossomed, and bore roses that were redder than rubies. Whiter than fine pearls were the lilies, and their stems were of bright silver. Redder than male rubies were the roses, and their leaves were of beaten gold.

He stood there in the raiment of a king, and the gates of the jewelled shrine flew open and from the crystal of the many-rayed monstrance shone a marvellous and mystical light. He stood

there in a king's raiment, and the Glory of God filled the place,
and the saints in their carven niches seemed to move. In the fair
raiment of a king he stood before them, and the organ pealed out
its music, and the trumpeters blew upon their trumpets, and the
singing boys sang.   (*W*, 233)

The staff, as in *Tannhäuser*, blooms from its barrenness. The mystical
glow of the Holy Grail shines forth from its shrine, just as it does in
Parsifal. Music resonates around the hero and ascends, up through
the voices of the boys which so moved Verlaine: "Et, ô ces voix
d'enfants chantant dans la coupole!" On up it ascends, up through
the blazing light from the dome. And one is left with the sense of
having observed the arrival of the long-awaited saviour: the one
who will now do away with all nightmarish pain, whether it be of
exploited Nibelung-like toilers, or of sufferers of Amfortas-like
deliriums. One is left, in short, with exactly the resounding sensation
with which one is left at the finale of Wagner's last work.

    Of course, Wilde could never have seen *Parsifal*, for Cosima
Wagner has placed an interdiction on its performance outside
Bayreuth, which through the 1890s was still observed. Nevertheless,
Wilde must have heard much about Wagner's *sacred festival play*, and
read about it, both what the French had written and what Shaw,
Moore and others were reporting from Bayreuth.[12] The mystique of
Parsifal at Bayreuth had an attraction for artists of the *fin-de-siècle*
much like that of *Tannhäuser* at Paris had for artists of the 1860s
(undoubtedly it was greater, considering how fashionable Wagner
had become in the interval).[13] This fact would not have been lost on
Wilde. And it seems entirely likely that rumours and recountings of
Wagner's final work could have inspired Wilde as he wrote "The
Young King", in much the same manner that rumours and
recountings of *Tannhäuser* may have inspired Swinburne as he wrote
"Laus Veneris".

THE ARTIST'S TRAGEDY

No one understood better than Wilde himself his turning from the
Tannhäuser of the Venusberg to the "good" Tannhäuser who
merges into a Parsifal figure. In *De Profundis* he presented the
process in detail and with much attention to the suffering of the
artist type. This suffering is likened to the cry of Marsyas, slain by

Apollo in an act of cruelty which marred that god's perfection (*L*, 490), much like commitment to the cruel law by which Siegmund must be slain marred Wotan's. This cry is one of accidie, the infection of *ennui* and morbidity of mind which had wasted Baudelaire;[14] that "disease of the will" for which Schopenhauer had designed the perfect philosophy, and Wagner the perfect dramatic exemplars in his Tristan and Amfortas and world-weary Wotan. The cry is discontent, plaintive, bitter, and unresolved as the *Sehnsuchtsmotiv*. Of all the arts it is best expressed by music:

> Music, in which all subject is absorbed in expression and cannot be separated from it, is a complex example, and a flower or a child is a simple example of what I mean: but Sorrow is the ultimate type both in life and Art. (*L*, 473)

The highest art will be an organic expression of Sorrow, a *Tristan*-like form in which outer music will match inner pain. And, as the highest art must be this expression of sorrow, the true Great Artist must live the role of the Great Sorrower:

> I see an . . . intimate and immediate connection between the true life of Christ and the true life of the artist, and I take a keen pleasure in the reflection that long before Sorrow had made my days her own . . . I had written in "The Soul of Man" that he who would lead a Christ-like life must be entirely and absolutely himself. . . . (*L*, 476)

The passage in "The Soul of Man under Socialism" (1891) to which Wilde here refers names Wagner, along with Shakespeare and a handful of others, as just such an artist:

> He who would lead a Christ-like life is he who is perfectly and absolutely himself! He may be a great poet, or a great man of science . . . a maker of dramas like Shakespeare, or . . . Wagner when he realized his soul is music. . . . (*W*, 1087)

As Wilde reaffirmed from his cell this extreme Romantic view of the artist, we might well ask how much he already knew of the letters from the exiled Wagner to August Roeckel (Wagner's imprisoned comrade of the 1849 Dresden rebellion), which he was shortly to request (*L*, 523). Did he perhaps know these words of

Wagner's: "I am an Artist, nothing else, and that is at once my blessing and my curse; otherwise I should have wished to have been a saint and to have ordered my life in the simplest way"?[15]
Did he know of the complaints of physical and spiritual isolation and suffering which Wagner so constantly voiced? And did he know of Wagner's equally characteristic self-rallying statements of recommitment to his divine artistic mission?

> For myself, I can no longer exist except as an artist; since I cannot compass love and life, all else repels me, or only interests me in so far as it has a bearing on Art. The result is a life of torment, but it is the only possible life. Moreover, some strange experiences have come to me through my works. When I think of the pain and discomfort which are now my chronic condition, I cannot but feel that my nerves are completely shattered: but marvellous to relate, on occasion, and under a happy stimulus, these nerves do wonders for me; a clearness of insight comes to me, and I experience a receptive and creative activity such as I have never known before.[16]

It seems likely that Wilde had either read these letters already or had them described to him, and that he requested them because he realized how well their lamentations matched his own feelings. But, whatever Wilde might have already known of the letters, the point is that in *De Profundis* he came to share with Wagner the conviction that the life of the artist must be one of sacred suffering; also the desire, expressed after pages of purgative complaint and self-pity, to turn these artist-sufferings into greater and clearer art than he has ever before produced.

De Profundis is perhaps Wilde's greatest tragic work; and it is in this sense that echoes of *Tannhäuser*, *Tristan*, the *Ring*, *Parsifal* and Wagner's philosophy and life are so readily suggested by it. Wilde projects a scenario in which, instead of putting on the persona of a Tristan or Wotan, he casts the artist himself in the role of tragic hero. Then, in the attitude of self-discovery necessary to the tragic hero, he observes his own pathetic fall:

> My business as an artist was with Ariel. You [Douglas] set me to wrestle with Caliban [Queensberry]. Instead of making beautiful coloured, musical things such as *Salomé*, and the *Florentine*

Tragedy, and *La Sainte Courtisane*, I found myself forced to send long lawyer's letters. (*L*, 492)

His flaw, which prevented him from reaching the musical ideal with consistency, was, as he states it, an inability to isolate himself sufficiently from philistine Life; also, implicity, an inability to resist the temptation to reduce Art to the status of a "looking-glass" for philistine Life, whereby he produced the more frivolous and shallow, if more commercially successful, art of the comedies. At last, having fallen and recognized his flaw, he declares his willingness to become what he could not be before imprisonment: an artist in total creative commitment and monastic isolation, seeking not "the articulate utterances of men and things", but "The Mystical in Art, the Mystical in Life, the Mystical in Nature – this is what I am looking for, and in the great symphonies of music, in the initiation of Sorrow, in the depths of the Sea I may find it" (*L*, 509).

CONCLUSION

The *Angst* of Tristan, the commitment to a Symbolist ideal like that of the Wagnerian French – such motifs echo and fade away. In the end Wilde failed to make his full Parsifalian turning, or to develop the discipline and solitude proper for the art of the future he envisioned. Why? "This century", he wrote, "bids me to alter my name . . . where even mediaevalism would have given me the cowl of the monk" (*L*, 510). Modern life, so we are encouraged to read in the myth of the artist to which Wilde was applying the sad finishing touches, had no more place for the "good" Tannhäuser in pilgrim's cowl than for the "evil" Tannhäuser of the Venusberg. Yet, in time, the myth, like Tannhäuser, would triumph. The flowering staff, sign of the knight's ultimate redemption, bloomed on at least two occasions in Wilde's last letters.[17] It also appeared prominently in *The Ballad of Reading Gaol* (1898), at the moment when, using an image that well befitted an artist whose ideal was a music of words, Wilde envisioned a flower blooming triumphantly not out of the mere earth above a murderer's grave, but out of the sinner's mouth itself:

> Out of his mouth a red, red rose!
> Out of his heart a white!

> For who can say by what strange way,
>   Christ brings His will to light,
> Since the barren staff the pilgrim bore
>   Bloomed in the great Pope's sight?

(*W*, 855)

In the case of Wilde we have noted the following points of connection with Wagner: (1) Identification with the Tannhäuser myth; (2) blithe references and allusions encouraged by the social vogue for Wagner; (3) belief in the mystical power of music to awaken memories and unconscious desires; (4) a musical aesthetic and aspiration to create a new musical prose; (5) the use of leitmotiv and chromatic progression; (6) a dramatic singleness of purpose; (7) the theme of Absolute Passion as absolutely destructive, parallel to *Tristan*; (8) a focus on male chastity and the Christlike leader, parallel to *Parsifal*; (9) the point of view of the artist as hero/martyr/ Christ, his role as the highest spiritual undertaking, and his fate to be solitary and at odds with philistine life. These motifs are typical of the English nineties as a whole. We shall find them resounding in various metamorphoses in works of the others to be discussed – including the Modernists.

4 Symons

Arthur Symons was first introduced to Wagner's music as an adolescent. An amateur musician himself, he went through a period of intense musical awakening, similar perhaps to that which the young Nietzsche had experienced. Unlike Nietzsche, the young Symons did not immediately become a devotee of the composer of *Tristan* to the exclusion of all else.[1] As he matured, his primary interests were poetry and his English poetic predecessors, Browning in particular. It was not until after he travelled to the Continent with Havelock Ellis, met the celebrated French literary Wagnerians, and went to Bayreuth for the first time that Wagnerian motifs began to appear in his writing. This was in the period 1894–5, the time of Wilde and *The Yellow Book*, then of Wilde's trial and the general recoiling from all who were associated with Wilde in the public mind. These included Aubrey Beardsley, who had done the illustrations for *Salomé*, and to a lesser extent Symons himself. Both men were excluded, along with other declared Decadents, from *The Yellow Book*, to which they had been contributors.

It was a time of crisis for the Decadent artist in general, and for Symons personally. Like Dorian Gray, he had lived the Decadent mode to the point at which the only choices left seemed "the pistol or the foot of the cross". Symons's crisis was brought on, at least exacerbated, by an affair with a half-Spanish dancer, Lydia, which finally had to be broken off, apparently unsatisfactorily for Symons. Lydia became the poet's model for his characteristic *femme fatale*, the type that as the dark Venus was to haunt his final works, and that appeared in exaggerated form in such poems as "Vampire", written at this time:

> Intolerable woman, where's the name
> For your insane complexity of shame?
> Vampire! white bloodless creature of the night,
> Whose lust of blood has blanched her chill veins white,
> Veins fed with moonlight over dead men's tombs;
> Whose eyes remember many martyrdoms.[2]

If Lydia provided the live outline of the Decadent female, other versions of the type suggested ways to fill out her features. And in Symons's women one might frequently hear echoes of Baudelaire's and Villiers's women; of Wagner's Venus and Kundry ("whose eyes remember many martyrdoms"); and, most apparently here in "Vampire", of Swinburne's Venus with her "lust of blood".

In this as most things Symons was the consummate Decadent. Moreover, ín his "pioneering" study *The Symbolist Movement in Literature* he was the man most responsible for bringing the aesthetics of the Wagnerian French into English letters, for the Modernists as well as for his own generation.[3] These things make Symons a central figure in our study. The irony is that Symons himself lived out the Modernist years among ghosts of the past, a lonely survivor of "the tragic generation" carrying on its enthusiams for Wagner and Swinburne and the French Decadent gods long after they, and he, had fallen out of fashion. In this chapter we shall consider the significance of Wagner to English Decadence and Symbolism as evidenced in Symons's career, his magazine *The Savoy*, his attempt at a Tristan drama, his mature criticism, and his personal myth and breakdown. Some of what we shall discuss has been taken up by A. Guy Randall in his thesis "The Poetic Drama of Arthur Symons", the most considerable work on Wagner and Symons to date.

THE SAVOY I: BEARDSLEY

While Symons was lingering in the pain of his broken affair with Lydia, other prominent Decadents were scattering in the wake of Wilde's trial. John Gray, who may have been one model for Dorian Gray and whose *Silverpoints* (1893) contained "some of the first translations into English of French *symboliste* verse", was in the process of becoming a Catholic priest.[4] Beardsley, who was himself to convert to Catholicism in a few years' time, had for the moment gone to Dieppe, a city to which Symons also found his way at the end of the summer of 1895. This mini-exile proved fortunate for both men. In Dieppe they decided to launch a magazine which, they declared, would not be a mouthpiece for any single artistic movement;[5] but *The Savoy* was from the first regarded as having taken up Decadence where *The Yellow Book* left off. The first issue appeared in January 1896. It struck an immediate tone of hostility towards the English bourgeois morality which had sent Wilde to

jail, and of contrasting admiration for things Continental –
particularly French. Beardsley set this tone in the first pages with a
poem written and set in Dieppe, "The Three Musicians". In this a
soprano "lightly frocked", a "slim gracious boy", and a Polish
pianist

> stroll along
>> And pluck the ears of ripened corn,
> Break into odds and ends of song,
>> And mock the woods with Siegfried's horn,
> And fill the air with Gluck, and fill the tweeded tourist's
>> soul with scorn.
>
> (*S*, 1, 65)

The musicians' undisguised intention is to shock the tweeded
Englishman with their behaviour. This includes, we should note,
the breaking-out into Wagner's anarchist hero's motif. It ends with
the soprano and the boy copulating in full view.

The poem was *risqué*, but tame in comparison to the "novel"
which Beardsley had also begun in Dieppe. The original title of this
work was *The Story of Venus and Tannhäuser* and the subject the erotic
one that had fascinated Wilde, Swinburne and Baudelaire. According to Annette Lavers, Beardsley "unquestionably felt that he was
much more suited to be the hero of the story than many of those who
had chosen it before him";[6] and he set about with gusto to ornament
Wagner's framework with a series of "polymorphous perverse"
fantasies told in the manner of the French *ancien régime*. The
publisher of *The Savoy* balked. Beardsley thereupon expurgated the
most erotic passages, changed the characters' names, and published
the story serially under the more obscurely Tannhäuserian title of
Under the Hill. In this revised version the most extensive reference to
Wagner is to *Rheingold*, another work of which Beardsley considered
writing a full-length parody. His characterization of *Rheingold* as a
"brilliant comedy" does indeed sound the parodistic note, as does
his linking of Wagner to the pulpit and the Wagnerian aesthete to
priests. But the synopsis of *Rheingold* which Beardsley gives through
Abbé Fanfreluche's eyes is marked by the deep appreciation that
he, like Symons an accomplished amateur musician, felt for all of
Wagner's works.

Once more he was ravished with the beauty and wit . . . the
music that follows the talk and movements of the Rhine-maidens,

the black hateful sounds of Alberic's love-making, and the flowing melody of the river of legends. The feverish insistent ringing of the hammers at the forge, the dry staccato restlessness of Mime, the ceaseless coming and going of the troup of Nibelungs, drawn hither and thither like a flock of terror-stricken and infernal sheep, Alberic's savage activity and metamorphoses, and Loge's rapid, flaming tongue-like movements, make the tableau the least reposeful, the most troubled and confusing thing in the whole range of opera. How the Abbé rejoiced in the extravagant monstrous poetry, the heated melodrama, the splendid agitation of it all!   (*S*, II, 192–5)

Celebration of what convention regarded as the most "troubled and confusing" and delight in whatever was "least reposeful" came to Beardsley even more naturally than to Baudelaire or the young Swinburne. His extreme impulse to *épater le bourgeois* was an aspect of Beardsley's personality for which his more reverent co-editor later felt moved to apologize.[7] This impulse was perhaps most apparent in the distortions of his sketches. And his Wagner sketches, many of which were published in *The Savoy*, are fine examples. His "Siegfried" is knock-kneed, thin-limbed, and clad in a highly-ornamented almost Roman costume. His "Isolde" is more grotes-que than beautiful and has more in common with his own, and Wilde's, Decadent Salomé than with Wagner's passionate heroine. His "Wagnerites at a Performance of Tristan and Isolde" are black-gowned plump versions of this Isolde/Salomé/*décadente*. And his sketches of *Rheingold* portray a conniving Oriental-looking Wotan, and a mocking, smirking Loge whose features seem rather like those of the caricatures of Wilde which lurk in the backgrounds of the *Salomé* sketches. Indeed, none of Beardsley's Wagner sketches portrays its subject in less than a startling and strangely distorted manner – unless perhaps it is the one of the Rhinemaiden Flossihilde, which appeared in the final issue of *The Savoy*, several issues after Beardsley had abandoned serialization of *Under the Hill*, unable to work on because of his terminal illness.

THE SAVOY II: NIETZSCHE

Regarding Wagner in *The Savoy* beyond Beardsley, we should note the articles of Havelock Ellis. Ellis, as we have seen, shared in the general Wagnerism of the day; and he brought the *Meister* to bear on a number of subjects. One of these was Zola, of whom Ellis claimed in *The Savoy*'s first issue,

> Zola seems to have been the first who has, deliberately and systematically, introduced . . . *leit-motiv* into literature as a method of summarizing a complex mass of details, and bringing the impression of them before the reader. (*S*, I, 70)

Ellis's main interest in the period of *The Savoy* however was Nietzsche; and his articles on the German philosopher were pioneering. In part reviews of translations of three works, including *The Case of Wagner*, which had recently appeared, the first translations of Nietzsche into English, Ellis's articles focus a great deal on Nietzsche's relationship to Wagner, whose name to *The Savoy* audience was as well known as his errant disciple's was not. The first article begins by mentioning Nietzsche's early passions for music and poetry: "At the age of ten appeared his taste for verse-making, and also for music, and he soon began to show that inherited gift for improvisation by which he was able to hold his audience spell-bound" (*S*, II, 82). It then proceeds to trace Nietzsche's Wagner-passion from the "discovery" of the score of *Tristan und Isolde* in 1859, through the rhapsodic praise of *The Birth of Tragedy from the Spirit of Music* (1872) and "Richard Wagner at Bayreuth" (*Thoughts out of Season*, 1876), to the reaction which set in after the first festival and led to the famous "flight from Wagner".

This flight Ellis chooses to interpret as primarily a function of Nietzsche's chronic ill-health: "At Bayreuth [he] was forced to realize the peril of his position as he had never realized it before. He could no longer disguise from himself that he must break with all the passionate interests of his past" (*S*, II, 89). After the break with Wagner, Ellis continued, Nietzsche took up

> the position of a gouty subject who is forced to abandon port wine and straightway becomes an apostle of total abstinence. This remedy seems to have been fairly successful. But the disease was in his bones. Impassioning interests that were far more subtly poisonous slowly developed within him, and twelve years later flight had become impossible, even if he was still able to realize the need for flight. (*S*, II, 90)

We have seen the association of music, passion and destruction in the works of Swinburne and Wilde. Perhaps we can discern it in the careers of Baudelaire and Laforgue, whose early deaths followed shortly after discovery of the music of Wagner. It was becoming an increasingly common theme in European literature of the day – in Tolstoi's "Kreutzer Sonata" for instance; also Mann's early stories such as "Little Herr Friedemann" (1897), in which the hero is sped to destruction by the experience of Wagner and the attentions of a Decadent *femme fatale* at a concert. And, though this association predated Nietzsche and his madness by many years, Nietzsche and his fate nevertheless gave compelling new emphasis to it. The fact was not lost on Ellis. And, though critical of Nietzsche's later ideas, he responded sympathetically to the overarching myth of the Great Tragic Life, which Nietzsche no less than Wilde had cultivated in his demise.[8]

Ellis's last lines enwrap his subject in an aura of heroic transcendence through the martyrdom of madness: "A period of severe hallucinatory delirium led on to complete dementia, and he passes beyond our sight" (*S*, II, 94). And one can hardly help but wonder how much Arthur Symons, reading this, might have been moved, either immediately or later as he approached his own breakdown, by the idea of the Great Tragic Life his former flatmate projected.[9] The artist Symons always aspired to be would have been, like Nietzsche or Baudelaire, one of the great *voyants* of the age. But the artist Symons actually became never seemed quite able to find the perfectly original insight or form of expression thus to distinguish himself. And could not this Symons, type of the Decadent artist-*manqué*, have perceived in the idea of the Great Tragic Life the mirage of an alternative path towards his wish-destiny? The speculation may seem fantastic. But in fact Symons's eventual "tragedy" would share qualities with Nietzsche's, Baudelaire's and even Wilde's. And, though he minimized the accomplishments of two of these precursors (he would maintain that Nietzsche's ideas had been anticipated by Blake and that Wilde's only truly great work was *The Ballad of Reading Gaol*),[10] it seems entirely likely that the myths of such outstanding artist/martyrs of the Decadent era could have effected his quest for his own myth in some way.

THE SAVOY III: "MUNDI VICTIMA"

In the final issue of *The Savoy* we come upon a morbid yet strangely impressive lamentation entitled "Mundi Victima". This Symons seems to have intended as a sort of swansong – of Decadence in general perhaps, of the last great journal of the English Decadence at any rate. The poem evokes the doom that was hovering over the remaining figures of that Decadence: the fatally ill Beardsley, whose drawing "A Répétition of 'Tristan and Isolde'" immediately precedes the poem, and of course Symons himself. The poem does not refer directly to Wagner, but the presence of the Beardsley drawing encourages one to identify the broken lover who is speaking with Wagner's tragic hero. So too does the inscription of the *Sehnsuchtsmotiv* on the next page:

The imagery and mood of "Mundi Victima" are often remarkably anticipatory of those of *The Waste Land*; and, without at present speculating on whether Eliot might have borrowed hearts of silence or handfuls of dust or rats' feet from Symons, we might note that a plethora of typical motifs from the end of Romanticism are deposited in this rather overlooked poem and could easily have been salvaged at a later date.[11] Among other things to be found in the "heap of broken images" is this amalgam of fragments of Christian mysticism, *Tannhäuser* and *Parsifal*:

> The world is made for dutiful restraint.
> Its martyrs are the lover and the saint,
> All whom a fine and solitary rage
> Urges on some ecstatic pilgrimage
> In search of any Holy Sepulchre.
>
> (*S*, VIII, 21)

A few lines later we come upon an image of the outsider which might call to mind both the Dutchman of Wagner's early opera and the eternal stranger in a hostile world that Siegmund is in *Die Walküre*:

> The lover is a lonely voyager
> Over great seas and into lonely lands,
> He speaks a tongue which no man understands,
> Much given to silence, no good citizen.
>
> (*S*, VIII, 21)

The outsider and wanderer, Siegmund; the martyr, Tannhäuser;

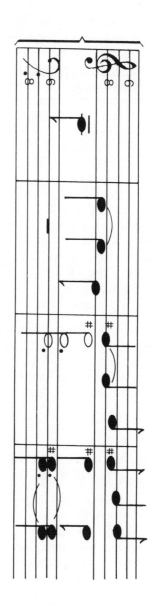

the tragic lover, Tristan; the sex-wounded dying man, Amfortas – these are the myths with which Symons, or his speaker in "Mundi Victima" at any rate, wishes to identity himself.

Like so many of Wagner's heroes and their imitators, Symons's speaker seems to be heading irrevocably towards renunciation of the struggle and Tristan-like transcendence into a beyond of blissful nothingness. But finally he wishes for some way to reattach to the world:

> Say not that I have left you to your fate,
> That I have made my own life desolate,
> Casting adrift upon a shoreless tide,
> While you, blind, shipwrecked, and without a guide.
>
> (*S*, VIII, 22)

And so he turns, in what can only seem a desparate act, to embrace the one thing which had given his existence vitality and meaning, the very Decadent ideal of which the entire poem has been an arraignment: "Folly, the comforter", a creature at least as carelessly destructive as Swinburne's Venus. He proposes to "drink every poison life has found". He promises to "light and exterminate" his desire "in Folly's fire". Then, in a tumultuous and tormented finale which echoes and inverts earlier visions of the Romantic century (notably the Spirit of Shelley's West Wind) he cries,

> Take me and make me yours: I am yours. O take
> The sacrifice of soul and body, break
> The mould of this void spirit, scatter it
> Into the vague and shoreless infinite,
> Pour it upon the restless arrogant
> Winds of tumultuous spaces; grant, O grant
> That the loosed sails of this determinate soul
> Hurry it to disaster, and the goal
> Of swiftest shipwreck; that this soul descend
> The unending depths until oblivion end
> In self-oblivion, and at last be lost
> Where never any other wandering ghost
> Voyaging from other worlds remembered not,
> May find it and remind of things forgot.
>
> (*S*, VIII, 26–7)

PARSIFAL AND MYSTICISM

Such a poem as "Mundi Victima" has a finality to it. One almost feels it incumbent upon the author to live out its implications and exit from the stage in all the flame and glory he has conjured. Perhaps part of Symons wished to make such an exit. If so, that part did not get its way. Instead, in the wake of the demise of *The Savoy*, Symons set out travelling the Continent seeking, as if a latter-day Gérard du Nerval, new artistic sensations and *raisons d'être*. At this time, as Randall says, "The theme of wandering appeared in Symons' poetry as a figurative search for a Parsifal-type figure."[12] Indeed, Symons's travels took him in 1897 for a second time to Bayreuth, where he saw for the first time Wagner's "sacred festival play". "The performance," he wrote later in an article for *The Dome*, "seemed to me the one really satisfying performance I had ever seen in a theatre".[13] And he recorded his impressions in a poem:

> Rose of the garden's roses, what pale wind
> Has scattered these flushed petals in a hour,
> And the close leaves of all the alleys thinned,
> What re-awakening wind,
> O sad enchantress banished to a flower?
>
> Parsifal has out-blushed· the roses: dead
> Is all the garden of the world's delight,
> And every rose of joy has drooped its head,
> And for sweet shame is dead;
> Sweet joy being shameful in the pure fool's sight.
>
> (*W*, II, 108)

The scattering of petals (an image which had also appealed to Verlaine, whose "Parsifal" sonnet is echoed here) so impressed Symons that he mentioned it as well in the article for *The Dome*. Then, taking similar images from the first and third acts of Wagner's drama, he went on to make a comparison that revealed his developing interest in mysticism:

> At times one is reminded of the most beautiful drama in the world, the Indian drama *Sakuntalá*: in that litter of leaves, brought in so touchingly for the swan's burial, in the old hermit

watering his flowers. There is something of the same universal tenderness, the same religious linking together of all the world in some vague enough, but very beautiful, Pantheism.[14]

Collaboration with Arnold Dolmetsch on songs for a production of the above-mentioned Indian drama was one of Symons's numerous artistic activities after returning to England. This might help explain why he couches his praise of *Parsifal* in terms of a drama of Eastern mysticism. So too might his renewed study of the French Decadents: of the "essentially Eastern" philosophy of Villiers, for instance, in which Verlaine had perceived "the formula for our century". Other elements might have been his close association at this time with Yeats, who had steeped himself in Madame Blavatsky's quasi-Tibetan dogma and felt a passion for Sufi poetry comparable to Wagner's;[15] also the mysterious presence of the young Indian "princess" Sarojini Chattôpadhya, "the Magic of the East", during long evenings of conversation about mysticism and art in the rooms Symons and Yeats shared at Fountain Court.[16] But, as we have noted in connection with the French, a major attraction of *Parsifal* lay in its synthesizing of Eastern and Western mysticism. And, beyond his attractions to the Eastern qualities of the work, Symons was also sufficiently impressed with its atmosphere of mediaeval Christian legend to make a "pilgrimage" in the summer of 1898 to Montserrat, the monastery outside Barcelona by which Wagner's Montsalvat may have been partly inspired. There Symons was moved to another poetic reverie on Parsifalian themes, this one revealing vague pantheistic feelings that might have been either Eastern or Western:

> Peace waits along the hills;
> I have drunk peace,
> Here, where the blue air fills
> The great cup of the hills,
> And fills with peace.
>
> Here, where the Holy Graal
> Brought secret light
> Once from beyond the veil,
> I, seeing no Holy Graal,
> Seek divine light.

$$(W, \text{II}, 85)$$

In the end however, the only mysticism in which Symons could put faith was neither precisely Eastern nor Western, but the more general and inclusive mysticism which he discerned to stand behind Symbolist art. He was on the point of putting this into words when he wrote the poem above; for at that time he was busy transforming an article he had written in the early 1890s, "The Decadent Movement in Literature", into a major critical book. The ultimate reservation of belief in other more exclusive and religious systems of mysticism which he was to state in *The Symbolist Movement* was foreshadowed in the concluding sentences of the article on *Parsifal* in *The Dome*:

> I think it is beside the question to discuss how far . . . Parsifal himself is either Christ or Buddha, and how far Kundry is a new Magdalen. Wagner's mind was the mind to which all legend is sacred, every symbol of divine things to be held in reverence; but symbol, with him, was after all a means to an end, and could never have been accepted as really an end in itself. I should say that in *Parsifal* he is profoundly religious, but not because he intended, or did not intend, to shadow Christian mysteries. His music, his acting, are devout, because the music has a disembodied ecstasy, and the acting a noble rhythm, which can but produce in us something of the solemnity of sensation produced by the service of the Mass, and are in themselves a kind of religious ceremonial.[17]

Art which, like that of *Parsifal*, synthesizes the great traditions of mysticism could hold off the doom towards which Decadence led: the dead-end of sensual indulgence in the Venusberg, the pain and lamentation of an Amfortas, the self-immolation of the speaker of "Mundi Victima". Such art alone could free one of "the great bondage" of the fear of death – so Symons wrote in his famous conclusion to *The Symbolist Movement*. In that book Art achieves the status of religion for Symons; and, not surprisingly considering the place of *Parsifal* in guiding Symons to his faith, Wagner is the presiding spirit throughout.[18]

A SYMBOLIST *TRISTAN*

"Between Wagner's *Gesamtkunst* and Mallarmé's *grimoire* Symons derived his own theatre of the soul", Randall tells us;[19] and, fresh

from his Wagner-experience at Bayreuth, Symons made his first
attempt to write for the stage. His primary focus by the turn of the
century had turned to theatre, and much of his vision was
foreshadowed by (again) that article on *Parsifal* in *The Dome*.[20]
Symons's ideal was a synaesthetic, quasi-religious theatrical experience in which all elements would contribute to a single artistic
and spiritual effect. Movement would be stylized and the human
personalities of the actors removed in so far as possible. Words
would be spoken only when essential and then only in the form of
poetry. "I do not see why people should ever break silence, on the
stage, except to speak poetry", Symons wrote. Perhaps he was
echoing Mallarmé's dictum, "Words are only of value as a notation
of the free breath of the spirit." In any case the influence of
Mallarmé's static ideal, and of Maeterlinck's wish to create
"drames pour marionettes", is clear in Symons's theory. The
essential difference between it and those of the French Symbolists
may be ascribed to admiration for Wagner that actually exceeded
theirs: "Here's the picture completed, awaiting only, for its ideal
presentment, the interpretative accompaniment of music, which
Wagner will give it." Symons regarded music as the proper
completion of the ideal theatrical art. Here he parted company with
Mallarmé, who was finally more a worshipper of the Word than a
synaesthetist and wanted music fully incorporated into poetic
speech once again.[21]

At the same time as he was propounding his dramatic theory,
Symons was also translating works by Gabriele D'Annunzio.
D'Annunzio was a devoted Wagnerian who, well before George
Moore or Thomas Mann, had begun to make use of Wagner in the
novel. Symons was among the first in England to note this fact. He
was particularly impressed with D'Annunzio's treatment of the
Great Love Story in *Trionfo della Morte*; and, in his introduction to
the translation of *The Child of Pleasure*, he strayed from his topic to
praise it:

> *Antony and Cleopatra, Tristan and Isolde*: it might have seemed as if
> nothing new could be said on a subject which is the subject of
> those two supreme masterpieces. But D'Annunzio has said
> something new, for he has found a form of his own, in which it is
> not Antony who is "so ravished and enchanted of the sweet
> poison" of the love of Cleopatra, nor Tristan who "chooses to die
> that he may live in love", for the sake of Isolde, but two shadows,

who are the shadows of whatever in humanity flies to the lure of earthly love. Here are a man and a woman: I can scarcely remember their Christian names, I am not even sure if we are ever told their surnames; and in this man and woman I see myself, you, every one who has ever desired the infinity of emotion, the infinity of surrender, the finality of possession. Just because they are so shadowy, because they may seem to be so unreal, they have another, nearer, more insidious kind of reality than that reality by which Antony is absolutely Antony, Tristan so absolutely heroic love. These live in themselves with so intense a personal or tragic life that they are for ever outside us; but the lovers of *Trionfo della Morte* might well be ourselves, evoked in some clouded crystal, because they have only so much of humanity as to have the desires, and dangers, and possible ecstasies, and possible disasters, which are common to all lovers who have loved without limitation and without wisdom.[22]

Symons thought of himself as one who had "loved without limitation and without wisdom", with Lydia. This had been the primary theme of his creative efforts as a Decadent poet, "Mundi Victima" being a fine example. The Beardsley sketch and musical notation introducing that poem encouraged us to identify its speaker with Tristan. And here again in this introduction to *The Child of Pleasure* we are encouraged to identify (besides ourselves) Symons with Tristan, as with the tragic lover of *Trionfo della Morte*.

It was with the background of such identifications that Symons came to apply his newly acquired theory of Symbolist drama to the Great Love Story. His *Tristan and Iseult* was conceived after the 1898 journey to Bayreuth and composed in 1902–3 after another trip to the Continent, which included an experience of *Tristan* at the one theatre outside Bayreuth that had incorporated Wagner's design, the Prinzregententheater in Munich. This was also the time of publication of *Plays, Acting, and Music*, a "book of theory" on theatre which opened with the article "Nietzsche and Tragedy" and ended with "Notes on Wagner and Bayreuth".[23] Nietzsche's adolescent favourite of Wagner's works was clearly Symons's primary inspiration for his own attempt at the drama. He probably also consulted Wagner's source, the mediaeval epic of Gottfried von Strassburg, which had recently been translated into English by Jessie Weston.[24] Arnold's Tristan poem and Tennyson's idyll (which Weston described in her preface as "incomparably the worst version of the story ever written") were probably of less interest to Symons than

Tristram of Lyonesse, whose creator Symons had long admired. Like Swinburne's poem, Symons's play has the two Iseults;[25] and in some respects Symons's work follows Swinburne's in matching the English versions of the tale better than Wagner's. Still, Symons's preference is indicated by a statement he was to make in his "Beethoven" essay: "There are poems of Swinburne which attempt to compete with music on its own ground, *Tristram of Lyonesse* for example, and they tire the ear which the music of Wagner's *Tristan* keeps passionately alert" (*W*, IX, 133).

We might suppose from this comment that Symons's intention in his own *Tristan* was not to compete with music but rather, like Maeterlinck, to try to achieve through the artifices of Symbolist drama the effect Wagner had achieved through music. If so, then we might ask what led him to believe that his drama could escape the deficiency he implied was to be found in *Pélleas* when he made the comment that *that* drama had only become successful on stage once completed by Debussy's music (*W*, IX, 185). Indeed, in undertaking his Symbolist drama, Symons seems to have disregarded both his instinctive scepticism of the Mallarméan emphasis on the power of the Word alone, and his belief stated in the article for *The Dome* that only through the final touch of music did the ideal theatrical art become complete. Perhaps Symons entertained hope that some Debussy would appear to transform his mere words into a Wagnerian finished product. No doubt he envisioned some sort of music to attend production, something spare like that which Yeats was conceiving for his plays perhaps. Even so, considering his accurate intutition that Symbolist drama was largely doomed without music, his undertaking seems less a careful artistic calculation by the critical intelligence which had produced *The Symbolist Movement* than an act of wish-fulfilment by the Decadent lover and aesthete of the early 1890s.

This is not to say that Symons does not bring some new insights and a characteristic intensity to his subject. Indeed, the metaphysical significance of Iseult's words at one point resonates beyond that of Wagner's *Liebesnacht* to that of the Kiss which stands at the centre of *Parsifal*,[26] and demonstrates a perception of the paradoxical nature of passion much like that expressed in Nietzsche's famous remark, "People actually kiss that which plunges them . . . into the abyss":[27]

> Tristan, it is my life
> Your lips drink up: I cannot bear your lips:

> I feel them to the marrow of my bones.
> O I would be a fire and burn your lips,
> O I would be a beast and eat your lips,
> I would annihilate their sweetness. Now
> My blood is all an anguish of desire.
> Speak, slay me, do not kiss me. Kiss me now!
>
> (*W*, vi, 62)

Further, the play has many arresting dramatic moments – the one at the end of the *Liebesnacht*-scene for instance, in which King Mark reappears in a righteous rage and breaks Tristan's sword over his knee, an act calling to mind the confrontation between Wotan and Siegfried. But in the best moments even Symons's originality is called into question by suggestions of D'Annunzio and Maeterlinck.[28] And over the whole work hovers the inescapable question of how the playwright, without the resources of music, could hope to add anything to the scenes of passion which Wagner had so memorably portrayed. Symons in short, however talented, could not match in mere words Wagner's *Liebestod*. Nor had he much chance even to match Swinburne's final discursus on Fate, in which his predecessor's long lines – for all their prolixity and straining after the musical effect – had done an admirable job of depicting the heave of the waves, the movement of the brooding skies, and the cosmic resonances of the tragedy.[29]

THE WAGNERIAN CRITIC

The love-potion that drives one mad, the immortal passion of a Tristan – these pieces the seventy-five-year-old Symons would still be trying to fit together to form the myth of his career.[30] A few years after the writing of *Tristan and Iseult* he was to go mad indeed. In the meantime, however, he was still sustaining himself with the worship of Art he had arrived at in the period of *The Symbolist Movement*. As a critic the Edwardian years found Symons in his prime. His scope included all the obvious arts and some others as well. His ideals – Symbolist, Wagnerian and synaesthetic – were clearly defined. His prose sounded the Paterian music (as times perhaps even a little too rhapsodically). One commentator of the period described him as a Baudelairean critic,[31] and this he surely was, though not so self-consciously so as he was to become in the 1920s. He ascribed to

Baudelaire's doctrine of the correspondence of the arts and applied it frequently; he wrote in the personal and impressionistic manner that had characterized *Richard Wagner et "Tannhäuser" à Paris*; and he quoted from that book frequently, his favourite phrase being: "It would be prodigious for a critic to become a poet, and it is impossible for a poet not to contain a critic."[32] Inasmuch as Baudelaire had used this phrase to justify Wagner's theorizing (and inasmuch as Baudelaire's most important theoretical work was itself about Wagner), it might have been more accurate for the commentator to have described Baudelaire as a Wagnerian critic, and Symons one as well. In Symons's case, at any rate, the designation seems apt.

His most important book of the decade was *Studies in Seven Arts* (1907) and the most extensive essay in it "The Ideas of Richard Wagner". This essay begins by recommending Baudelaire's study, which "said the first and last word on many of the problems of Wagner's work" (*W*, IX, 150). It then proceeds to paraphrase and condense the major ideas of Wagner's *Artwork of the Future* and *Oper und Drama*, contending that:

> Everything else in his theoretical writing is a confirmation, or a correction, or (very rarely) a contradiction, of what is to be found in these two books; and their thorough understanding is essential to any realization of why Wagner did what he did. (*W*, IX, 154)

The assertion does not seem altogether accurate. Symons had probably not studied Wagner's prose works by the time he wrote the *Parsifal* article for *The Dome*; but that article, so brief yet so full of insightful discovery and original thought, demonstrates what seems ample instinctive understanding of "why Wagner did what he did". The essay in *Studies in Seven Arts* certainly offers more of Wagner's ideas, and in much more readable form than to be found in Wagner's own prose; but the scholarly approach required a sacrifice of the sort of personal excitement that had characterized Symons's earlier piece. Only towards the end of the essay, when he leaves off paraphrasing and talks about Wagner in general terms, does Symons begin to give an idea of the enormous non-rational and evocative power of Wagner's music over him. "Music cannot think, but she can materialize thoughts," he quotes in a phrase calling to mind that picture of Mallarmé composing poems on unrelated subjects while the Wagnerian orchestra "dictated" (*W*, IX, 174).

"Music, [Wagner] shows us, blots out civilization like sunlight blots out lamplight" (*W*, IX, 189).

Such a blotting-out could not fail to appeal to an artist who remained essentially the anti-bourgeois, world-weary Decadent at heart; and at the end of the Wagner essay Symons was moved to conclude, "At the beginning of the twentieth century, may we not admit that the typical art of the nineteenth century, the art for which it is most likely to be remembered, has been the art, musical and dramatic, of Richard Wagner?" (*W*, IX, 195). In the essay which followed, "The Problem of Richard Strauss", Symons criticized Wagner's successor for what amounted to an attempt to reverse this process of "blotting-out". Strauss has a propensity to explain his music programmatically: to say, "Here you see Zarathustra ascending the mountain"; or, "Here you see *der Held* vanquishing his carping critics." This destroys the impulse to that Mallarméan free-association to which music should naturally give birth. It is not only in programme-notes that Strauss does this but also in the music itself, which is constructed as a web of allusions and demands that the listener pay strict attention, often with the result that he seems to be listening to a collection of footnotes: "He is able, it is true, to convey something approximating an idea; but it is conveyed, after all, by association of ideas, not directly, and is dependent on something quite apart from the expressive power of the music itself" (*W*, IX, 200). Strauss's allusive technique makes an appeal to the intellect that can catch and arrange the quotations. It does not appeal to the emotions and "materialize" the type of mystical reverie that the equally allusive prelude to *Parsifal* can:

> Turn from the opera music of Strauss to the opera music of Wagner, and what is the result? I play twenty pages of the piano score of *Feuersnot*, and as I play them I realise the immense ingenuity, the brilliant cleverness, of the music, all its effective qualities, its qualities of solid construction, its particular kind of mastery. Then I play a single page of *Parsifal* or of *Tristan*, and I am no longer in the same world. That other flashing structure has crumbled into dust, as if at the touch of an Ithuriel's spear. Here I am at home, I hear remote and yet familiar voices, I am alive in the midst of life. I wonder that the other thing could have detained me for a moment, could have come, for a moment, so near to deceiving me.   (*W*, IX, 212–13)

RETURN TO DECADENCE

This opinion sheds an interesting light on Symons's own aesthetic myopia. His creative ideal was to produce emotional ecstasy, like that of Verlaine's poetry or Wagner's music. And, while his poetry was also allusive in its way, its allusions were no more intended to stand out from the whole and be regarded as such than the echoes of Mendelssohn and Liszt and his own earlier works in Wagner's *Parsifal*. The poet steals, he does not borrow, as Eliot would say. Strauss's method is like the Poundian method Eliot would use in *The Waste Land*: an arrangement of allusions which stand out distinctly and demand some degree of individual recognition before the work as a whole can be fully understood. This method creates a more intellectual and mechanical, less impressionistic and emotive effect than the one Symons admired. The distinction explains not only Symons's resistance to the Modernist method he perceived in Strauss; but also the increasingly obsessive preoccupation with nineteenth-century art and inability to "*MAKE IT NEW*", to use Pound's phrase, by which Symons could be led in the 1920s to cite Kipling and Henley and a few other equally conventional rhymers as the best poets of the day, while completely ignoring the author of *The Waste Land*.[33]

Symon's "Beethoven" essay, which immediately precedes the Wagner and Strauss essays in *Studies in Seven Arts*, begins with a reference to Wagner and appears to be to some extent a summary of Wagner's own 1870 study of his German predecessor, a work which Symons found one of Wagner's most appealing. The summary, like those in the Wagner essay, reveals little of significance about Symons's own aesthetic. But one subsequent comparison between Beethoven's music and Wagner's provides a revealing insight on the metamorphosis of the Romantic ideal in the course of the nineteeth century:

> The animal cry of desire is not in Beethoven's music. Its Bacchic leapings, when mirth abandons itself to the last ecstasy, have in them a sense of religious abandonment which belongs wholly to the Greeks, to whom this abandonment brought no suggestion of sin. . . . In the music of Wagner's Venusberg we hear the cry of nature turned evil. Pain, division of the soul, reluctance, come into this once wholly innocent delight in the drunkenness of the senses; and a new music, all lascivious fever and tormented and

unwilling joy, arises to be its voice. But to Beethoven nature was
still healthy, and joy had not begun to be a subtle form of
pain.   (*W*, IX, 131–8)

The idea implied here is like the one suggested by the finale of
"Mundi Victima": that the abandonment of the self to a free-flying
spirit which is such a joyful process in Shelley has become for the
Decadent Romantic an abandonment to a supernatural demon –
Folly, a spirit who can only lead to inevitable destruction.

In this expression of the idea, as in "Mundi Victima", we can see
the type of split that characterizes the vision Wilde is led to by the
overture to *Tannhäuser*: Classical Beauty, followed hard upon by the
destruction of one who has abandoned himself to that "Amour de
l'Impossible". In this expression, as in "Mundi Victima", Symons
himself appears to have perceived clearly that the plunge into the
depths of passion, the Wagnerian Venusberg and Baudelairean
other world of "evil" and the supernatural, is destructive: an
abandonment of real joy, a self-condemnation to an existence of
"burning burning" – that subtle form of pain which rendered
Swinburne's knight frenzied and insomniac. One might have
expected Symons, having perceived the danger so clearly, to have
shed some of his intense devotion to the Wagnerian disposition and
to have moved towards a more technical appreciation of more
rational forms. But Symons was still the Decadent, still one who
adhered to the Paterian dictum that the artist must *feel* with the
burning intensity of the "hard gem-like flame". This is finally
Symons's hubris, and that of all Decadents: to long for that type of
joy which is a "subtle form of pain", to want to "kiss that which will
destroy him". And, though Symons appears to have understood
what Ellis had written that Nietzsche had recognized at Bayreuth –
that the Wagnerian alchemy of music and passion could be terrible
and destructive – he would not recoil as Nietzsche had.

MADNESS

The fact is that at the time he was finishing these essays for *Studies in
Seven Arts* Symons was again approaching the doom towards which
he had seemed to be drawing in the 1890s when Wagner and Yeats
and the religion of Symbolist art had intervened. At that time music
seems to have provided a balm for him, to have performed the

curative function that Wilde ascribed to it. Now however it seems to have begun to perform the opposite function: to hasten the listener towards the abyss:

> The sounds torture me: I see them in my brain;
> They spin a flickering web of living threads,
> Like butterflies web of living threads,
> Nets of bright sound. I follow them, in vain.
> I must not brush the least dust from their wings:
> They die of a touch; but I must capture them,
> Or they will turn to a caressing flame,
> And lick my soul up with their flutterings.
>
> (*W*, II, 223)

This poem gains impact because it has the autobiographical veracity that "Mundi Victima" did not: the doom *was* approaching, the music *was* tormenting him. The following summer Symons stopped for a few days in Venice. He was on his way to Rome, where he hoped that, with Eleanora Duse willing, he would at last have his *Tristan* performed. But, there in the city where Wagner had written the last act of *Tristan* and had died two decades later, the sounds of music came to torment Symons more fatally:

> The gondoliers' hoarse shouting comes violently through the music. Two or three phrases, poignant and piercing, monotonous and profound, rise suddenly out of the luminous night of waters. It was this cry that Wagner heard from the balcony on that fortunate night when he found the melody for his shepherd's pipe. Inspiring, disconnected scraps of song, harsh expressive voices, abrupt pauses and repetitions, but with a strange fantastic beauty; songs that decorate and illumine the night, cries out of the depth of the secret heart of Venice, songs instinctive and remote, melancholy and passionate, what strange and obscure secrets you conceal![34]

So Symons was to recall in the chronicle of his madness. The description continues: images of "crimes and carnality" flash across the man's mind; of dark dungeons against which the waters strike with "a monotonous plash"; of chains, of bars, of prisons, of "odious beauty", of acts of cruelty. The images come in a fury as he hears the sounds of music, the rhythms of the great city of decay which

English poets such as Byron and Browning and fictive heroes such as the lover of *Trionfo della Morte* had known so well. Hellish visions come with the music. Then, suddenly, the victim is wandering, crazed as the unforgiven Tannhäuser on his way back from Rome, through the Italian *campagna* which he found so beautifully captured in the novels of D'Annunzio. Vagrant, he is arrested, manacled, thrown into a dungeon which, by his account, held terrors exceeding that of any normal prison, and a filth no doubt exceeding that of the English jails which Wilde had complained of in his *De Profundis*.[35] There he goes mad. And his madness intensifies so that, for some time after his release, he is helpless and incoherent; shut away in institutions and expected to die, as Nietzsche had died, after a few years of wasting frenzy.

Perhaps posterity would have viewed Symons as the martyr/ *voyant* he styled himself had he too "passed beyond our sight" as a madman. Symons, however, clung to life. He recovered and lived on to brandish his experience of madness, comparing himself now and again to Gérard du Nerval, reliving Decadent "memories and desires", writing impressionistic "studies" of great artists he had known, and publishing previous unpublished works with the encouragement of John Quinn (the American patron now best remembered for his help to the Modernists of the Pound era). Old works thus published included *Tristan and Iseult*; also a collection entitled *Lesbia and Other Poems*, most of which were inspired by Symons's original beloved, Lydia. The name given this collection was derived from the heroine of Swinburne's long "novel", *Lesbia Brandon*, the story of another Decadent *femme fatale* with whom Symons apparently saw his own merging. Whether in the form of Iseult or Lydia, Swinburne's Lesbia or Venus or Faustine, Rossetti's women or Baudelaire's,[36] this female was to dominate Symons's imagination throughout his later years. And hovering not far behind her seem always to be Wagner's fiery Venusberg and its decadent goddess: the pagan Venus who is transformed at the end of the career into the part-Spanish, part-Oriental, inscrutable Kundry.

CONCLUSION

Symons's major critical book of the later years was *Charles Baudelaire, a Study*. This ends with ostentatious mention of the fact that

Swinburne's autographed copy of *Richard Wagner et "Tannhäuser" à Paris* has been sitting icon-like on Symons's desk throughout his work. Symons's study contains one of the most apt demonstrations of how the obsession of his later years tended to synthesize the various Decadent fantasies over which his mind had lingered; and to distort, while at the same time bringing strange flashes of critical insight to, the critical investigation at hand. From discussion of the young Baudelaire's travels (which he is probably in error to assume reached their originally intended desination of India)[37] Symons drifts into this reverie:

> Certainly his imagination found in the East a curious fascination, with an actual reawakening of new instincts; and with that oppressive sense of extreme heat, as intense, I suppose, as in Africa, which makes one suffer, bodily and spiritually, and in ways more extraordinary than those who have never endured those tropical heats can possibly conceive of. There he may have abandoned himself to certain obscure rites that to him might have been an initiation into the cults of the Black Venus. And, with these hot suns, these burning midnoons, these animal passions, the very seductiveness of the nakedness of bronze skin, what can I imagine but this: that they lighted in his veins· an intolerable flame, that burned there ardently to the end?
>
> For in his *Wagner* (1861) he writes: "The radiant ancient Venus Aphrodite, born of white foam, has not imprudently traversed the horrible darkness of the Middle Ages. She has retired to the depths of a cavern, magnificently lighted by the fires that are not those of the Sun. In her descent under earth, Venus has come near to hell's mouth, and she goes, certainly, to many abominable solemnities, to render homage to the Arch-demon, Prince of the Flesh and Lord of Sin." He finds her in the music where Wagner has created a furious song of the flesh, with an absolute knowledge of what in men is diabolical. "For from the first measures, the nerves vibrate in unison with the melody; one's flesh remembers itself and begins to tremble. *Tannhäuser* represents the eternal combat between the two principles that have chosen the human heart as battle-field, that is to say, of the flesh with the spirit, of hell with heaven, of Satan with God."[38]

There are echoes of many old and new interests of Symons's career: of Blake, of the mediaevalism of Wagner and the Pre-Raphaelites and Yeats, of the Eastern fascinations of the Parnassian French, of the self-exile of Rimbaud to African mysteries, of the rank heat of Conrad's *Heart of Darkness* and his Malayan jungles,[39] to name but a few. With a symphonic sweep of his impressionistic imagination, Symons manages to harmonize these all into an ominous motif that had been sounding in the work of others of the last Romantics: the subtle attraction of the jungle, of primitivism, of decay – the very motif, complete with Eastern jungle imagery, which had lured Mann's synthetic representative of the European artist of the age to his destruction in that city whose name sounds so much like Venus.

Such passages often reveal more about the critic than about his subject; and Symons's later criticism was dismissed by Modernists as dated, eccentric, undependable. Still, for his early critical works he merits a central place in our study: *The Symbolist Movement in Literature*, with its emphasis on the importance of Wagner to the French; *Plays, Acting, and Music* and *Studies in Seven Arts*, with their Wagnerian celebrations of the composite artwork and the Symbolist theatrical ideal. Symons should further be noted for his efforts to promote an atmosphere in literary London of the 1890s like that which the Wagnerian French had generated in Paris in the 1880s – this through his editorship of *The Savoy*, his evenings of aesthetic discussion at Fountain Court, and his tireless investigation of foreign developments in all the arts. Symons's efforts provided important encouragement to the Wagnerian novel-writing of Moore and the Symbolist theorizing of Yeats. He himself, moreover, provided a dramatic model of the old Decadent for the Modernists of a later generation. Throughout his life and art, Symons remained fascinated with the Wagnerian types of the neurotic-yet-beautiful Venus and the Tristan longing for love-death. These fascinations led him not only to certain beautiful but ill-advised experiments in his art (the attempt at English Symbolist drama in *Tristan*), but also to a pathetic denouement in madness and nostalgia in his life. As in the case of Nietzsche (or perhaps more accurately that of Ludwig II of Bavaria), Symons demonstrated an acute case of that tendency latent in many Wagnerians to that kind of sickness which is brought on by increasingly intolerable contrast between the real world and an ideal vision awakened by music and High Art. In this respect above all Symons must be reckoned as an important predecessor to the author of *The Waste Land* – a poem built, as we shall see, on this typical *fin-de-siècle* motif.

5 Shaw

Shaw styled himself as something of a Decadent when the English Decadence was at its height. He could write a letter showing a passion to play the wounded lover worthy of an Arthur Symons:

> Miserable, ill-starred woman, what have you done? When my need was at its highest, my weariness at its uttermost, my love at its holiest, I found darkness, emptiness, void. I cannot believe now that we shall ever meet again. Years have passed over me – long solemn years: I have fallen in with my boyhood's mistress, Solitude, and wandered aimlessly with her once more, drifting like an unsatisfied moon. Tears have fallen from my heart. . . .[1]

But Shaw had little taste for lingering in such Shelleyan dejection. And, when he wrote to the same woman in this vein thirteen years later, it was clear that he had lapsed into a playful moment of nostalgia and was being for the most part facetious: "I am . . . a relic of a bygone phase of affectation marked by Yellow Books, Keynotes novels, Beardsley, John Lane and other dusty relics of the day before yesterday."[2] Such remarks were not characteristic of Shaw, not even to this onetime "beloved", Florence Farr. Most of his letters to her were filled with lectures on how to speak properly on stage, and admonitions to clear her mind of her "psaltery" and the other "fresh artificialities and irrelevances" in which Yeats was simultaneously encouraging her.[3] Shaw was as fascinated as Yeats with the timbre and pitch of the actress's voice, and would cast her in his plays with such considerations in mind. Still, the "musical" speech which he saw as proper was not the mystical ideal sought by his more Francophile contemporaries.

Decadent aesthetics were never wholly congenial to Shaw.[4] He was the most outspokenly Wagnerian man-of-letters of his day, but his plays did not exhibit the poetical type of Wagnerism of Symons's *Tristan* or Wilde's *Salomé*. With his compatriot Wilde Shaw shared a liking for the fantastic, and the "artificialities" of the comedy-of-

manners. But, after Wilde fell and the Decadent bubble burst, Shaw
did not join in the progress towards a Symbolist movement in
English towards which Wilde's theoretical pronouncements
harked. Perhaps this was because Shaw had not begun his career as
a poet, and looked to Ibsen and Turgenev as foreign precursors
rather than to the French. In any case, while Symons and Yeats
were applying Symbolist theory to English drama, Shaw developed
predominantly in the direction towards which his juvenile novels
had tended: towards Symbolism's theoretical antithesis,
Naturalism. To consider Shaw in this study then is to leave the 1890s
and their Decadent/Symbolist experiments for the most part
behind, and to consider Wagner and literature from the point of
view of a maverick whose great moment was the Edwardian era. We
shall look at the relationship of Wagner to Shaw's public persona,
his philosophy, his plays, and his politics. No study on specifically
these subjects has been written. William Beard's thesis "*John Bull's
Other Island*" makes some interesting indications about the use of
Wagnerian method in one of Shaw's plays. Other sources which I
have found helpful include Sir Oswald Mosley's article "Wagner
and Shaw: A Synthesis", and the observations of Katharine Worth,
who has recently published *The Irish Drama of Europe from Yeats to
Beckett*.

YOUNG SHAW AND HIS WAGNER

Hesketh Pearson's official biography of Shaw, closely supervised by
the aging playwright, seems to share with the autobiography
Wagner dictated to his wife at an equally advanced stage in his
career the calculated lack of objectivity of a successful artist
concerned with his "myth". Still, it provides an authoritative
account of the facts of Shaw's early years. His mother, unhappy in
her marriage to a "drunken teetotaller", retreated into study of
music under G. J. V. Lee, a vocal enthusiast with a variety of
advanced interests and unconventional theories.[5] From this surrogate father the young Shaw derived not only his vegetarianism
and habit of sleeping with the windows wide open, but also his love
of music. Art took the place of religion for the Irish boy, and music
the premier place among the arts. In particular Shaw was attracted
to Beethoven and Mozart, whose *Don Giovanni* he learned by heart;
also to Gounod's *Faust*, for he delighted in "the sardonic vein of

Mephistopheles". The youth was "opera mad", and took up piano in order to accompany himself as he sang the vocal scores he had saved up to buy. One of these was *Lohengrin*. The purchase of this score in his nineteenth year constituted Shaw's introduction to Wagner. Presumably the libretto was in English; for, as Shaw confessed to Pearson years later, he could never learn foreign languages.

Music was the prime interest the young man took to London when his family moved to that city in the late 1870s. The interest was quickly joined by one in literature and one in politics. The first led Shaw to write five novels between 1879 and 1883, all of which failed to be published; the second to his celebrated founding role in the Fabian Society. Politics became the prime interest by the mid-1880s. Through it Shaw developed friendships with (among others) the future Theosophist Annie Besant, the aging Pre-Raphaelite William Morris, and the theatre critic and Ibsen-translator William Archer. Archer's impression of Shaw in the reading room of the British Museum sums up the thirty-year-old's dialectic of interests: "[He] read Marx's *Das Kapital* in the intervals of studying the orchestral score of *Tristan und Isolde*."[6] By the later 1880s music had regained sufficient primacy in the dialectic for Shaw to take up writing music criticism for *The Star*, under the pseudonym Corno di Bassetto. In 1890 he moved on to *The World*, where, under his own initials, he wrote the same for four more years – that is, until he had his first *succès d'estime* as a playwright with *Arms and the Man*, produced through the patronage of Miss Annie Horniman, a fellow-Wagnerian and also patron to the young Yeats. In 1894 Shaw moved on to become drama critic for Frank Harris's *Saturday Review*. There he stayed until 1898, by which time playwriting had come to occupy his full attention.

As a music critic Shaw aggressively espoused the cause of Wagner, lambasting not only the philistines who did not accept the "music of the future", but also many of those who did for what he regarded as the wrong reasons. He recommended the journal of the London Wagner Society, *The Meister*, to his readers and considered the translations of Wagner's *Prose Works* by its editor to be "admirably done". At the same time he criticized that journal, as he likewise criticized the Bayreuth Wagnerians, for "an evident indisposition to provoke hostility . . . an indisposition to which the Meister himself was not at all subject".[7] The impression of Wagner as above all an agitator runs throughout most of Shaw's writing on the subject. And in one of his final pieces as a music critic he painted a picture of the *Meister* as a Daniel trapped in a world of philistine beasts – a quasi-psychological explanation for why Wagner had become this agitator type:

> I have seen Richard Wagner, who was so vehemently specialized by Nature as a man of genius that he was totally incapable of anything ordinary. He fought with the wild beasts all his life; and when you saw him coming through a crowded cage, even when they all felt about him as the lions felt about Daniel, he had an air of having his life in his hand, as it were, and of wandering in search of his right place and his own people, if any such there might be. When he had nothing else to do he would wander away to the walls and corners, apparently in search of some door or stairway or other exit from the world, not finding which he would return disconcerted, and either sit down in desperation for a moment before starting off on a fresh exploration, or else – being a most humane man – pet one of the animals with a little conversation.[8]

An alien artist whose genius both justifies and stimulates malcontent and abnormal behaviour – this was Shaw's Wagner; not the "artist of decadence" whom Nietzsche had depicted as happily ensconced amid fawning disciples at Bayreuth. Yet, no less than Nietzsche's, this picture tells as much about the psychology of the author as of his subject.

Shaw's Wagner was a moderately humane manic Siegfried trying to hammer his way out of Mime's cave and onward to his destiny: the Wagner who could say, "My business is to make revolution wherever I come!"; not the Wagner who would confess that, as a revolutionist, he was "involved in error".[9] Shaw combated the silk-dressing-gowned version of Wagner generally offered by the popular press, and played down those qualities so often noted by Decadents: the Tristan-like suffering, the impulses to erotic and Christian love, the Buddhistic longing for peaceful transcendence. Shaw propagandized the side of Wagner he wanted to see – so much is evident from a comparison of Wagner with his favourite English Romantic, Shelley, in an article for the *Fortnightly Review*:

> Shelley and Wagner were arch-voluptuaries . . . in whom intense poetic feeling was the permanent state of consciousness; nevertheless they were indifferent to most of the pleasures of the

senses. They were apostles of water-drinking and vegetarianism; had an utter horror of violence and sport.[10]

Indifference to the pleasures of the senses, vegetarianism, aversion to alcohol – the facets of personality emphasized here, as in the case of the Daniel characterization of Wagner, so closely match facets of Shaw's own personality that it seems almost as if the budding playwright, not yet fully assured of his own stature, were saying, "Look here, I am the same type as these great ones, Shelley and Wagner!" The idea gains credence when we consider it in the light of another early linking of Shelley and Wagner. This occurs in the most overtly Wagnerian of all Shaw's creative works, one of those unpublished novels, *Love among the Artists*.[11]

The hero of *Love among the Artists* is a young composer, Owen Jack, whose *avant-garde* works meet with an opposition from the Establishment much like that with which Wagner's had met. Jack himself is a revolutionary who alienates his superiors and demands from his orchestras more than they are willing to give. His *magnum opus* is a Wagnerian rendering of Shelley's *Prometheus Unbound* which, like *Tristan und Isolde* at Vienna in 1859, is destined to be abandoned as too unconventional and difficult. Only after interminable rehearsals and cancellations is the work produced; the audience reacts with a mixture of philistine indifference and jeering; and the composer storms from the theatre in triumphantly defiant protest. In Jack's revolutionary *opus*, drawing as it does on Shaw's two favourite Romantic precursors, we might see a foreshadowing of what the young writer himself wished to create; likewise in Jack a glimpse of the type of artist he aspired to become. Clearly Shaw's attitude towards Shelley and Wagner at this early stage in his career partook of idolization of "artist-fathers". At a later stage, when he came to write *The Perfect Wagnerite* in 1898, Shaw had become sufficiently confident of his own artistic stature to take both precursors to task.

AGAINST LOVE

Pearson tells us that Shaw's object in writing his essentially political study was "to prove Wagner a sound Shavian".[12] To be a "sound Shavian", as would become increasingly evident in the mature Shaw's plays, was to be not only a Fabian socialist but also a believer in the quasi-Darwinian doctrine of "the Life Force".[13] To the extent that Shelley and Wagner anticipated that doctrine, Shaw accorded them praise in *The Perfect Wagnerite*. What he now criticized them for were the final messages of their *magna opera*:

> *Prometheus Unbound* is an English attempt at *The Ring* . . . Both works set forth the same conflict between humanity and its gods and governments, issuing in the redemption of man from their tyranny by the growth of his will into perfect strength and self-confidence; and both finish by a lapse into panacea-mongering didacticism by the holding up of Love as the remedy for all evils and the solvent of all social difficulties.[14]

With Shelley Shaw was willing partially to excuse this "lapse" into Love because of the poet's youth; also because he regarded Shelley's brand of Love as "a sentiment of affectionate benevolence that has nothing to do with sexual passions". With Wagner however Shaw was not so lenient, for he saw Wagner's brand of Love as calculatedly erotic:

> Wagner sought always for some point of contact between his ideas and the physical senses, so that people might . . . feel them through the infection of passionate emotion. Dr Johnson kicking the stone to confute Berkeley is not more bent on common sense concreteness . . .   (*PW*, 65)

Though normally the champion of "common sense concreteness", Shaw disapproved of this manifestation of it. The eroticism of the music which finishes *Siegfried* and resounds throughout *Götterdämmerung* is "expressed with a frankness and forcible naturalism which would possibly have scandalized Shelley". Further,

> It is clear enough that such love as that implied by Siegfried's first taste of fear as he cuts through the mailed coat of the sleeping figure on the mountain, and discovers that it is a woman; by her fierce revolt against being touched by him when his terror gives way to ardor; by his manly transports of victory; and by the womanly mixture of rapture and horror with which she abandons herself to the passion which has seized on them both, is an experience which it is much better, like the vast majority of us, never to have passed through, than to allow it to play a more than recreative holiday part in our lives.   (*PW*, 66)

The mature Shaw was in many respects as prudish as his late-Victorian bourgeois audiences. In *The Perfect Wagnerite* this Shaw went on to maintain what he had intimated in that *Fortnightly Review* comparison of Shelley and Wagner: that Wagner himself was essentially just as prudish too:

> It did not play a very large part in Wagner's own laborious life, and does not occupy more than two scenes of *The Ring. Tristan and Isolde*, wholly devoted to it, is a poem of destruction and death. *The Mastersingers*, a work full of health, fun and happiness, contains not a single bar of love music that can be described as passionate. . . . *Parsifal* makes an end of it altogether.
>
> (*PW*, 66–7)

As a counterbalance to the popular view of Wagner as an "arch-voluptuary", this argument may have had merit; so too the pointing-out of the strong puritan strain throughout Wagner's works, particularly the later ones. On the whole however, the argument must seem exaggerated and one-sided. The two "passionate" scenes in the *Ring* in question are presumably the love-duets between Siegmund and Sieglinde in the first act of *Die Walküre*, and between Siegfried and Brünnhilde in the last act of *Siegfried*. But what about the duets between Siegmund and Sieglinde in the second act of *Die Walküre*, and Siegfried and Brünnhilde at Daybreak in *Götterdämmerung*? The fact is that passion stands behind almost every scene in the *Ring* from the one in which Alberich tries to catch a Rhinemaiden all the way to the one in which Gutrüne poses her love for Siegfried against that of Brünnhilde. Thus the serious reader of *The Perfect Wagnerite* must realize that, whatever the merits of Shaw's reading of the *Ring* as an anarchist/socialist allegory, his overall view of a "sound Shavian" Wagner is based on a loaded anti-Romantic argument.

Shaw dismissed the ideology of the *Ring* after the second act of *Siegfried*; at which point, he contended, Wagner lapsed back into non-philosophical grand opera. This famous contention is the subject of Mosley's essay on Shaw and Wagner.[15] Like Chamberlain before him, Mosley takes the view that *Parsifal* represented the natural completion of the allegory begun in the *Ring*;[16] and he opines that if Shaw had perceived this he could not have dismissed the third act of *Siegfried* and *Götterdämmerung* so facilely. According to Mosley, Wagner recognized while composing *Siegfried* that a hero possessing a fearless will alone was insufficiently equipped to succeed in the world, and thus would be doomed to the sort of tragic end Siegfried comes to in the land of the Gibichungs. To succeed, a hero must possess, beyond a fearless will, a divine intimation of Love. It is this that allows Parsifal to distinguish the treacherous intentions of Klingsor and Kundry, where Siegfried could only fall victim to those of Hagen and Brünnhilde; and that gives Parsifal's journey a goal from the first, where Siegfried's never had any greater purpose than the testing of his will. *Götterdämmerung* thus, far from being mere grand opera, is the crucial transition piece in a larger continuum: as the flames burn the body of the hero on whom the world's salvation depended, the orchestra offers the theme of Love in explanation of what was lacking in the old hero which must be sought in the new. In this way is anticipated the coming of the second hero: *Parsifal* come to resolve the tragic chaos of the *Ring*.

Nowhere does Shaw show sympathy for this concept of love which Mosley and others regarded as so essential to Wagner's philosophy. Of the ultimate message of the *Ring*, it is only in life that Shaw could put faith: "The only faith which any reasonable disciple can gain . . . is not in love, but in life itself as a tireless power which is continually driving onward and upward" (P*W*, 67). Of *Parsifal* Shaw was laudatory; but he seems to have found its metaphysic obscure: "This *Parsifal* is a wonderful experience. . . . The impression it makes is quite independent of liking the music or understanding the poem. Hardly anybody has the slightest idea of what it all means."[17] At heart what Shaw may have found uncongenial was the idea of Love as self-transcending sympathy, which Wagner had first espoused in *Tristan* and for which Schopenhauer had provided the philosophical definition:

This can occur because *another* can actually become the final concern of *my* willing – as I am myself its usual concern: that is to say, because I can desire *his* weal and suffer *his* woe as acutely as though they were my own. But this necessarily presupposes that I can actually participate sympathetically in *his* pain . . . as otherwise only my own. Which, in turn, demands, however, that I should for a certain time become *identified with him*: demands, that is to say, that the final distinction between me and him, which is the premise of my egoism, should, to some degree at least, be suspended. And since I am not actually *in the skin* of that other, it can only be through my *knowledge* of him, his image *in my head*, that I can become to such a degree identified with him as to act in a way that annuls the difference between us[18]

Parsifal carries the knowledge of Amfortas's pain in his head throughout his journey through the waste lands; at the crucial moment of the kiss, when he cries out "Amfortas!", he becomes identified with his precursor; in this manner he makes Amfortas the sole concern of his willing, as Tristan and Isolde have made each other the sole concern of theirs. This metamorphosis of Will into Love is one of the things which that devout proponent of the Will, Nietzsche, had found repellent in Wagner. And Shaw appears to have followed Nietzsche in this, as in other opinions.

No doubt Shaw saw Wagner's brand of love as akin to that vague Romantic spiritualism which, whether expressèd in Baudelaire's *Fleurs du mal* or Wilde's reveries on "Amour de l'Impossible", seemed only to hasten the Decadents towards the abyss. In any case, such love cannot be found in Shaw's mature works. When we look for it in his lovers, we quickly discover that these are no longer lovers of the Romantic type – rather, characters with rational affections for one another. We find no merging of identity, no eclipsing of the self to make another the concern of one's willing. As a matter of fact, we usually find self-conscious resistance of Jack Tanner to Ann in *Man and Superman*, for instance, which is based on outspoken suspicion of Romantic love. Such suspicion is perhaps justified in the all-too-human "real" world through which Shaw moves his mortals. In order to achieve distinction in such a world, they must develop invulnerable and single-minded wills; and what character bent on developing such a will can afford to loose himself into self-transcending passion? Thus, in place of Romantic affairs, Shaw's "lovers" engage in relationships: teacher and student like Caesar and Cleopatra, messiah and disciple like Dubedat and his wife, master and servant like Tanner and (as he might have it) everyone else. Relationships based on the need of one party for an exemplar and the other for an admirer, one for art and the other for money, and so forth – these in the end are the anti-Romantic Shaw's types of "love".

PLAYS: WAGNERIAN BRIC-À-BRAC AND ASPIRATION

Considering the divergence of Shaw and Wagner on ultimate matters, it should not be surprising to find that the relevance of

Wagner to Shaw's plays is often superficial. We find bric-à-brac here and there: a timely mention of a Wagner-performance in *Mrs Warren's Profession* (1894),[19] a fanciful assessment of Wagner's place in the history of art in *Fanny's First Play* (1910). We find also minor and usually ironic parallels between Shaw's characters and Wagner's, as in the Tanhäuser identifications in *Overruled* (1912). It is rare to find a more ambitious attempt at producing a Wagnerian character or situation. One case may come in *The Philanderer* (1893), where Wotan figures in the original description of Charteris (*P*, 32); and, like Wotan, Charteris has terrible arguments with his mate; and, like Wotan ànd Fricka, the two talk about swearing oaths (*P*, 34); and, like the *Ring* in general, there is much concern about Old and New Orders in the finale (*P*, 60). Another case may come at the start of *Caesar and Cleopatra*, where Caesar rushes on stage in front of the sphinx and declares himself to be a wanderer, a fugitive and a stranger to the race of men in terms reminiscent of Siegmund (and to a lesser extent of Wotan). This tempts one to look for further parallels as the play develops. Perhaps such parallels exist; if so, I have not found them. Possibly Shaw intended some development at the outset which he later abandoned. More likely the Wagnerian motif came to his mind when he was pondering how to achieve the desired heroic effect in his introduction, and he used it in a manner that might be designated an imitation more properly than an allusion.

The most arresting instance of such imitation is the death-speech of Louis Dubedat in *The Doctor's Dilemma* (1906). This Shaw lifted almost verbatim from a story about a dying musician which the young Wagner had written at the nadir of his fortunes in Paris:

I believe in God, Mozart and Beethoven, and likewise their disciples and apostles; – I believe in the Holy Spirit and the truth of the one, indivisible Art; – I believe that this Art proceeds from God, and lives within the hearts of all illumined men; – I believe that he who once has bathed in the sublime delights of this high Art, consecrate to Her for ever, and never can deny Her; – I believe that through this Art all men are saved, and therefore each may die for Her of hunger; – I believe that death will give me highest happiness; – I believe that on earth I was a jarring discord, which will at once be perfectly resolved by death. I believe in a last judgement, which will condemn to fearful pains all those who in this world have dared to play the huckster with chaste Art, have violated and dishonoured Her through evilness of heart and ribald lust of the senses; – I believe that these will be condemned through all eternity to hear their own vile music. I believe, upon the other hand, that true disciples of high Art will be transfigured in a heavenly fabric of sun-drenched fragrance of sweet sounds, and are united for eternity with the divine fount of all Harmony. – May mine be a sentence of grace! – Amen![20]

Shaw shortens this speech and, as Dubedat is a painter, substitutes the names of great painters for Mozart and Beethoven. On the basis of this clear connection we might go on, as E. B. Adams does, to regard Shaw's most fully developed artist-hero as a picture of Wagner as well as of Edward Aveling, the contemporary artist usually cited as the model. To support this theory Adams compares Dubedat's opinions and behaviour to other pieces in Wagner's *A German Musician in Paris*, and the argument is persuasive.[21] Dubedat is not an effete decadent, but a ruthless and dedicated artist: an alien in his world of beastly doctors and philistines, a man of single-minded will, a believer in the Shavian creed. In short, Dubedat is a logical development of the Wagnerian type Shaw had portrayed in Owen Jack and described in his early critical writings.

In Shaw's longer and more ambitious plays, he seems to have been consciously trying to match the great metaphysical epics of his favourite Romantics. *Heartbreak House*, written during and about World War I, has been called Shaw's *Götterdämmerung*; and it is filled with the type of lamentation, death-wishing and attraction to destruction that characterizes that drama of the *Ring* which Shaw had formerly dismissed as grand opera. We can see this particularly in the finale, where the characters collect on the porch of a Sussex country-house to watch fire-bombs burning in the distance. As Katharine Worth has pointed out, *Heartbreak House* demonstrates a debt to Wagner and grand opera throughout. The close of Act I, for instance, attempts an operatic effect: it is "a regular trio". It is no accident either that in Act II Hesione draws Mangan out into the garden, remarking that there is moon and that it is like the night in *Tristan und Isolde*. "Shaw and Wagner were alike in moving from 'brave new world' optimism to attacks on the decadent Establishment," Worth says; "and the *Tristan* allusion in *Heartbreak House* points up the debasement of the romantic ideal which is so ironically presented throughout the play."[22]

Two others of Shaw's most important plays, *Man and Superman*

(1903) and *Back to Methuselah* (1921), set out to present in detail the Shavian counter-creed to the Love of *Prometheus Unbound*, the *Ring* and Romanticism in general. In the dream section of *Man and Superman* Shaw's Don Juan rejects the sensual pleasures of Hell for the puritan philosophizing of Heaven – an act which the Devil, himself the consummate aesthete, compares to the rejection of Wagner by Nietzsche:

> THE STATUE:. . . . Who in the deuce is [Nietzsche]? . . .
>
> THE DEVIL: Well, he came here first, before he recovered his wits. I had some hopes of him; but he was a confirmed Life Force worshipper. It was he who raked up the Superman, who is as old as Prometheus; and the 20th century will run after this newest of the old crazes when it gets tired of the world, the flesh, and your humble servant.
>
> THE STATUE: Superman is a good cry; and a good cry is half the battle. I should like to see this Nietzsche.
>
> THE DEVIL: Unfortunately he met with Wagner here, and had a quarrel with him.
>
> THE STATUE: Quite right, too. Mozart for me!
>
> THE DEVIL: Oh, it was not about music. Wagner once drifted into Life Force worship, and invented a superman called Siegfried. But he came to his senses afterwards. So when they met here, Nietzsche denounced him as a renegade; and Wagner wrote a pamphlet to prove that Nietzsche was a Jew; and it ended in Nietzsche's going to Heaven in a huff. And good riddance too.   (*P*, 389)

Thus, in Shaw's Dante-like scheme, Wagner is placed in an *inferno* of all-too-pleasant non-philosophical aestheticism. At the same time, Nietzsche along with what Shaw regarded as the best of Wagner's ideas, Siegfried and his will and the derivative cult of the Superman, is placed in an ascetic *paradiso*. Thence Shaw, in his persona of Don Juan, ascends to ponder extensively on the Life Force.

The eventual result is *Back to Methuselah*. In this cycle of plays the creed of the Life Force achieves the status of dogma; and aestheticism and passion are looked on as ludicrous signs of weakness, and parodied with a vengeance. Thus the ritual in the Temple of the Oracle in Act III of *The Tragedy of the Elderly Gentleman*, with its resonances of *Parsifal* and the Mass and Symbolist drama, degenerates quickly into a farce. The pair of Romantic humanoids whom some young artists-of-the future creates in *As Far As Thought Can Reach*, Ozymandias (Shelley again presumably) and Cleopatra, behave with absurd pretensions that lead to disaster and proceed quickly to a death orchestrated by mock-passionate music and *Tristan*-like outbursts such as "How could either of us live without the other?"[23] These things give Shaw's spokesmen, the long-lived all-wise Ancients, their perfect opportunity to lecture the young on the follies of art and passion. Thus, having rejected such typical Wagnerian motifs (and most moral activities other than philosophizing), Shaw ends his *magnum opus* with a soliloquy by Lilith, goddess of the Life Force itself. In this he reiterates the governing idea of the plays, and of his career: that, no matter what may happen from one human epoch to the next, Life will keep on *ad infinitum*. Commentators have suggested that Lilith is a version of Wagner's Erda, and that *Methuselah* as a whole is Shaw's answer to the *Ring*. This may be so. But, with its lack of sympathy for the Romantic metaphysic of Love and its persistent focus on that one semi-Darwinian idea in which Shaw could "put faith", this cycle of dramas seems to have little more in common with Wagner's than the fact that it too constitutes a world-historic epic.

UNENDING DRAMA

While Shaw's plays mock that type of Romanticism which had reached its apotheosis in Wagner, his dramatic theory and achievement developed in a way not at all dissimilar to those of his youthful idol. As we have noted, Shaw had sufficiently little of the Paterian in him to compose with the poetical/musical intent which distinguished *Salomé* or Yeats's *Shadowy Waters*. Still, music remained the premier art for the mature dramatist as much as it had been for the "opera-mad" youth, and Shaw conceived his art as "a music of ideas"; or, as Edmund Wilson puts it, "a music of moralities".[24] Shaw focused his action and dialogue around one central idea, weaving all other ideas into it, harmonically as it were, in a manner analogous to the system of *Tristan* whereby all elements are developed around the *Sehnsuchtsmotiv*. Shaw gave lengthy metaphysical speeches on the subject of his central idea, arias of a kind, to his Tanners and Caesars and other principle spokesmen, in a manner which certainly bears relation to Wagner's technique with Wotan.[25] In general, Shaw showed great daring in bringing the metaphysical idea to the forefront of an essentially Naturalistic theatrical genre, which in the hands of Pinero and others had been more simply designed to entertain. The example of Wagner, with Ibsen, was Shaw's inspiration in this. But even as he did it, Shaw was diverging from his precursor in a crucial way.

Where Wagner had carefully calculated his form so as to bring the *Sehnsuchtsmotiv* to musical and dramatic resolution in the *Liebestod*, Shaw conscientiously abjured such calculation and brought his central ideas to no absolute conclusions. Where the Life Force of the *Ring* meets with opposing forces of destruction and disappears in the end but as a vague hope of some future awakening, the Life Force of *Back to Methuselah* progresses without meeting any serious opposing forces throughout Shaw's cycle and reveals itself in the end to have the same constant vitality that it had in the beginning. Here lies the revolutionary uniqueness and perhaps weakness of Shaw's art: as his idea of the Life Force was endless, so too his dramas of ideas became endless. The theory was that, after "unending melody", why not unending drama? The problem, which Shaw with his virtuoso skills in dialogue often successfully transcended, was that the very nature of drama – Art, not Life – is to build towards a conclusive ending. Liberated from the traditional concept of an ending, it becomes possible for drama to drift, as Mahler's unending symphonies of Shaw's same post-Wagnerian era sometimes seem to drift, towards the shoals of endless tedium; and, indeed, while many *avant-garde* Edwardians were eager to acclaim Shaw as "the Great Liberator" of drama, some critics with a longer perspective came to regard him in some respects as drama's great enemy. "The new anarchy of construction is all very well when it liberates a Shaw; it is not at all well when it liberates half-baked disciples of that master and pretenders to a new gospel of cosmic message."[26]

So one commentator was to observe from the perspective of the 1930s. By that time Shaw's success had reached truly Wagnerian proportions. Years of lionization by Granville-Barker and others at the Royal Court had allowed Shaw an artistic licence comparable to that which Wagner had enjoyed in Ludwig II's Munich. Productions of his plays at the Malvern Festival looked to be leading towards the annual Shaw Festival on the Bayreuth model for which H. V. Nevison and other disciples were calling.[27] The German translations of Siegfried Trebitsch had made Shaw's plays well known in central Europe, and by 1929 they had become so sought-after on foreign stages that *The Apple Cart* was premiered in Poland. Still, it could be said of Shaw the dramatist, as of Wagner the musician, that the revolution he had started, because of its spurning of ultimately desirable traditional forms, was running swiftly towards excess, confusion, dead-end. Shaw himself would say this about Wagner. And it seems altogether fitting (and was probably amusing to the lifelong disciple of Nietzsche) that, just as there had been those who had prophesied that the Great Liberator of melody would lure European artists-of-the-future into an "unending sea" where they would lose their footing, so too there were modern Cassandras who proclaimed that the Great Liberator of English drama would lead young English dramatists-of-the-future "on the rocks".

SOCIALISM TO THE DICTATORS

"In company with Shelley, Wagner, and Ibsen, I was a social reformer and doctrinaire first, last, and all the time", Shaw commented to his biographer.[28] He was never content to be an artist alone, and saw his type as blessed with special powers of prophecy and insight, heir to Shelley's principle that the poet is "the unacknowledged legislator of mankind". Wagner, who had been driven from Ludwig II's Munich largely because of suspicions that he was directing the King's policies, had arrived at the same Shelleyan principle independently:

> Where the statesman despairs and the politician is helpless, where the socialist torments himself with impracticable systems, and even the philosopher can only interpret, never foretell, because the phenomena before us can only display themselves in an unconventional form, not to be brought evidently before the senses, the clear eye of the artist will discern the forms by which the desire for what alone is true, his desire for humanity, will be fulfilled.[29]

The position was common enough among artists of the greater period we are discussing. We have seen it in Wilde, will see it again in Yeats, and will see it begin to decay and be transformed in Lawrence and Eliot. The case of Shaw provides an obvious instance of it, as Shaw was an early Fabian and lifelong socialist. Shaw's brand of socialism was, like Wagner's, grounded in a concept of romantic individualism peculiar to this type of artist: an eccentric and paradoxical brand of socialism which perhaps had found its best expression in Wilde's "The Soul of Man", a work Shaw admired and tried to convince his Fabian brethren to publish, along with Wagner's "Art and Revolution" and Morris's *News from Nowhere*.[30]

Throughout their careers both Shaw and Wagner engaged in polemicizing, often at risk to public acceptance of their art. Both had two periods of particular activism, the first in their thirties, the second in their final phase of development. Wagner's revolutionary pamphlets of the early 1850s and Shaw's Fabian speeches of the 1880s belong to the first period, while Wagner's more extreme pronouncements of the *Bayreuth Blätter* and Shaw's idealization of the dictators to the second. In general it might be said that both were concerned with bringing on a bright new socialist day in the first period, and on uprooting a decadent Establishment in the second. Both experienced a progression, related to a deterioration of faith in human nature, from optimism in the first to cynicism in the second. Both continued to use the rhetoric of socialist revolution, replacing Old Orders with New, and combating the related evils of democracy and international capitalism and cultural decadence throughout their careers. According to Chamberlain, Wagner found the root-causes of decadence to be: (1) money and property; (2) deterioration of blood; and (3) influence of meat-eating and alcohol.[31] Shaw agreed in large part with the first, thus was a socialist; in some part with the second, thus was a proponent of eugenics; in full with the third, thus was a vegetarian and teetotaller. Shaw was the first of the artists we are discussing to stand in serious opposition to the pan-European phenomenon of Decadence, thus to be in accord with that Nietzschean side of Wagner which believed in what Chamberlain refers to as "a doctrine of regeneration".[32]

Thus the similarities. The differences betweeen Shaw's politics and Wagner's derived principally again from the incompatibility of "Life" and "Love": Shaw's anti-Romantic realism and Wagner's Romantic utopianism. Wagner's social vision was ever that of the creator of *Lohengrin* and *Parsifal*; his impulse to bring the "real" world into focus in his ideas was largely limited to recognition of the new force of the emancipated Jews in European life; and race-theory became the central feature of his politics as a result. Shaw's social vision was by contrast that of the creator of *Widower's Houses* and *Major Barbara*; and his impulse to found his ideas on the facts of "real" life led to a broad knowledge of social conditions as demonstrated in those plays, the willingness to compromise demonstrated by his adherence to Fabian "gradualism" through most of his career, and the suspicion of utopianism of any sort demonstrated by his criticism of that vague millenial communism believed in by Wagner and other precursors of the mid-century.[33] Shaw recognized that such yearnings had neither the economic nor organizational strength to succeed. He was simply a more serious socialist than Wagner. His socialism did not veer off into fanatical nationalism. Nor did he share with Wagner, nor with Yeats, who must be seen as a good Wagnerian in this respect, the impulse to romanticize his homeland and its *Volk*. And, though he shared the artist's belief in the cult of individual genius, he did not entertain romantic dreams of the Good King like the Wagner of *Lohengrin* or Wilde of the fairy-tales.

For Shaw such visions were those of silly amateurs. His own belief could only be posited in a socialist oligarchy based on merit. Only when he saw that fail before his eyes with the Ramsay MacDonald governments did he determine that the credible alternative was an individual of ruthlessness and efficiency: Siegfried, not Parsifal, transformed into the twentieth-century man-of-action, the dictator – Mussolini, Stalin, Hitler. In a passage of his biography which was no doubt Shaw-inspired, Pearson indicates just how much this attraction to the dictators grew out of respect for the flamboyant, no-nonsense, artist-*cum*-reformer persona Shaw had cultivated for himself as a young man:

> In literary London . . . Shaw seemed a unique and scandalous phenomenon, whereas, having assimilated Marx and Henry George, anticipated Ibsen and Nietzsche, and taken his fellow-townsman Wilde seriously, he was simply in the forefront of a revolution in morals. This had not as yet seized political power in Germany, Italy, Russia and Turkey, nor incidentally stained its triumphs by shedding oceans of blood and by innumerable blunders and ineptitudes. Nowadays, up against Lenin and Stalin, Hitler and Mussolini, Ataturk and Rhiza Khan, Shaw seems a very harmless old gentleman.[34]

Harmless old gentleman as he may have seemed to Pearson and himself, the aging Shaw was, in many of his pronouncements, even more that ruthless agitator type, modelled on his Wagner, than he had been as a young man. And in this connection we might valuably ask whether Wagner himself, with his belief in Love and his Schopenhauerianism and his conviction that in the end politics was "quite fruitless",[35] would have gone nearly so far as Shaw in enthusiasm for the dictators. Certainly it is fair to assume that Wagner would have approved the idea of suppression of the Jews, which struck Shaw as counter-productive.[36] But in general it seems that, like Yeats, Wagner would soon have wearied of fascist agitations and retreated to the "ivory tower" of the music-room at Wahnfried.

Shaw's active interest in the dictators on the other hand continued largely unabated through the 1930s. Later, while the Holocaust was in full progress, he would be met in Hyde Park carrying a volume of *Mein Kampf* and comparing it to Calvin's *Institutes*, Marx's *Capital* and Smith's *Wealth of Nations* as an "epoch-making" work.[37] Some might wish to find the origins of this enthusiasm in the avidity with which a younger Shaw had read Wagner's *Prose Works* in the 1890s, or the favour with which he had reviewed Chamberlain's *Foundations of the Nineteenth Century* in 1911.[38] More properly, I think, it should be attributed to the disillusionment the apparently "realist" Fabian had suffered through years of watching "gradualism" fail to achieve its objectives. In his vision of socialism in England Shaw seems in fact little less of a idealist than Symons in his vision of Symbolist drama in England. And, once Shaw's ideal vision had been shattered, he like Symons began to veer off in an unsocial and unfortunate direction. Improbable as the comparison might seem, Shaw's highly personal political creed of the 1930s shares with Symons's defiantly unmodern aestheticism of the same period marks of a kind of breakdown: a breakdown resulting from the impact of a youthful Wagnerian dream against an all-too-human modern reality.[39]

CONCLUSION

Shaw's Methuselah-like longevity allowed him to observe the reactions to Wagner over even more decades than this study covers. His 1935 introduction to the collected music criticism he had written as Corno di Bassetto offers a memorable summation of the changes in those reactions, both in general and in Shaw himself:

Only his early works were known or tolerated [then]. Half a dozen bars of *Tristan* or *The Mastersingers* made professional musicians put their fingers to their ears. The Ride of the Valkyries was played at the Promenade Concerts, and always encored, but only as an insanely rampagious curiosity. The *Daily Telegraph* steadily preached Wagner down as a discordant notoriety-hunting charlatan in six silk dressing-gowns, who could not write a bar of melody, and made an abominable noise with the orchestra. In pantomime harlequinades the clown produced a trombone, played a bit of the pilgrims' march from *Tannhäuser* fortissimo as well as he could, and said "The music of the future!" The wars of religion were not more bloodthirsty than the discussions of the Wagnerites and the Anti-Wagnerites. I was, of course, a violent Wagnerite; and I had the advantage of knowing the music to which Wagner grew up, whereas many of the most fanatical Wagnerites (Ashton Ellis . . . was a conspicuous example) knew no other music than Wagner's, and believed that the music of Donizetti and Meyerbeer had no dramatic quality whatever. . . .

Nowadays the reaction is all the other way. Our young lions have no use for Wagner the Liberator. His harmonies, which once seemed monstrous cacophonies, are the commonplaces of the variety theatres. Audacious young critics disparage his grandeurs as tawdry. When the wireless strikes up the *Tannhäuser* overture I hasten to switch it off, though I can always listen with pleasure to Rossini's overture to *William Tell*, hackneyed to death in Bassetto's time. The funeral march from *Die Götterdämmerung* hardly keeps my attention, though Handel's march from *Saul* is greater than ever. Though I used to scarify the fools who said that Wagner's music was formless, I should not now think the worse of Wagner if, like Bach or Mozart, he had combined the most poignant dramatic expression with the most elaborate decorative design. It was necessary for him to smash the superstition that this was obligatory; to free dramatic melody from the tyranny of arabesques; and to give the orchestra symphonic work instead of rosalias and rum-tum; but now that this and all the other musical superstitions are in the dustbin, and the post-Wagnerian harmonic and contrapuntal anarchy is so complete that it is easier technically to compose another *Parsifal* than another Bach's Mass in B Minor or *Don Giovanni* I am no longer a combatant anarchist in music, not to mention that I have learnt that a successful revolution's first task is to shoot all revolutionists. This means that I am no longer Corno di Bassetto.[40]

As a young man Shaw determined to see Wagner as the social agitator, the Great Liberator of musical forms, the creator of Siegfried and proponent of the will; not as the exponent of the Romantic "Love-panacea", the Schopenhauerian renouncer of Will, the silk-dressing-gowned Decadent, the precursor of Symbolist "fog", or indeed most of those things the *Meister* had been considered to be by Shaw's contemporaries of the 1890s. Thus self-deceived, Shaw aspired to be the type of artist he had defined in this Wagner. As a dramatist he modelled his forms after the composer's "unending melody". He called his works "dramas of ideas" rather than of "situations".[41] And, like Yeats, to whom in most respects he must be seen as an antipode, he took on the Wagnerian attitude that the theatre was a quasi-religious institution; even agitated for a theatre in England on the model of Bayreuth. However, as the twentieth century progressed, the aging Shaw, ever concerned with moving "onward and upward" (which meant further and further from all attachments to the nineteenth century), became more strident in his opposition to Romantic aestheticism and passion, and something less of a "violent" Wagnerian as a result.

Shaw succeeded in the ambitions of the creator of Owen Jack, and no doubt the example of his Wagner helped along the way. Shaw, however, was not a great literary Wagnerian in the style of most of those we are discussing. He was not primarily a poet; nor a stylist of Mallarméan/Paterian "musical" type; nor a synaesthetist critic in the manner of Baudelaire, Swinburne, Wilde, Symons, Moore or Yeats.[42] Shaw made no serious attempt to penetrate ancient legends in the manner of Wagner and most of these others, nor to adopt the mythic voice except in a style which attached evidently to the bourgeois accents of his chosen country.[43] Nor did Shaw share in the pervasive Schopenhauerian yearning for detachment from Life and retreat into the High Art of "l'art pour l'art". That he was a political Wagnerian is open to question, and a philosophical Wagnerian to serious debate. Still, to the extent that he was these things, and a literary Wagnerian after an idiosyncratic style, we might call him a Wagnerian of a second type: one who much like Nietzsche eschewed Decadent Romanticism, and claimed Wagner as his "sound Shavian" precursor in a tradition of "heroic vitalist" art and idea.[44]

6 Moore

As a young man George Moore went to Paris to become a painter. After a few years he decided to turn his talents to writing instead and published two volumes of poetry, *Flowers of Passion* (1878) and *Pagan Poems* (1881). Both of these owed much to *Les Fleurs du mal*. So much is evident from the titles of the first and of a number of poems in the second: "Spleen", "Ode to a Beggar Girl", "À une poitrinaire", "A Parisian Idyll", "Sappho", "The Corpse", and so forth. The poems also have imagery in common with the Pre-Raphaelites, as can be seen in the following lines, which might have been inspired by a Hughes or a Waterhouse:

> With linkèd hands we went
> Unto the tiny lake of mountain born,
> And bathed unwatched amid the flowers.
> She was a vision of voluptuousness,
> And o'ver the water streamed her wondrous hair.[1]

Much of the imagery also anticipates that of the Symbolists: moons floating amid the leaves, stars appearing between the clouds, the weary tune of fountain waters.[2] As we have seen, such *Pélleas*-like atmospherics owed much to Wagner, particularly the Wagner of the *Liebesnacht*. Moore had met French Wagnerians such as Villiers de l'Isle-Adam by this time, but apparently knew little of Wagner himself. Still, the spirit of Wagner is omnipresent. Significantly, considering the mix of Wagner and Catholicism which Moore was to make in his most overtly Wagnerian experiment, *Evelyn Innes* (1898), we should note the Parsifalian merging of passion and spirituality in "Ginevra" in *Flowers of Passion*, a playlet set in a "ruinous" old convent full of mysterious music and the songs of nuns.

Moore's poems were contemporary with Wilde's and occupied much the same place in a career which, after their publication, developed along lines not dissimilar to Wilde's for some years. In

1880 Moore moved to London. There he busied himself writing
Naturalistic novels and critical articles on French subjects. These
included beyond Naturalism, Impressionism, "Les Décadents" and
À rebours. The influence of Huysmans's novel was apparent in the
successful memoir of his days in Paris, *Confessions of a Young Man*,
which was published in London in 1888 and also serialized in Paris
by Edouard Dujardin's *Revue indépendente*. The Moore of *Confessions*
was still not "rotten with Wagnerism";[3] but he had so thoroughly
adopted the style of the French as to claim that Schopenhauer had
provided "the philosophy of the book", and to refer to the Wagner
sonnets of Mallarmé and Verlaine. The latter's "Parsifal" he
quoted in full, saying of it:

> In English there is no sonnet so beautiful. . . . The hiatus in the
> last line ["Et, ô ces voix des enfants chantant dans la coupole!"]
> was at first a little trying, but I have learned to love it. . . . The
> charm is that of an odour of iris exhaled by some ideal tissues, or of
> a missal in a gold case, a precious relic of the pomp and ritual of
> the arch-bishop of Persepolis.[4]

Also in 1888 Moore published a novel, *Spring Days*, in which "an
experience of *Tristan and Isolde* force[d] its way through the
surface".[5] This was the first of Moore's many prose representations
of Wagner performances. It is similar to such passages in Mann's
early novels, only delivered in a tone of aesthetic rapture rather than
ironic detachment. So much was typical of this perennial enthusiast.
After *Spring Days* Moore became a full-blown literary Wagnerian –
as William Blisset pointedly puts it, "The rudderless skiff of Moore's
prose enter [ed] the Wagnerian whirlpool."

Moore was to go on to apply Wagner to the novel more
systematically than any other writer in English. As Blisset indicates,
Moore's experiments were often more bold then successful; and we
shall discuss them more briefly than similar experiments in the
epoch-making works of James Joyce, which benefited from them. In
this chapter we shall take up Moore's Wagnerian theory of the
novel, various instances of that theory at work, and finally,
indications of the similarities between Moore and Joyce. Some of
these similarities have been touched on by Blisset in "George Moore
and Literary Wagnerism", the pioneer work on the subject.
Richard Cave's recent *Study of the Novels of George Moore* also covers
much of the material contained in this chapter, which Cave read in

thesis form in 1976. Cave emphasizes the Wagnerian achievements of *The Lake* and *The Brook Kerith*, which he considers to be Moore's masterpiece. I have dealt with these later novels more briefly as a result.

A WAGNERIAN NOVEL IN THEORY

The beginning of the 1890s found Moore continuing to write Naturalistic novels and articles on French art. But by then the grip of Wagner was firmly upon him: "Wagner's operas are now my great delight and relaxation. I daresay I do not understand but what does that matter?"[6] Asides about Wagner crept into articles ostensibly about painting, sometimes threatening to take them over and obliging the author to apologize before returning to the designated topic.[7] As a critic Moore had developed a synaesthetic point of view and tastes like Baudelaire's. A description of Wagner coming from this period sounds as if inspired by one of Baudelaire's passages on the great French "colourist", Delacroix:

> Wagner was the greatest of colourists; his palette was . . . rich in sunset crimson and prophetic gold, nostalgic azure, eager pink, clear and sudden greens. . . . He cannot enchant us with pure line, like Ingres; he cannot construct like Michael Angelo; he can only heap colour upon colour.[8]

Further on in the same article Moore commented, "Wagner reminds me of the dark-eyed Bohemian who comes into a tavern silently, and, standing in a corner, plays long, wild, ravishing strains . . . ." In this he might have been giving an impression of the taciturn Baudelaire himself, ready to recite a melodious "flower of evil" to the café literati. Clearly this fanciful Wagner of Moore's is far from the revolutionary agitator and artist of the Will whom Shaw was simultaneously promoting. Alien to bourgeois convention, this Wagner is nevertheless no neurotic Daniel trying to claw his way out of a lion's den; he is an alien of a traditional type as old as the gypsy, the Wandering Jew, the mediaeval troubadour.

This Wagner of Moore's was the inscrutable Bohemian so dear to café poets from Baudelaire's youth in the 1840s to the 1870s, when Verlaine was *prince des poètes* and Moore an aspiring young Irish artist in Paris. This Wagner was Romantic and French in the manner Nietzsche derided; evoked by a reverie "after *Parsifal*", not socio-political exegesis of the *Ring*. This Wagner, as Moore pictured him in an 1897 article for *The Musician*,[9] was also a divinely blessed *literary* dramatist. At his nativity a good fairy had promised that he would be the greatest writer of all time. But then a jealous black fairy had come along and rendered him unable to write; so the good fairy returned and blessed him with "the gift of expression . . . the musical power." Wagner's musical genius was the result of a stifled literary impulse, Moore thus contended. And, with an enthusiasm comparable to that of the Bayreuth devout,[10] he went on to claim that, at least in *Parsifal*, Wagner was a greater story-teller than Shakespeare. Indeed, Wagner was such a first-rate literary dramatist that the entire *Ring* would surely make a successful play spoken in the original German verse, *without* the music!

From Wagner as a great literary artist to Wagner's art as a great literary model is not an enormous leap; and, by the time he came to write this article, Moore had begun to make it. In an age in which music was considered the highest of the arts, several novels about music had been attempted. None, however, according to Wagner critic and biographer Ernest Newman elsewhere in *The Musician*,[11] had successfully captured the "psychology of the musician himself". There was Tolstoi's "Kreutzer Sonata", but it was imperfect. There were Balzac's stories "Gambara" and "Massimilla Dona", which were well done; but they were fifty years old. Of contemporary works in English of any merit there was only Stanley Makower's *The Mirror of Music*, a story of "a young girl in whom there is hereditary music-madness, and who conceives all her experience under the form of music". Newman's article summed up the challenge confronting the novelist of the day who might wish to write a music-novel. No doubt Moore read it – *The Musician* was a small magazine with which Moore was associated throughout its brief career. No doubt it encouraged him that he was embarked on a milestone work in his Wagnerian novel, *Evelyn Innes*.

In an "interview" in one of the final issues of *The Musician*[12] Moore took up the subject of music and literature himself and stated his intention to create a new form of novel, no longer purely Naturalist, but psychological. One of his models was Dujardin, with whom he was corresponding frequently and of whose Wagnerian novel he was to write, "In *Les Lauriers* you have discovered *the* form, the archetypal form, the most original in our time; but the psychology is a little 'naturalist'."[13] Another major model was

D'Annunzio, whose work Moore had recently discovered, through Symons probably. In the "interview" in *The Musician* Moore praised the Italian's psychological technique: "He has revived [psychology]. In mid-century the soul was forgotten for the spectacle of things of which man had once been the centre; in naturalistic literature man's soul was adrift in the stream of things." This Baudelairean antipathy for "things" (Naturalist reality and bourgeois materialism) and predilection for intense psychological investigation into the individual "soul", combined with the "exquisite fluidity of the execution", were the respects in which D'Annunzio's art so closely resembled Wagner's. Moreover, D'Annunzio had adapted a vital technique:

I think I see in it an attempt to write by means of motives. Flaubert has done this, but he did it unconsciously. D'Annunzio has done something to systematize this new method. And I do not see why literature should not partake of the musical art of Wagner. . . . Wagner was the first musician who marauded literature, but in the middle of the century the habit of the novelist was to maraud the territory of the painter; naturalistic literature chose the most objective of the arts; the psychological novelist will chose the most subjective music. In D'Annunzio the bias is very decided. The very artifice [leitmotiv] which I depreciate as a violation of the border he employs unhesitatingly. Although we are told very little about the personal appearance of the woman in "L'Intrus" we are constantly referred back to her pallor – she is as pale as a chemise . . . then she is pale as the wall against which she is leaning; further on she again becomes pale as her chemise; then she is as pale as muslin; later still you can only distinguish her hands from the sheets by the blue veins; the comparison is again varied, and he finally returns to the original key – she is pale as her chemise. The employment of such a trick by a less skilful writer would be intolerable, but I do assure you that D'Annunzio saves himself. . . . Never once did I regret the repetition of the phrase, so exquisitely is it used – just in the right place, just at the right moment it comes in, like the love motive of the Valsungs – always exquisitely modulated, suggesting or completing the sensation . . . .

The blue vein might call to mind the blue vein which stands out from the temple of Detlev Spinnel when he is excited in Mann's *Tristan*; or the modulation of the repeated phrase describing O'Connor's nervous rolling of his cigarettes in Joyce's "Ivy Day in the Committee Room". Certainly both Mann and Joyce would attempt in such early tales to perfect the technique which Moore recognized here in D'Annunzio. It may well be the most serviceable technique that any writer was to adapt from Wagner's music to literature; and, if D'Annunzio was the first novelist to "systematize" it,[14] Moore was the first to do so self-consciously in English. This he did most apparently in *Evelyn Innes*, but in gestures grander yet than those of his Italian model. The example of the "pale chemise" cited from "L'Intrus" is a small descriptive motif, rather like the drag-footed marching phrase by which Wagner characterized Mime. Regarding the "employment of such a trick by a less skillful writer . . . intolerable", Moore judiciously left it for artists-of-the-future like Joyce. For his own use he took that larger type of Wagnerian motif which, like Alberich's curse or the *Sehnsuchtsmotiv* or Amfortas's pain, is no mere descriptive emblem but rather a central psychological *motive*-force. Coyly at the end of his "interview", Moore revealed to readers of *The Musician* that the major motifs of his soon-to-be-published music-novel would be the heroine's conflicting loves for her father, her lover and her art; also the "motive of destiny".

A WAGNERIAN NOVEL IN PRACTICE

As a music-novel *Evelyn Innes* is flawed. In spite of his consultations with Arnold Dolmetsch, Moore remained ignorant of many technical matters.[15] Thus the first chapter ends with a description of "wailing chords" from Mr Innes's virginal; and, as Blisset points out, who has ever heard "wailing chords" from a virginal?[16] Of course, if one is not a trained musician such incongruities can easily be overlooked; and in respect to Moore it is surely more significant *what* is being played than *how*. The "wailing chords" Mr Innes induces from his virginal are those of a sacred motet from Vittoria; and his comment to his daughter, "That is where Wagner went for his chorus of youths in the cupola", is the Parsifalian note on which the first chapter ends.[17] Thus Moore's most extended Wagnerian outing begins. "Moore uses Wagnerian parallels [in *Evelyn Innes*] as often as James Joyce was to use Homeric parallels [in *Ulysses*],"

Blisset tells us; "but without Joyce's appearance of system."[18] I
disagree. True, there is no chapter-by-chapter system like the one
by which Joyce would make the Citizen into the Cyclops, or Bella
Cohen's brothel into Circe's den. Still, there is an obvious
overarching system of parallels in Moore's novel: to the chronological development of Wagner's *oeuvre*.

At an early stage Evelyn is like Senta, a young woman living with
her doting father, through whom the man of her dreams is
introduced into her life. Her response to this man is much in the
spirit of Senta's response to the legendary Dutchman: "Though he
represented to her the completely unknown, she seemed to have
known him always in her heart; she seemed to have been waiting for
knowledge of this unknown and the rumour of the future grew loud
in her ears" (*E*, 14). Fittingly this "Dutchman", Sir Owen Asher,
has a yacht; and, on one occasion when he is off cruising, Evelyn,
Senta-Like, dreams of him "borne on top of a huge wave, clinging to
a piece of wreckage, alone in the solitary circle of the sea". When
Asher returns from his actual uneventful Mediterranean cruise,
Evelyn tells him of this dream; he is unimpressed; and not long after
the *Dutchman* parallels fade to be replaced by those to *Tannhäuser*.
From a superficial point of view Evelyn's association to Wagner's
second major work is made by the fact that she begins studying the
role of Elisabeth. From a psychological point of view the significance is that she is now confronted with the Tannhäuser-dilemma
herself: whether to elope to the Continent with Asher and become
an opera-star, or stay at home with her father and the devout
Catholicism of her girlhood. For some time she is suspended, her
Venusberg alternative represented by amorous trysts, her Elisabeth
alternative by the life of the nuns whom she visits. Finally, rather
more like Swinburne's knight than Wagner's, she opts for the
Venusberg; and the nuns fade away like the song of Wagner's
pilgrims:

> The nuns! Strange were their renunciations! For they yielded the
> present moment, which Owen and a Persian poet [presumably
> the Sufi, Hafiz] called our one possession. She seemed to see them
> fading in a pathetic decadence, falling like etiolated flowers, and
> their holy simplicities seemed merely pathetic. (*E*, 91)

We hear echoes of Verlaine on *Parsifal*, possibly also of Symons;
then we move on to Wagner's third major work, *Lohengrin*. Evelyn has

eloped with Asher; now the dilemma becomes whether or not to marry. *Lohengrin*, with its theme of ill-fated marriage, provides counterpoint much as we saw it doing in *Dorian Gray*. Evelyn and Asher go to a performance of the opera, which so bores them that they cannot sit through it. Soon after they decide not to marry, and the *Lohengrin* parallel fades. *Tristan und Isolde* thereupon surfaces, and it is not only Wagner's version that Moore seems to have in mind here. For, in a reversal of the older versions in which there are two Iseults, Moore gives Evelyn two Tristans: the more passionate older lover, Asher; and a more chaste new companion, Ulick Dean. Isolde is Evelyn's most important role both onstage and off. For years she studies Wagner's drama, worries about her amours, and experiences feverish moments in which the two come together like this:

> The score slipped from her hands and her thoughts ran in reminiscence of a similar scene which she had endured in Venice nearly four years ago. She had not seen Owen for two months, and was expecting him every hour. The old walls of the palace, the black and watchful pictures, the watery odours and echoes from the canal had frightened and exhausted her. The persecution of passion in her brain and the fever of passion afloat in her body waxed, and the minutes became each a separate torture. . . . She had cast a frightened glance round the room, and it was the sceptre of life that her exalted imagination saw, and her natural eyes a strange ascension of the moon. The moon rose out of a sullen sky, and its reflection trailed down the lagoon. Hardly any stars were visible, and everything was extraordinarily still. The houses leaned heavily forward and Evelyn feared she might go mad, and it was through this phantom world of lagoon and autumn mist that a gondola glided. This time her heart told her with a loud cry that he had come, and she had stood in the shadowy room waiting for him, her brain on fire. The emotion of that night came to her at will, and lying in her warm bed she considered the meeting of Tristan and Isolde in the garden, and the duet on the bank of sultry flowers. (*E*, 156)[19]

After *Tristan* in the chronology of Wagner's works comes the *Ring*; and, as Evelyn's long association with Isolde begins to fade, *Ring* motifs indeed begin to resound. I shall not enumerate these in detail. Moore himself must have sensed that the process was becoming tedious; for not long after the Brünnhilde/Wotan interviews between Evelyn and her father, the system starts to loosen and dissolve. This is at the point in Evelyn's progress when she begins to turn from her lovers and career towards "the foot of the cross". Naturally, as her career as a singer comes to a close, the importance of Wagner to the novel must diminish. Still, we find moments when a Wagner association appears to illuminate Evelyn's dilemmas:

> She twisted in her fingers a letter which she had received that morning from Mademoiselle Helbrun. She was staying at the Savoy Hotel, and had just returned from Munich. Evelyn felt she would like to hear about her success as Frika and how So-and-So had sung Brünnhilde, and the rest of the little gossip about the profession. She would like to lunch with Louise in the restaurant, at a table by the window. She would like to see the Thames, and hear things that she might never hear again. But was it possible that she was never going to join again in the tumult of the Valkyrie? She remembered her war gear, the white tunic with gold breastplates. Was it possible that she would never cry their cry from the top of the rocks; and her favourite horse, the horse that Owen had given her for the part, what would become of him? (*E*, 385)

Evelyn goes to have lunch with her erstwhile Valkyrie sister at the Savoy by the Thames, Moore's counterpart to the fiery rock by the Rhine. But, like Brünnhilde in the scene in *Götterdämmerung* when Waltraute beseeches her to violate her newly taken vows and return the ring, Evelyn does not succumb to her sister-singer's entreaties – in this case to return to the stage and perform her great roles again, in Munich and at Bayreuth.

Gradually, then more swiftly, Evelyn's future becomes clear. She does not opt, as Swinburne's knight finally does, for the Venusberg, but, like Wagner's, for her Elisabeth-alternative, the Church. At the end of that "interview" for *The Musician* in which he had previewed the leitmotivs of his novel, Moore stated that the most important would prove his heroine's religious impulse, which "could be treated as Wagner treats the Love Feast motive in *Parsifal* as a foundation for the motive of salvation". It is no accident that, as Evelyn makes her turning, motifs from Wagner's last, quasi-Catholic work begin to appear: "She had seen on the stage the outward show of men who had renounced the world – the pilgrims in *Tannhäuser*, the knights in *Parsifal*, but this was no outward show.

The women she was now witnessing had renounced the world" (*E*, 431). The meaning of renunciation, its mysticism, has eluded her always until now: "The explanation seemed to have come to her. Yes, it is by denial of the sexual instinct that we become religious" (*E*, 467). Thus, renouncing sex and the world, Evelyn like Parsifal becomes a member of a sacred order. She takes on the new name of Sister Teresa because "the extraordinary vehemence and passion, the daring realism" of that saint remind her of Vittoria, whose motet her father had long before identified as the source for Wagner's "voix des enfants" (*E*, 460). On that Parsifalian note, we remember, *Evelyn Innes* began. Shortly after striking it again, the volume ends.

PARSIFAL YEA AND NAY

Though the system of *Evelyn Innes* is a loose chronological progress through all of Wagner's works, *Parsifal* finally has more to do with the heroine's progress from sex and the world to the Church than any other. From the first Owen Asher envisions Kundry as the crowning role of Evelyn's career, and it is with this in mind that he takes her to the Continent to make her a star. Kundry is the one Wagnerian role that Evelyn cannot feel within her. Nevertheless, she goes ahead with Asher's plan for many years. It is only when confronted with the point of view of the "fallen Wagnerian", Ulick Dean, that Evelyn realizes that she will never play Kundry, and that her career must end as a result. To Dean *Parsifal* is a "revolting hypocrisy" and Kundry "the blot on Wagner's life":

> In the first act she is a sort of wild witch, not very explicit to any intelligence that probes below the surface. In the second, she is a courtesan with black diamonds. In the third she wears the coarse habit of a penitent, and her waist is tied with a cord; but her repentance goes no further than these exterior signs. (*E*, 191)

Not only is Dean unable to share the Decadent fascination for this type of *femme fatale*; he cannot appreciate Parsifal's brand of the heroic either:

> Now, if we ask ourselves what Siegfried did, the answer is, that he forged the sword, killed the dragon and released Brünnhilde. But if, in like manner, we ask ourselves what Parsifal did, is not the

answer, that he killed a swan and refused a kiss and with many morbid, suggestive and disagreeable remarks? (*E*, 191)

In general these criticisms sound much like Nietzsche's, both in style and content; and it seems likely that Nietzsche, as well as the oft-cited Yeats,[20] was Moore's model for Dean at this point. Some years later Moore was to contend, "There is very little of Nietzsche in me."[21] But the passage of *Human, All-too-Human* that he would thereupon paraphrase shows that Moore was familiar with Nietzsche *contra* Wagner: "We shall not meet again, and if we do, of what use? We are like ships; all and sundry destinies and destinations." Moore has Dean paraphrase the same passage in his farewell to Evelyn (*E*, 415).

The Case of Wagner appeared in English while Moore was at work on *Evelyn Innes*. This probably explains the sudden appearance of the anti-*Parsifal* attack. How much this attack represents Moore's true position is, however, a more complicated matter. In the first volume of his memoir, *Hail and Farewell* (1911–14), Moore was to recall commenting to Siegfried Wagner at Bayreuth: "I've heard [*Parsifal*] many times, and it makes no personal appeal as do the other works."[22] Combined with the fact that he has that old Kundry-enthusiast Asher come round to Dean's point of view in the last part of *Evelyn Innes*, this would suggest that the mature Moore had indeed swung towards Nietzsche's position – in contrast to the extravagant enthusiasm the slightly younger Moore had voiced for Wagner's last drama in his article "After *Parsifal*". But this is not the whole matter. The more mature Moore was to make extensive and affectionate identifications between his friend Edward Martyn and Wagner's "guileless fool" throughout *Hail and Farewell*.[23] And, as a seventy-year-old, Moore would undertake a major reworking of the Parsifal-legend entitled *Peronnik the Fool* (1924). The preponderance of evidence therefore suggests that, whatever his objections to Wagner's version, he was fascinated by the idea of Parsifal throughout his career: end and middle as well as beginning.

Moore's problem with Wagner's treatment centres primarily on this issue of renunciation, which is the dominant issue of *Evelyn Innes* in the end, and a theological question that would occupy Moore at other times. Into Dean's mouth Moore puts an observation, reminiscent of Shaw's comment on Wagner's erotic "concreteness", as to why Wagner had chosen Parsifal of the various "subjective heroes" he considered dramatizing:

> In neither Christ nor Buddha did the question of sex arise, and
> that was the reason that Wagner eventually rejected both. He
> was as full of sex – mysterious, subconscious sex – as Rossetti
> himself. In Christ's life there is the Magdalen, but how naturally
> harmonious, how implicit in the idea, are their relations, how
> concentric; but how excentric . . . are the relations of Parsifal to
> Kundry. . . . A redeemer is chaste, but he does not speak of his
> chastity nor does he think of it; he passes the question by. The
> figure of Christ is so noble, that whether God or man or both, it
> seems to us in harmony that the Magdalen should bathe his feet
> and wipe them with her hair, but the introduction of the same
> incident in *Parsifal* revolts.   (*E*, 192)

This argument is Dean's most original and convincing, and at a
glance it would seem that Moore was in agreement with it. On the
other hand, Evelyn herself is no less self-conscious than Wagner's
hero about the necessity of renouncing sex, and this would seem to
make Moore's work as a whole confirmation of the artistic aptness of
the very sexual focus to which Dean objects in Wagner's. Artistic
aptness, however, is not the whole point; nor was *Evelyn Innes*
Moore's last word on the matter. Evelyn Innes does indeed become
"chaste" like Parsifal, and a "saviour" to her convent through the
proceeds of her concerts; but, then, at the end of the second volume
of her story, *Sister Teresa* (1901), Evelyn finally recants her
renunciations, leaves her sacred order, and returns to the world.
This final turnabout reveals Moore's most characteristic feeling
about Wagner's last work: he found its situation fascinating and
germane to the themes with which he was most concerned; but he
could not ultimately accept its "moral" of renunciation, either of
sex or of the world.[24]

LOHENGRIN AND *THE LAKE*

Wagner has a smaller place in *Sister Teresa* because Evelyn is no
longer an opera-singer. Only towards the end of the volume, when
she begins to reconsider her decision to become a nun, does Wagner
return to her thoughts, stirring "memory and desire":

> Every day she found it more difficult to think of God, more
> difficult to keep her lovers out of her mind, and the music that she

used to sing for their delight. One day she began to play the prelude to *Lohengrin* from impulse and to see what an effect it would have on Veronica [a sister nun], and when she had finished she asked her for her idea of it.

"It seemed to me", she said, "as if I stood waiting on some mountain top, somewhere where there is no boundary. The dawn seemed to be breaking, light seemed to increase, the rays grew brighter, and my soul seemed to be waiting amid the increasing light."

"Yes, it is that, Veronica – that is a very good description; how did you think of it?"

"I did not think it. . . . I felt like that. . . . Oh, Sister, that music is not like our life here. . . . It is far away. You used to sing that music, and yet you came here."

"Perhaps I came to escape from it, Veronica."

The prelude to *Tristan* and the "Forest Murmurs", and the Rhine Journey could not but trouble the quiet souls of Sister Elizabeth and Sister Veronica, and Evelyn knew that in playing this music to them she was doing a wicked thing. But a strange will had taken possession of her and she had to obey it. She stopped in the cloister to remember that she had saved the convent, and now she wished to destroy it.[25]

As is often the case in Mann's novels, this music now appears as the potentially destructive force Nietzsche recognized it to be. Evelyn realizes that it is a hostile force to "quiet" lives, and that for her to play it is "wicked". She almost imagines herself to be possessed by the Mannian devil, but stops short of describing her reborn erotic/ Dionysian impulse in such terms. Instead she merely calls it a "strange will", and aptly so. The impulse to break out into the world now moving her is analogous to the will of a Siegfried, not, any longer, the renunciatory love of a Parsifal. This will to live, unlike Shaw's in that it is stimulated by the memory of old lovers, is the dominant motif on which the two-volume novel ends. The motif is muted, however; made to harmonize with the opposite strains of Evelyn's regret about abandoning the convent, apprehension about entering the outer world, and residual desire to withdraw and purify her soul.

It is significant that *Lohengrin* is what Evelyn chooses to play on the eve of her departure. The story of the son of Parsifal who leaves a sacred order for the world, is unable to live amid human imperfection, and returns to the sacred order ultimately might be seen as an emblem of Evelyn's career of oscillation between the sacred and real; and its tragic tones suggest the pathos we might be moved to feel for her inability to find a satisfactory place in either. "What I like best of all Wagner now is *Lohengrin*", Moore wrote to Dujardin as he was completing *Sister Teresa*.[26] The preference had significance for his own condition as well as that of his heroine. *Lohengrin* was conceived a few years after Wagner's return to his homeland from self-imposed artistic exile in Paris, and its themes reflect his disillusionment on realizing that the perfect atmosphere for his art which he had hoped to find on coming home was in fact lacking. *Sister Teresa* was completed about the time that Moore returned to Ireland after years of artistic exile, with grand hopes for an Irish literary renaissance and the place of this own art in it. Like Wagner's, Moore's hopes were gradually deflated. His dramatic collaboration with Yeats turned out unsatisfactorily; his efforts to rechannel Martyn's theatrical talents fared little better; and his own published work during the half-decade of repatriation was limited to a book of humble stories, *The Untilled Field* (1903). To say that Moore became disillusioned in Dublin in the manner of Wagner in Dresden would be to overstate it. Still, the Moore who came to write *The Lake* (1905) was a Moore who, like Wagner, was again distancing himself from his homeland.

   The Lake owes much to Wagner. Moore was reading the composer's correspondence with Mathilde Wesendonck as he worked; it moved him deeply and may have inspired his efforts.[27] The novel is formed as a correspondence between an "agitated" priest and a sophisticated young woman who writes about her lovers, her experiences of theatre in London and Bayreuth, and her travels on the Continent. The situation is a reversal of Evelyn Innes's story, in which the exciting world of a young Evelyn is now seen from the point of view of one of those "quiet" souls who has renounced it. As with *Sister Teresa*, *Lohengrin* in the Wagnerian work with which *The Lake* finds its most subtle connection. Moore was to write years later:

   The Lake would not be as it was if I had not listened to *Lohengrin* many times. . . . The pages in which the agitated priest wanders about a summer lake recall the silver of the prelude. The sun shining on the mist, a voice . . . heard in vibrant supplication, is the essence of the prelude.[28]

The Lake contains none of the direct references to Wagner's work to be found in *Sister Teresa*. Still, Moore's conscious attempt to let its spirit shimmer behind the activities of the lonesome priest points up his perception of the intrinsic connection. Like its predecessor, *The Lake* shares with *Lohengrin* themes of the gulf between the sacred and real worlds; the eternal human lot of waiting for the lover/saviour; and the inner anguish of a type who tries to live a life of spiritual purity, while at the same time longing for a flesh-and-blood beloved.

UNENDING NARRATIVE AND THE LATER MOORE

Sister Veronica's description of the prelude to *Lohengrin* echoes that passage in *Richard Wagner et "Tannhäuser" à Paris* where Baudelaire quotes Berlioz's "magnifique éloge en style technique" and is moved to a prose reverie of his own.[29] The image of growing light which Sister Veronica uses is the very image around which Baudelaire's reverie revolves; and her description, and Evelyn's reaction to it ("Yes, it is that, Veronica"), confirms Baudelaire's point that Wagner's music was so particularly suggestive as to evoke similar visions in different minds. Whether or not this echo of Baudelaire was conscious, the passage testifies to Moore's lifelong desire to capture the spirit of Wagner's music in his prose. Blisset quotes the young Moore of *Confessions* to this effect:

> Wagner made the discovery . . . that an opera had much better be melody from beginning to end. The realistic school following on Wagner's footsteps found that a novel had much better be all narrative – an uninterrupted flow of narrative. Description is narrative, analysis of character is narrative, dialogue is narrative; the form is ceaselessly changing, but the melody of narration is never interrupted.[30]

Blisset then goes on to contend that Moore's ambition was to "obtain in narrative the equivalent of endless melody"; and with this I must agree. As we have seen, Moore sought to achieve both the psychological insight of D'Annunzio and the symbolical suggestiveness that Mallarmé had preached, and that Symons and Yeats were pursuing in their experiments with drama. These Moore wanted to synthesize with the principles of Naturalism on which he had constructed his early novels to create the perfect modern prose: a synthesis of psychology, symbolism, and naturalism – in short, the very elements Wagner had so successfully brought together.

In *Evelyn Innes* Moore did not achieve this ideal: it was too naturalistic still. In *The Lake*, with its slow, sensual, beautiful prose, Moore came considerably closer. As Cave says, *The Lake* strikes a most satisfying balance between Dujardin's staccato "monologue intérieur" and a Wagnerian continuity of movement;[31] and those pages which recall the "silver" of the prelude to *Lohengrin* are fine evidence. But, significantly, of *The Lake* Moore's biographer was to write:

> The book in its slow movement foreshadowed the work of his later period (*The Brook Kerith, Héloïse and Abélard* and *Aphrodite in Aulis*). It was the turning point in his writing, and the first of his books of which the complaint was made that he seemed to be more interested in manner than in content.[32]

The complaint has much truth. *The Lake* marked Moore's farewell to contemporary naturalistic subject-matter in the novel. Subsequently he turned to myth and legend, where plot and character were already provided and attention could be more completely devoted to stylistic presentation. Cave suggests that this turn may have been inspired by Wagner; and, like Wagner's, Moore's treatment of old legends contained significant modifications of traditional characters and plots. Still, as Wagner's most remarkable contribution to the legends he used was his musical settings, so Moore's would be his "musical" prose settings. The medium, in short, was much more the message than in early naturalistic works such as *Esther Waters* and *Rienzi*.

Moore's fanciful impression of Wagner as a great literary story-teller before a musician found its personal complement in his view of himself as a great musical-prose stylist before a story-teller. But musical method is only suited to the story-teller's art up to a point. And, as musical style increased its importance *vis-à-vis* naturalistic tale in his later works, Moore proceeded towards the ranks of Gertrude Stein and other synaesthetic literary pioneers, whose works would often provide examples of what *not* to attempt.[33] "I read about thirty pages of *The Brook Kerith*. It began to dawn on me that there was no mortal reason why Moore should not keep going on like that for fifty thousand pages, or fifty million for that matter."[34]

Thus Shaw, whose own works were no great examples of brevity, would report in 1916 on reading the book Moore considered to be his masterpiece. Masterpiece or major folly, *The Brook Kerith* went further than any previous Moore novel to achieve a narrative equivalent to Wagner's "unending melody"; and to read its long sentences in long paragraphs unbroken by dialogue, or sudden shifts of emphasis, or technical surprises of any sort, is to experience the effect Nietzsche complained of in Wagner's music – that is, of entering the sea and proceeding until one loses one's footing and drowns. Moore himself of course recognized this aqueous "unending" quality in his work: he had, after all, consciously sought it. But Moore would have characterized it in more appealing terms. As Hone says: "His writing aimed at continuity and suggested to the reader the movement of a stream . . . in summer."[35]

If the example of Wagner lured Moore into the stylistic experiment of *The Brook Kerith*, it may also have provided the idea of its subject. Like "Jesus of Nazareth", the subject of that article in which Moore had claimed that Wagner was a great *literary* artist, *The Brook Kerith* was a retelling of the life of the historical Jesus. Its immediate origin was a play Moore composed in 1910, *The Apostle*, on the subject of Joseph of Arimathea, whom Wagner had identified as the figure from whom Titurel had received the holy relics of the Grail Order. The atmosphere of a "Pre-Raphaelite Galilee" was inspired by a "pilgrimage" Moore made in 1914 to the Holy Land. Another important impetus came from Dujardin, whose Wagner-enthusiasm had been joined since the turn of the century by a fascination for the Jesus legend. Following Renan, Dujardin had become an exegete and published several works on the subject, notably *La Fleuve chrétien*, in which he argued that the legend may have been in part a conflation of ancient fertility myths. Following Dujardin, Moore dabbled in a bit of exegesis himself and, after a time, came to the conclusion that Jesus had never "existed on this earth". Dujardin was amused. Moore was a novelist not an exegete, he commented; and he predicted that the novelist's instinct would override scholarly opinion in any work Moore might undertake on the subject.[36] So it did. *The Brook Kerith* presented a Jesus who, like Wagner's sacred heroes, had "progressed through pantheism to the verge of Buddhism": a "shepherd mystic" who was also a Schopenhauerian.[37]

Like Wagner's Parsifal, Moore's Jesus was "meant to personify an ideal of moral beauty".[38] Similar idealism was apparent in others of his last creations, Heloïse and Peronnik for instance. Indeed, such idealism in treatment of such legendary subjects continued to be the direction in which the "rudderless skiff" of Moore's musical prose proceeded for the remainder of his career. Exceptions to this were the non-fiction pieces, the memoirs. But, even in *Hail and Farewell*, Moore's most entertaining outing, evidence of the Wagnerian aspirations is apparent. The style of this massive work, composed and published between *The Lake* and *The Brook Kerith*, was also musical, developing motivally and in largely unbroken "unending narrative". Interest is sustained by lively recountings of people and events during the period of Moore's return to Ireland. But, as Cave tells us, the trip to Bayreuth which forms the central event in the first volume (*Ave*) "establishe[d] Wagner's achieved artistic ideal as the standard against which all the Irish characters, events and results [were] to be measured".[39] Given what for Moore was a virtually unmatchable standard, it is easy to see why he could not maintain sufficient sympathy with the day-to-day struggles of the Irish literary renaissance to remain in his homeland after publication of *The Lake*. As Cave goes on to say,

> No prophet is held with honour in his own country and Yeats had written that "the Irish genius would in the long run be distinguished and lonely". The very writing of *Hail and Farewell* has severed all Moore's natural ties of friends, family and kin. Exile is his only future.
>
> By adopting a mythical status which is both outrageous and absurd, Moore has exposed the perennial weakness of the Irish mind: its very faculty for myth-making.[40]

MOORE AND JOYCE

The Lake was dedicated to Dujardin, and Blisset reminds us that Dujardin is now best remembered for the fact that Joyce cited his *Les Lauriers* as the model for the method of *Ulysses* (1922). Dujardin seems a rather distant figure for Joyce to have cited, but Dujardin's friend George Moore seems a close and likely influence indeed. Like the young Moore, the young Joyce left Ireland for Paris with the ambition of becoming a great "artist", and the immediate intention of supporting himself by writing articles on French art for English magazines. Like Moore, his first publication was a volume of

imitative aesthetic verse. Like Moore, his first success was with a
book describing his early artistic development. Like Moore, his
mature ambition was to write a new sort of novel that was musical
and psychological, and that synthesized post-Wagnerian Symbolism with Naturalism.[41] Moore was the most influential Irish
novelist before Joyce; and it should not come as any surprise that
Joyce imitated Moore, parodistically at times, even stole motifs
outright from him.

An arresting instance of such theft may be found in the Siegfried
motifs that Joyce weaved into the finale of *A Portrait of the Artist as a
Young Man* (1916). At one point Stephen Dedalus and his friend are
hailed across a green by the birdcall from Act II of Wagner's
drama.[42] Later, at the climax of the book, Stephen makes his famous
declaration, "I go for the millionth time to encounter the reality of
experience and to forge in the smithy of my soul the uncreated
conscience of my race."[43] As Blisset has discovered, the same motifs
had been present in *Hail and Farewell*, the last two volumes of which
appeared while Joyce was hurrying to complete his novel for
serialization. On more than one occasion Moore recalled hailing
Edward Martyn by whistling motifs from Wagner up at Martyn's
window. More striking still is Moore's fantasy, complete with
Joycean anti-Catholic bias and allusions to Parnell, that he was the
one destined to "forge the uncreated conscience" of the Irish
race:

> Ireland has lain too long under the spell of the magicians, without
> will, without intellect, useless and shameful, the despised of
> nations. I have come into the most impersonal country in the
> world to preach personality . . . personality for all except for
> God; and I walked across the greensward afraid to leave the
> garden, and to heighten my inspiration I looked toward the old
> apple-tree, remembering that many had striven to draw forth the
> sword that Wotan had struck into the tree about which Hunding
> had built his hut. Parnell, like Sigmund, had drawn it forth, but
> Wotan had allowed Hunding to strike him with his spear. And
> the allegory becoming clearer I asked myself if I were Siegfried,
> son of Sigmund slain by Hunding, and if it were not my fate to
> reforge the sword that lay broken in halves in Mimi's cave.
>
> It seemed to me that the garden filled with tremendous music,
> out of which came a phrase glittering like a sword suddenly
> drawn from its sheath and raised defiantly to the sun.[44]

Moore had returned to Ireland to "preach personality" (the creed also of Wilde, one of Stephen Dedalus's better-remembered Irish forbears), and to write the prose of race: to forge the Nothung that Stephen was to brandish in *Ulysses*, the prose that Stephen-as-Joyce was later to write.

These common Wagnerian motifs are only a hint of the similarities between Moore and Joyce. There are also the evidence of Joyce's debt to *Evelyn Innes*: his story "Eveline" is about a young girl trying to decide whether to elope with her lover to foreign continents of opportunity or stay home with her father and her Catholic upbringing, the very Tannhäuserian dilemma we have seen Evelyn confronting after meeting Owen Asher; his *Ulysses* has a structural system of parallels like that of Moore's novel, as we have noted; and Joyce's novel is among other things about a female singer (Molly as a debased Evelyn) who is suspended between two men and preoccupied with question of sex. Further resonances of Moore include the long stretches of discussion about Dante and Aquinas and various aesthetic and philosophical questions of the day, particularly in Part v of *Portrait* and the Library chapter of *Ulysses*. These recall the second volume of *Hail and Farewell* (*Salve*), in which appear John Eglinton and Oliver Gogarty, two characters whom Joyce was to include in *Ulysses*, the former as himself and the latter as Buck Mulligan. Finally, we might consider Stephen's encounter with the girl on Sandymount Strand at the end of Part iv of *Portrait*, and Bloom's prurient observation of another bold young woman (Gerty MacDowell) on the beach in a central chapter of *Ulysses*. Both exhibit a type of eroticism characteristic to Moore, and either might have been inspired by the passage which ends the central chapter of *Salve*:

> I . . . strayed fifty yards. . . . I saw . . . three girls. . . . On seeing me they laughed invitingly; and, as "if desiring my appreciation, one girl walked across the pool, lifting her red petticoat to her waist, and forgetting to drop it when the water shallowed, she showed me thighs whiter and rounder than any I

have ever seen, their country coarseness heightening the temptation. She continued to come towards me. A few steps would have taken me behind a hillock. They might have bathed naked before me, and it would have been the boldest I should have chosen, if fortune had favoured me. But Yeats and Edward began calling, and, dropping her petticoats, she waded from me.

What are you doing down there, George? Hurry up! Here's the hooker being rowed into the bay, bringing the piper and the story-tellers from Arran.[45]

CONCLUSION

Thus was Moore drawn away from the Bloom-like fantasies and Joycean reality which held such strong appeal for him towards music and legend, in this case the realm of Yeats and old Celtic Ireland rather than of Wagner and pan-European myth. Though in later years he distanced himself from this Ireland, the vignette provides an apt representation of the denouement of Moore's long career. And one is tempted to observe that, had he not been drawn away to such realms (to the writing of *The Brook Kerith* and *Peronnik the Fool*, for instance), Moore might have captured the world of *Ulysses*, Irish reality in post-Wagnerian prose, long before James Joyce took the opportunity. On the other hand, it should be said that Moore was a *fin-de-siècle* aesthete to the end; and *fin-de-siècle* aestheticism, as we shall see, had only a distant relationship to *Ulysses*. Moore's experiments of the later years in 'musical" prose were in a sense a return to the ideals he had shared with the French of the 1880s, and English associates such as Symons of the 1890s. Unlike Symons, however, and perhaps more like his compatriot Shaw, Moore was ever concerned with taking these ideals a stage or two further. And in this respect his final experiments share in the Promethean daring with which he had forayed into Naturalism, *À rebours*-like memoir, and psychological fiction in English as a younger man.

Succeeding or failing, in constructing a Wagnerian system of parallels in *Evelyn Innes* or pursuing "unending melody" in *The Brook Kerith*, Moore advanced the Wagnerian movement in novel-writing to logical and instructive conclusions. From these it would proceed to more full and satisfactory assimilation in works of more Modernist younger writers. The fact makes it possible to describe

Moore as a synthetic figure. Wagner was a (perhaps *the*) principle influence on Moore, as he had been on many whose influence Moore had also felt, and as he was to become in differing ways on many whom Moore anticipated. Besides Joyce, Moore's influence was to be felt by such lesser figures as Charles Morgan and David Garnett;[46] also, as we shall see, by D. H. Lawrence. It might even have reached budding novelists beyond the confines of the language. There is, for instance, much common ground between Moore and Mann. The longest works of each, *Hail and Farewell* and *Joseph and His Brothers*, both begin, as does Proust's *A la recherche du temps perdu*, with "overtures".[47] All three books are subtly marked by techniques and motifs from Wagner throughout.

7 Yeats

The Flying Dutchman and *Lohengrin* were produced in Dublin in Italian in 1877, and excerpts from other Wagner works were given in concert in the following years.[1] Wagnerism in Dublin however was never the phenomenon it became in Paris in the 1880s or London in the 1890s, and what Wagnerism developed was inspired as much by the reputation of the man as by performances of his works. Here was a revolutionary artist who had created passionate dramas out of a body of Celtic and Norse myths which had been largely neglected since the twelfth century. The dramas were mystical, pagan and vaguely Catholic at the same time; and their premiere in a theatre built especially for their production marked the cultural birth of a new nation. Such a reputation could hardly help but appeal to the culturally and nationally deprived Irish. And Wagnerian subjects found their way into Dublin intellectual journals, from that of the Theosophical Society, which invoked Wagner's name frequently, to the Catholic conservative *Dublin Review*, which published articles on two of Wagner's mediaeval sources, Walther von der Vogelweide and the *Nibelungenlied*.[2]

The Theosophical Society was attracted to the mysticism of Wagner, the more academic *Dublin Review* to the mythic tradition he had revived. Both things were of interest to the young Yeats, who had begun his career as poet of the "Celtic Twilight" and then proceeded, like his countrymen Wilde and Shaw and Moore, to spend much of his time in the more sophisticated aesthetic milieu of London. There in the 1890s Yeats absorbed the styles of Pater and the Wagnerian French. Under their influence his work, which had been sensual from the first, became self-consciously "musical" in the Decadent manner.[3] Unlike his friends Symons and Beardsley, Yeats was no musician; nor is there evidence that he spent much time in concert-hall or opera-house. He was "tone-deaf", Moore and others tell us.[4] But, as Katharine Worth states, "This curious irony was compensated for, surely, by the extreme delicacy of his ear for verbal sounds and rhythms." Worth calls Yeats "the most musical poet writing in English in this century".[5] The century she refers to is the twentieth. But before the century had even turned Yeats was already demonstrating this quality: the poems of *The Wind among the Reeds* (1899) and prose of such fables as "Rosa Alchemica" (1897) must rank with the finest examples of verbal music from the entire period.

Worth's recent book, *The Irish Theatre of Europe from Yeats to Beckett*, explores the relationship of Yeats's mature drama to Wagner and Wagnerians, particularly Symons and Maeterlinck. In this chapter we shall also take up the relationship of Wagner to Yeats's early ideas and his persona as an artist. The chapter will be brief for two reasons. First, Yeats never "experienced" Wagner like many of his contemporaries, and never proclaimed himself a Wagnerian after their flamboyant fashion. Secondly, many of the Wagnerian motifs to be found in Yeats have already been discussed in reference to others, notably Wilde and Symons in those sections of their chapters dealing with the artist and with Symbolism. No works on Wagner and Yeats as such have been published, but Worth's first three chapters cover the essentials admirably. Helpful indications have also been given by Blisset in his article on Moore, and Randall in his thesis on Symons.

IDEAS OF GOOD AND EVIL

The Wind among the Reeds and "Rosa Alchemica" come from the period in which Yeats was most involved with magic and mysticism, through the Order of the Golden Dawn.[6] It is also the period in which he was living at Fountain Court with Symons, contributing articles on Blake to *The Savoy*, and assisting in Symons's study of the Symbolists. Clearly this was a formative time. In it Yeats began to search for definition of his own artistic intentions among movements of the earlier nineteenth century, and the yet-more-remote past. His discoveries produced numerous articles. These he collected in 1903 to make up his first major critical volume, *Ideas of Good and Evil*. The book praises a number of Romantic artists whom the maturing poet considered his precursors. Prime among these is Blake, who, Yeats pointed out, had never found a satisfactory mythology, because of the age he had lived in: "Had he been a Catholic of Dante's time he would have been well content with Mary and the angels; or had he been a scholar of our time he would have taken his symbols where

Wagner took his, from Norse mythology."[7] In his pantheon Yeats also included Goethe, who has been said to have a closer "affinity" to Yeats than any other poet;[8] Shelley; Keats of the Odes; Blake's follower Calvert; Rossetti, who "painted in moments of intensity when the ecstasy of the lover and the saint are alike" (*I*, 50); Wagner, whose imagination had made "the Scandinavian tradition . . . all but the most passionate element in the arts of the modern world" (*I*, 202); Mallarmé; the Symbolist dramatists Villiers and Maeterlinck; D'Annunzio; William Morris; the young Ibsen; and, at a distance, Nietzsche, "whose thought flows always, though with an even more violent current, in the bed Blake's has worn" (*I*, 140).

Some similarities between these artists should be pointed out. With the possible exception of the reactive Nietzsche, they were all synaesthetists either in theory, like Shelley and Mallarmé; or in practice, like Blake and Rossetti and Wagner. Again with the possible exception of Nietzsche, they were all symbolists: concerned with evoking and exploring a world beyond conscious reality and contemporary life, behind the naturalistic description and superficial word – a world where dimensions of space and time spread out towards the infinite and the imagination could be free to roam to other moments in its history, all the way back to its "earliest picture dreamings". These artists all applied a personal order to experience that stood in place of the order previously applied from outside by church, state or Enlightenment philosophy. Each of these personal orders shared to some degree in an "amoral" attitude towards traditional values – a sharing suggested by the title *Ideas of Good and Evil*, which recalls the spirit of Blake's title "The Marriage of Heaven and Hell", of Nietzsche's title *Beyond Good and Evil*, and of Wagner's harmonizing of strains of the "evil" Venusberg music with the "good" Pilgrims' Chorus in the finale of *Tannhäuser*. These artists who questioned traditional morality, broke through old conventions towards new forms, and sought new worlds based on personal symbolisms were bound together in a philosophical tradition that also included Theosophy and the new Schopenhauerian "Buddhism", the experiments of the mediaeval alchemists, and the Gnostic rituals and love-epics of the twelfth century. They belonged, in short, to a tradition of heterodox thought that deviated from Western authority systems.[9]

The art of Yeats's chosen grew out of "the reaction against the rationalism of the eighteenth century . . . mingled with a reaction

against the materialism of the nineteenth century" (*I*, 204). It was
high Romantic art with immediate roots in the German *Aufklärung*,
the thought of Schelling for instance, and back further to such
figures as Jacob Boehme, on whom Blake had drawn (*I*, 118). This
art had attachments not only across time to the heresies of the
Middle Ages, but across space through traceable migrations of
Celtic myth and Moorish culture to the further East.[10] In terms
Ronald Gray uses in his *German Tradition in Literature*, it was art that
opened out into Nature Mysticism, that pantheism which can
discover divine spirit in all matter and proposes that the Universe
can be integrated within the Self; as opposed to Theistic Mysticism
(including orthodox Judiasm and Christianity), which regards all
matter as fallen, divine spirit as the property of God alone, and
Universal integration as possible only through a God who (except
for the saved) always remains outside the Self.[11] The goal of this art
was to synthesize the One out of the many, which among Germans
from Goethe to Yeats's contemporary Thomas Mann had been
sought through dialectical blending of antipodes – that process
which, as Mann would write, is achieved in music by harmony and
in writing by irony.[12] Such a goal proceeded from what Gray
unsympathetically refers to as "a sense than anything less than all-
embracing must be presumptuous".[13] It produced the world-myth
of Blake as well as that of Wagner; also the ambition of Mallarmé to
write "The Book".

IDEAS FOR AN IRISH THEATRE

In *Ideas of Good and Evil* Yeats placed himself squarely among these
artists and their tradition, and declared that he would carry on that
tradition in a new art using ancient Irish legends, which "have so
much of a new beauty that they may well give the opening century
its most memorable symbols" (*I*, 204). Even before publication of
the book Yeats had returned to Ireland, where he quickly became
the central figure in an Irish literary renaissance, focusing on his
dream of an Irish national theatre. Many of the figures around
Yeats at this time were Wagnerians. There was Moore; Edward
Martyn, who travelled with Moore to Bayreuth, and whose plays
The Heather Field and *Maeve* took motifs from Wagner; T. W.
Rolleston, who would adapt the Tannhäuser, Lohengrin and
Parsifal legends into poems, published as *Three Love Tales after*

Richard Wagner: Sacred and Profane Love (1920); also John Todhunter, a playwright who also published poetic versions of *Rienzi* (1881) and *Isolt of Ireland* (1916). Two even more important figures around Yeats, AE (George Russell) and Lady Gregory, were not known as ardent Wagnerians but possessed imaginations that "flowed in the same bed" that Wagner's had worn: that of fairy-tale, mediaeval legend, and myth. Most important of all perhaps was Miss Annie Horniman, who had helped Ashton Ellis translate Wagner's *Prose Works* in the 1890s and met Yeats soon after through the Order of the Golden Dawn. Miss Horniman became Yeats's chief patron and financial adviser in the early years of the Abbey Theatre. In encouraging him, she was apt to refer to the example of Wagner: "Work on as best you can for a year. . . . At the year's end do what Wagner did and write a 'Letter to my Friends' asking for capital."[14] Yeats agreed to work "in some such way" and supervised the growth of the theatre in close association with Miss Horniman, until misunderstandings led her to withdraw her support in 1910.

Yeats's dream of a theatre dated at least from his first association with Symons and exposure to Symbolist drama, particularly to Villiers's *Axël*, which he saw performed in Paris in 1894 and for years regarded as "a sacred book". Like Symons, Yeats developed an antipathy for the general English theatre-going audience. He felt instinctively that the type of drama he wished to create could have little success among "those quite excellent people who think Rossetti's women are 'guys', that Rodin's women are 'ugly', and that Ibsen is 'immoral', and who want only to be left at peace to enjoy the works so many clever men have made especially to suit them" (*I*, 180). This disenchantment was much like what Wagner had felt towards the audiences in pre-1849 Dresden, and expressed in "Art and Revolution" and *The Artwork of the Future*. To Yeats as to Wagner it seemed that there must be an alternative type of theatre where perfectly wrought, sincerely imaginative mythic drama could be performed for that elite who could truly appreciate it, and for the common *Volk* who might not understand fully but could feel its attachment to them through the stirring of deep racial memories. Yeats praised Bayreuth as a model theatre (*I*, 103). For many years he kept the ambition to build some sort of Bayreuth in Ireland himself.

At the outset of his career as a dramatist Yeats was at one with the 1890s and its aspiration to music, the most "colourist" (chromatic), least concrete, and most suggestive of the arts. He wished the verse of his plays to be spoken in such a way as to create a spell in which "the deep of the mind" might be apprehended.[15] Through training in the psaltery of Florence Farr and other such "artificialities", the actor would learn to speak "as if mere speech had taken fire and passed into song";[16] or, as Moore was later fancifully to put it, Yeats sought the effect of simultaneously "playing fiddle to the Arran Islanders, and reciting poetry to them".[17] The idea of mixing word and music in subtle rhythms that would produce an incantatory spell had come to Yeats from Wagner via the French and Symons. It was exactly the type of obfuscatory effect Nietzsche had predicted that young artists of the future would be lured into trying to achieve by that "Caligostro" of Bayreuth: "Rhythm casts a veil over reality; it causes various artificialities of speech and obscurities of thought; by the shadow it throws on thought it sometimes conceals it."[18] "Veil" is a word Yeats would later use to characterize the early phase of his career; and, as a Theosophist and mystic, it had become second-nature for him to want to seek shadow and obscurity. Like the depths of Finn MacCool's cave, central meanings would only become available to those who made the journey and penetrated the darkness.[19] Like the mystical rose of the Rosicrucians, the great secrets could be divined but not described.

Like an act of magic, the ideal "drama of the interior" would be *felt*, not just intellectually apprehended in a manner reducible to verbal explanation. We are certainly in the realm here of Maeterlinck's "static" ideal, with its emphasis on silences, pauses and emotionally pregnant movements. And Yeats laid down this directive: "Seek out those wavering meditative, organic rhythms, which are the embodiment of the imagination, that neither desires or hates, because it has done with time, and only wishes to gaze upon some reality, some beauty".[20] Seek out that atmosphere of quivering Buddha-like stillness that Wagner had achieved in the last act of *Parsifal*; then the drama might perform its functions of quelling hate and desire, opening the imagination, and evoking the Universal with its ineffable central meanings. As Mann would write of Wagner, the artist who does this has taken on the task of a priest: "An artist like Wagner, accustomed to dealing with Symbols and to elevating monstrances, must have ended by feeling like a brother of priests; indeed, like a priest himself".[21] Of artists of the future Yeats prophesied much the same: "[They] are about to take upon their shoulders the burdens that have fallen from the shoulders of priests, and to lead us back upon our journey by filling our thoughts with the essences of things, and not with things" (*I*, 210). "Essence" is a word suggested perhaps by Mallarmé and Yeats's ideal conformed fully with the spirit of Mallarmé's dictum that Symbolist theatre should take on the characteristics and functions of the High Mass. As Arland Ussher would comment, "The verse theatre was [Yeats's] true church."[22]

In focus and unity around the single overarching idea, Yeats's finest plays would match the achievement of *Salomé*, a work Yeats ever admired. *Salomé*, as we have seen, shared much with Wagner's *Tristan* in this respect; and in his first attempt at a drama for Irish production Yeats turned to another version of the ancient Celtic legend, the story of Diarmuid, who "ran off with Finn MacCool's bride, Grainne".[23] Uncertain perhaps of his dramatic talents, Yeats asked Moore to collaborate on the work. "An operatic text is what we should be writing together," the Wagner-enthusiast retorted;[24] and the product of the collaboration, *Diarmuid and Grania*, was distinctly Wagnerian in texture – what with horn calls, mortal wounds from a boar, lengthy dying reminiscences, funeral procession and pyre, rather more like *Götterdämmerung* than *Tristan*.[25] For the production Moore had Elgar compose some incidental music, which he praised for its "languorous rhythms" and harmonies.[26] In spite of this, the play was not a success. Hopes for production in London never bore fruit. Moore and Yeats quarrelled; plans for future collaborations were cancelled; Yeats wrote the play down from its high operatic pitch and published it as his own, *Where There Is Nothing* (1902).

THE SHADOWY WATERS

This false-start served to disenchant Yeats about imitating Wagner in the manner of Moore. It did not however dissuade him from projecting *Tristan*-like scenarios again. So much is demonstrated by *The Shadowy Waters*, a play Yeats had begun after seeing *Axël*, worked on sporadically during the period of *Ideas of Good and Evil*, and took up again in the summer of 1905, when he was staying at Lady Gregory's Coole Park. That summer was also when Symons was completing his long essay on Wagner, and Yeats wrote to his old Symbolist *confrère* that he was "waiting with a great deal of expectancy" for a copy.[27] Upon receiving and reading Symons's essay, Yeats wrote back to this effect:

The Wagnerian essay touches my own theories at several points, and enlarges them at one or two. . . . I have spent the entire summer rewriting *Shadowy Waters*. . . . In one place your Wagner essay helped me. A certain passage had always seemed wrong to me, and after I had rewritten it several times it was still wrong. I then came upon that paragraph where Wagner insists that a play must not appeal to the intelligence, but by being, if I remember rightly, a piece of self consistent life, directly to the emotions. It was just one of those passages which seemed to have no very precise meaning till one brings actual experience to their understanding. Your essay is a substitute for more volumes than anything of the kind I have seen, and I believe it has greatly pleased Ashton Ellis. At any rate I know it has pleased Miss Horniman who I think speaks as his voice.[28]

While it remains a matter of speculation where precisely Wagner's example proved helpful, it is clear that *The Shadowy Waters* partook of Wagner in many respects. Yeats himself was mindful of the connections right through production: he told Sturge Moore, who was doing the design, that the costumes should be in "Wagner's period, more or less".[29]

Like *The Flying Dutchman*, the play is set aboard a pirate ship sailing the northern seas. The captain, Forgael, is a dreamer who, both by choice and the supernatural power of the Fomorians (spirits of good and evil who rise bird-headed out of the bodies of dead men and fly away west), is fated to wander forever in search of the perfect woman. His crew is mutinous and ultimately deserts him to a phantom crew of Fomorians. In the meantime they capture another ship; kill the king who is on it; and bring his queen, Dectora, as a captive to Forgael. Like Isolde, whose betrothed was killed by Tristan, Dectora has ample reason to want to avenge herself on her captor. But, just at the moment when she might plunge a sword into him, she is struck by overpowering passion. The triumph of this passion is assured not by a love-potion, but by the equally magical strains of Forgael's harp: a version of Tristan's harp which, in the mediaeval version of the tale, had managed to save that hero from the vengeance of Queen Iseult and to awaken the passion of her daughter, Iseult the princess.[30] The role of the harp here is crucial. The spoken word breaks off and we are suddenly in the realm of aethereal music. As Worth says, "Yeats relies as much as Wagner on the power of music to suggest the transcendental nature of the sudden irrational passion that seizes the only half-willing lovers."[31]

Through his music, Forgael's perfection is revealed to Dectora. By her love, Dectora's perfection is revealed to Forgael. In the finale the harp, symbol of the art that has heretofore been Forgael's consolation for the perfect woman he has never found, burns. And, guided by the Fomorians, he and his queen sail into the mystic western twilight:

DECTORA: The world drifts away,
And I am left alone with my beloved,
Who cannot put me from his sight for ever.
We are alone for ever, and I laugh,
Forgael, because you cannot put me from you.
The mist has covered the heavens, and you and I
Shall be alone for ever. We two – this crown –
I half remember. It has been in my dreams.
Bend lower, O king, that I may crown you with it.
O flower of the branch, O bird among the leaves,
O silver fish that my two hands have taken
Out of the running stream, O morning star,
Trembling in the blue heavens like a white fawn
Upon the misty border of the wood,
Bend lower, that I may cover you with my hair,
For we will gaze upon this world no longer.
(*The harp begins to burn as with fire.*)
FORGAEL (*gathering Dectora's hair about him*):
Beloved, having dragged the net about us,
And knitted mesh to mesh, we grow immortal[32]

This finale is not precisely the tragic one of *Tristan*, but clearly it partakes of the spirit of the *Liebestod*. It is not quite the tragic one of *The Flying Dutchman* either, but it certainly recalls the image of Vanderdecken and Senta transcending over the western waves. It is not world-weary in precisely the Wagnerian fashion—Yeats's hero and heroine are seeking transcendence through liberation of their imaginations, not death.[33] Still, by the same sort of irony that transforms death into imaginative transcendence for Tristan and Isolde, the imaginative transcendence of Forgael and Dectora must be considered as a kind of death too: a death to their mortal beings – a final departure from the real world with its material ambitions, as personified in the mutinous crew.

BEYOND THE 1890s

In such a treatment of the mystical idea of transcendence, the poet of *The Wind among the Reeds* was probably more at one with the spirit of Wagner than any other artist we are discussing. Indeed, the resonances of *The Flying Dutchman* and *Tristan* are so striking that Professor Worth and I identified them in almost identical terms before we even knew of one another's work. Of course, it was Villiers's *Axël* that had provided the original inspiration for Yeats, and *The Shadowy Waters* follows that play more than Wagner in its obscure and systematic mysticism. As a statement of rarefied Romantic yearnings, *The Shadowy Waters* like *Axël* may have been a personal triumph. As a public production, it definitely followed Villiers's play in being almost impossible to bring off. When Yeats read the manuscript to Moore and Martyn at Coole, they predicted that no audience was going to be able to understand a drama so thoroughly on the level of symbol rather than action.[34] This proved to be the case at the Abbey; and the production was flawed by additional technical difficulties, such as the fact that the harp would not catch fire properly.[35] Yeats was disappointed, but not to be diverted from his high Romantic aspirations. He focused his next play, *Deirdre* (1906), on a theme of heroic passion similar to that of *The Shadowy Waters*, and of the Tristan legend, from which it also derived. Only after *Deirdre* received much the same lukewarm reaction did Yeats begin the process of distancing himself from this transcendentally moving but theatrically impractical type of subject.[36]

The lack of success of Yeats's most symbolical/mystical plays at the Abbey should not, however, be ascribed solely to intrinsic flaws. The major difficulties were external and twofold. In the first place, as John Eglinton was to recall,

> The heroic element seemed a little crestfallen on the Abbey stage, and the Irish heroes, impersonated by actors who had gained their renown in peasant parts, gave one the feeling that they had fallen on very evil times, especially when one thought of their Teutonic compeers moving amid the splendours of Wagnerian orchestration.[37]

In the second place, as Yeats gradually came to recognize, those Irish audiences whom he had imagined to have special capacities for appreciation of myth and oratory inherited from ancient times were in fact not so different from the English audiences he and Symons had spurned. They too responded more readily to the realistic and humorous and in the end wanted to be entertained or stirred into nationalistic passion, not set adrift in a shadow-world of myth and idea. In the theatre Yeats's response to these facts was to champion the more realistic plays of J. M. Synge. In his art it was to move from the precepts of *Ideas of Good and Evil*, reject the aesthetic mistiness of the 1890s in general, and make his own ideal harder and clearer. He read Nietzsche until his eyes went bad.[38] In terms echoing the sage of Sils Maria, he told Moore that he wanted to write "masculine" dramas which concentrated on "things" like the dramas of the ancients, not "ideas" like the "effeminate" art of the 1890s.[39] Moore was sceptical. Having fallen out with Yeats, he conceived that the poet's inspiration had dried up; and he proposed the novel theory that, because Yeats had never "gratified" his passion for Maud Gonne in the manner that Wagner had his for Mathilde Wesendonck, his art could only drift in the future further into Mallarmé-like obscurity.[40]

Brutal though Moore's assessement seems, it may have been in part correct about Yeats at this time. What Moore failed to recognize, however, is the extent to which Yeats would realize his own shortcomings and work to overcome them. While by no means abandoning Mallarméan ideals entirely, Yeats continued to dist-ance his work from the Symbolist shadows. In the next decade he let Ezra Pound's aggressive Modernism influence his style radically; and in Pound's translations of Japanese Noh dramas Yeats found the suitable models for his new "masculine" ideal. Classical as well as symbolical, hard and clear in line, aspiring to the statuesque rather than the musical – the Noh transformed Yeats's drama and his vision of the ideal theatre from an Irish Bayreuth to something more spartan and pastoral:

> Perhaps some day a play in the form I am adapting for European purposes shall awake once more . . . under the slope of Slieve-na-mon or Croagh Patrick ancient memories; for this form has no need of scenery that runs away with money nor of a theatre-building.[41]

In such a theatre Wagnerian noise and the Wagnerian habit of treating the voice as another instrument would not be found:

The human voice can only become louder by becoming less articulate, by discovering some new musical sort of roar or scream. As poetry can do neither, the voice must be freed from this competition and find itself among little instruments, only heard.[42]

Music was as essential to the Modernist playwright as it had been to the Paterian aesthete. But it was a type of music that came close to expressing interior stillness: the plaintive flute-solo of the third act of *Tristan*, not grand opera's pomp-and-circumstance or *Götterdämmerung's Stürm und Drang*.

THE CULT OF GENIUS

Yeats's lifelong dream of playing his dramas to a common folk free of "bookish" bourgeois *Kultur*-philistinism proved as naïve as Wagner's; and a good many of his plays, by his own intention in later years, never got further than the drawing-room coteries eager to work at understanding them. Yeats's equally lifelong aspiration to the aristocratic encouraged the development of such an elite; and a cult of the genius, led by Lady Gregory in Ireland and by admirers such as Pound's mother-in-law, Olivia Shakespear, in London, increasingly grew up around him. Moore recalls dinners at Coole when the guests would be required to wait at the table until the poet arrived, his tardiness giving rise to grave speculations as to whether he might have completed eight lines in the afternoon's work instead of the usual four or six.[43] Nietzsche, had he been in attendance, would doubtless have paled. The picture conjures up that of Wagner patronized by the Wesendoncks at Asyl, pampered by King Ludwig with Treibschen, and waited on by endless pilgrims to Bayreuth; and Lady Gregory in her role of cultivated protectress suggests something of Cosima Liszt von Bülow. Such comparisons are not entirely idle. Yeats himself on occasion invoked the example of Wagner to justify the type of artist he saw himself to be:

> The myth that artists create with ease and without great forethought which journalists have drummed into our heads has "created" in its turn a forgetfulness like that of soldiers in battle, so that journalists and their readers have forgotten that Wagner spent seven years arranging and explaining his ideas before he began his most characteristic work. (I, 166)

Taken on the whole the figure of Yeats may indeed have more in common with that of Wagner than any of the others we are discussing. Both were mystics whose unorthodox beliefs shared in that tradition of Western heresy and art outlined in *Ideas of Good and Evil*. Both, on the other hand, were practical men-of-the-theatre who spent years attending to routine business matters as well as to their art. Both were nationalists, at times to revolutionary extremes; both sought to awaken their nations to long-slumbering mythic heritages; and both became widely recognized as the greatest living artists of their nations at the very time that those nations were coming into being. On a deeper level, both were Romantics of the most passionate type, both lifelong seekers after the heroic, and both aspirants to the creation of a new religion based on the oldest standards of nobility of their races. In their own personalities both were continually divided between the sensualist and the man-of-fact, the illusionist and the architect, the scholar/critic and the man-of-action. Both lived their lives in symbiotic relation to their art, and conceived of that art as the battleground for the spiritual struggles of their souls. Both despised the "real" world and retreated to the hermetic realms of High Art, yet both felt continually compelled to return to that "real" world and pronounce and prophesy on its affairs.

Both Yeats and Wagner were egotists who wore their public personae as masks, yet through such projections came widely to be regarded as the representative geniuses of their time and place. Beyond these general similarities it might be pointed out that the Yeats of the later years when working on *A Vision* (1925; 37), like Shaw of *Methuselah* though very differently, shared with the Wagner of the *Ring* and *Parsifal* a hunger to divine an all-embracing cosmic order, and to define a system of continuity ruling the destinies of gods and men. It might also be noted that Yeats, like Wilde and Moore and Lawrence, as we shall see, shared with the Wagner of "Jesus of Nazareth" the need to deal in a personal way with issues of the Christ-myth; this being demonstrated first by the fable "The Crucifixion of the Outcast" (1894), for which the condemned Wilde had grateful words,[44] and later by the dramas *Calvary* (1917) and *Resurrection* (1931). In passing it should further be remembered that Yeats, like Shaw and Pound and Lawrence, shared with the inheritors of Bayreuth a fascination for the dictators. In Yeats's case this faded rather quickly. Nevertheless, it led at one point in the early 1930s to his donning of the blue shirt of General O'Duffy's Irish fascist movement.[45]

CONCLUSION

The personal similarities between Yeats and Wagner are important because Yeats, like Wilde (and really all those we are discussing with the possible exceptions of Joyce and Eliot), believed that the life of the artist was obliged to partake of artistic calculation itself. They should not, however, be allowed to distract from the more important similarities between Yeats's early art and ideas and Wagner's; nor the extent to which Yeats successfully distanced himself from what Joyce would describe as these "ninetyish" sympathies in later years. As events made Yeats less of an aesthete and more a man-of-action, the Wagnerian "fog" of *Ideas of Good and Evil* and *The Shadowy Waters* for the most part cleared, leaving the enduring Wagnerian inheritances of dramatic structure, emphasis on "the interior", and myth. As we have noted, the "Wagner-experience" had not imprinted itself on the psyche of the young Yeats as it had in the cases of Symons, Moore, and to a lesser degree Shaw. This, along with a remarkable capacity to renovate himself and his art, allowed Yeats alone of his contemporaries of the 1890s to transform into an acclaimed Modernist. As he did, Wagner came to be an increasingly dim figure in the twilight of the past: one of many artist-precursors invoked by an appreciative novitiate of a previous century, and recalled with patient irony in "The Trembling of the Veil".[46]

8 Joyce

In 1903 the twenty-year-old James Joyce, struggling in Paris to forge a destiny as a latter-day George Moore, wrote home to ask for his copy of Wagner's operas "*at once!*"[1] Clearly the young man was already familiar with the "Caligostro" of Bayreuth. Indeed, two years earlier he had given a lecture in Dublin on Ibsen's *When We Dead Awaken* in which he had identified Wagner, along with Ibsen, as the dramatic genius of the era. This lecture, Joyce's biographer Richard Ellmann tells us,

> is Joyce's strongest early statement of method and intention. His defense of contemporary materials, his interest in Wagnerian myth, his aversion to conventions, and his insistence that the laws of life are the same always and everywhere, show him to be ready to fuse real people with mythical ones, and so to find all ages to be one as in *A Portrait*, *Ulysses*, and *Finnegans Wake*. The exaltation of drama above all other forms was to be reformulated later in his esthetic system and, if he wrote only one play, he kept to his principles by making all his novels dramatic.[2]

The young Joyce was interested first and foremost in Wagner's mythic and dramatic technique, not in his music. Of course he knew the music well. An amateur tenor, he himself would sing a part in the quintet from *Die Meistersinger* in a concert in 1909.[3] But Joyce's first musical loves were the Irish songs his father had sung, and Italian arias such as "La ci darem la mano" from *Don Giovanni*, which he would make Leopold Bloom whistle throughout the day of *Ulysses*.[4] Often in Joyce's works one comes across evidence of Wagnerian myth and technique. Rarely does one hear the odd Wagnerian motif being whistled by one of his characters.

In his mid-twenties Joyce became increasingly cool in his remarks about Wagner. Undoubtedly this was part of a normal process of repudiating early immature opinions. More specifically, it may have come from a desire to distance himself from the men of the

1890s, who claimed such proprietary intimacy with things Wagnerian, and whose aesthetics in general the budding Modernist felt he had to outgrow. So much is suggested by Joyce's reaction on the occasion when Yeats took him to meet Symons:

> All the arts attracted [Symons]; in music he was a Wagnerian, and he played for Joyce the Good Friday music from *Parsifal*, remarking in a manner that seemed to Joyce 'ninetyish', "When I play Wagner, I am in another world". . . . Joyce, after sampling this remarkable sampler of artistic sensations, enjoyed the remark Yeats made to him when they were alone again. "Symons has always had a longing to commit the great sin, but he has never been able to get beyond ballet girls."[5]

Joyce's growing coolness towards Wagner may have been based further on the sort of intuition about the psychology of the common man that was to become the hallmark of his genius. This is suggested by a letter he wrote to his brother after a performance of *Götterdämmerung* in 1907:

> I went and tried to interest myself but was considerably bored. . . . The fault, I believe, is more mine than Wagner's but at the same time *I cannot help wondering what relation music like this can possibly have to the gentleman I was with in the gallery.*[6] [Emphasis added.]

The gentleman in the gallery was a genial Italian of middle age who struck up bits of conversation throughout the performance, graciously announced "Adesso viene Sigfrido" every time the hero entered, sang along incorrectly with various arias, "yawned much" and left before the finale. He was, in short, an Italian version of Leopold Bloom next to an earnest young Stephen Dedalus. Very likely his presence helped the future author of *Ulysses* to realize that no ordinary citizen of 1904 would wander around town whistling motifs from *The Ring* in the fashion of aesthetes such as Martyn and Moore. The common man of the new century would hardly be likely to whistle anything more ponderous or Teutonic than Mozart's "La ci darem".

Joyce's coolness towards Wagner continued to grow as he reached maturity. By 1908 he was calling his favourite *Meistersinger* "pretentious stuff";[7] and, by the time he had embarked on *Ulysses*, his public remarks about Wagner were occasionally hostile.

"Wagner puzza di sesso", he quipped at one point[8] – which may seem ironic when one considers that his own work was shortly to be banned as pornographic. The contemporary of Freud and D. H. Lawrence was no doubt registering his own distaste for the atmosphere of Victorian repression that clung to the eroticism of works like *Tristan*. But in general the irony of Joyce's anti-Wagner posture of this period is considerable. By the time he was seriously at work on *Ulysses* Joyce was becoming, after all, strikingly like Wagner not only in his ambitions but also in a number of his personal habits: love of luxury, irresponsibility with money, the penchant for self-advertisement, communications to friends soliciting patronage, submission of friendship to the cause of his own High Art, and so forth.[9] His frequent disparaging comments about other artists, Wagner included, often sounded reminiscent of Wagner's celebrated dismissals of his rivals. In this connection it is worth pointing out that, while Joyce was self-consciously cultivating the persona of the Great Artist, complete with disciples and cult-of-the-hero, Wagner was still the pre-eminent type of the Great Artist on which aspirants to the role might model themselves. Considering as much, it seems far from unlikely that, while rejecting Wagner publicly for obvious aesthetic reasons, Joyce was privately measuring his own behaviour against that of this titanic precursor.

In general Joyce's behaviour towards Wagner is exactly the behaviour, in exactly the pattern, that one would expect the developing Stephen Dedalus to exhibit towards an "artist-father": first reverence, then imitation, then competition, then repudiation, finally peaceful coexistence. A revealing instance of this "artist-son" behaviour in the competition/repudiation stage comes in a vignette from the time of composing *Ulysses*:

"I finished the Sirens chapter during the last few days. A big job. I wrote this chapter with the technical resources of music. It is a fugue with all musical notations: *piano, forte, rallentando*, and so on. A quintet occurs in it, too, as in *Die Meistersinger*, my favorite Wagnerian opera. . . . Since exploring the resources and artifices of music and employing them in this chapter, I haven't cared for music any more. I, the great friend of music, can no longer listen to it. I see through all the tricks and can't enjoy it any more."

The subject continued to occupy his thoughts. He read some of the Sirens episode to Ottocaro Weiss shortly before they went together to a performance of Wagner's *Die Walküre*. In the first act, when Siegmund sings the famous love song, "Winterstürme weichen dem Wonnemond" Joyce complained that the song's melodiousness was in bad taste and said to Weiss, "Can you imagine this old German hero offering his girl a box of chocolates?" During the intermission Weiss lauded the music with a fervor of a young Wagnerian. Joyce listened gravely and then said "Don't you find the musical effects of my Sirens better than Wagner's?" "No", said Weiss. Joyce turned on his heel and did not show up for the rest of the opera, as if he could not bear not being preferred.[10]

Thus Joyce the "artist-son", who had not yet received an acclaim to match that of the "artist-father". Some years later, when he did receive such an acclaim, Joyce's attitude would become more gracious. One of those precursors whom he would single out for credit was that old Wagner-enthusiast, Edouard Dujardin, whose *Les Lauriers sont coupé* Joyce had read on the boat when an aspiring young Irish artist making his first journey to Paris in 1902. *Les Lauriers*, Joyce declared at a literary luncheon in honour of the publication of *Ulysses*, had been the primary model for the "interior monologue" technique that he had employed with such signal success.

Old Dujardin, writing in thanks for being included at Joyce's luncheon, couched his reciprocal praise characteristically in a comparison to Wagner. The experience of reading *Ulysses* ranked with that of hearing the *Ring* for the first time, Dujardin effused: like Wagner's music, Joyce's prose created "le sentiment de nager dans un océan du spiritualité".[11] We might note a subtle irony in the use of phrase so reminiscent of Nietzsche's celebrated attack on Wagner's "unending melody"; but Dujardin surely did not intend any covert criticism. In a few years' time he himself would publish a book entitled *Le Monologue intérieur: son apparition, ses origines, sa place dans l'oeuvre de James Joyce*, in which he would accord Joyce's work much the same revolutionary status that he had once accorded Wagner's; also point out that, at least inasmuch as it had derived from his own *Les Lauriers*, Joyce's method had its origins in Wagner's music.[12] Neither this explicit association with Wagner nor the suggestion that his work created the sensation of "swimming in an ocean of spirituality" would seem to have been welcome to an artist as concerned with avoiding the "ninetyish" effect as Joyce. But, underneath the Modernist exterior, Joyce was undoubtedly more a man of the 1890s than he ever cared to admit. And the fact that he had dared to exhume the editor of *La Revue wagnérienne* in a Paris where the attitude towards Wagner had become as "estranged, belittling, [and] contemptuous" as it had once been "enthusiastic, favorable, [and] respectful" suggests ,that he had become considerably more confident about his relationship to his "artist-fathers"[13] – the acclaimed Great Artist of the present could now afford small gestures of homage to the past.

From the time of the triumph of *Ulysses*, Joyce's disparaging remarks about Wagner began to disappear; and during the later 1920s and the 1930s, while he was at work on a book which was in some sense the apotheosis of the musical ideal of the 1890s, he let his lifelong interest in Wagner and Wagnerian method flow as a subterranean current recognizable to all who might care to count the ways in which he could say "gutterdoomering" or "Wellhell",[14] or to "exagiminate" the *Ring*-like texture and scope of his most sublime yet pranksterish literary experiment. Our approach will be slightly less esoteric. In this chapter we shall discuss the Wagner parallels in Joyce's works, the relationship of Wagner's music to Joyce's technique, and the extent to which Joyce might be seen as an anti-Wagnerian artist in the terms Nietzsche set out. Blisset's "James Joyce in the Smithy of His Soul" has covered much of this territory; we shall go farther in some areas, however – notably with regard to *Chamber Music, Exiles,* and the factor of Nietzsche. Joseph Campbell's *The Masks of God: Creative Mythologies* is recommended to those interested in locating the many areas of spiritual affinity between Joyce and Wagner which are not made evident by direct allusion. In general the reader should be warned that, as we shall now be considering the most far-reaching and fully-assimilated aspects of Wagnerism in English literature, this chapter and the two that follow will be longer than their predecessors and the method somewhat less introductory.

* * *

CHAMBER MUSIC AND TRISTAN

Joyce's early volume of poems, published with the assistance of Symons in 1907, demonstrates the young writer's competence in the style of the previous generation. As Picasso absorbed and mastered the techniques of the Impressionists during the first years of the century, so Joyce absorbed and mastered the techniques of the Decadents and Symbolists. One needs only to read the first stanza of the first poem to hear echoes of Wilde and Symons and Moore:

> Strings in the earth and air
> Make music sweet;
> Strings by the river where
> The willows meet.[15]

One needs only to read the first lines of the second poem to mark the influence of "the poet of the Celtic Twilight", whose entire *oeuvre* Joyce had digested by the age of twenty-two:

> The twilight turns from amethyst
> To deep and deeper blue

The poetry of these precursors of the 1890s was Wagnerian in the general ways we have mentioned; and the poetry of *Chamber Music*, while containing no direct allusions to Wagner, is equally Wagnerian in mood and themes. In particular it resounds with echoes of *Tristan*. The theme of a magical and potentially tragic *Liebesnacht* is present in poems III and XXII, and implicit in others such as poem IV (which additionally begins, like Wolfram's song in *Tannhäuser*, with an invocation to the Evening Star).

The generally melancholy love-drenched atmosphere which pervades *Tristan* hangs over a number of other poems, XXVIII for instance:

> Gentle lady, do not sing
> Sad songs about the end of love;
> Lay aside sadness and sing
> How love that passes is enough.
>
> Sing about the long deep sleep
> Of lovers that are dead, and how
> In the grave all love shall sleep:
> Love is aweary now.

Indeed, the *Tristan*-like atmosphere hardly ever breaks to make way for the light-heartedness characteristic of the mature Joyce. The persona of Tristan himself, lying wounded and waiting on the castle ramparts by the grey waste sea, seems to appear in the penultimate poem of the collection:

> All day I hear the noise of waters
> Making moan
> Sad as the seabird is, when going
> Forth alone,
> He hears the winds cry to the waters'
> Monotone.
>
> The grey winds, the cold winds are blowing
> Where I go.
> I hear the noise of many waters
> Far below.
> All day, all night, I hear them blowing
> To and fro.

When the persona is not specifically like that of Tristan, it is generally suggestive of his larger Romantic type: the troubadour knight who seeks ennoblement by keeping his songs and sights on his lady and goddess Amor:

> He who hath glory lost, nor hath
> Found any soul to fellow his,
> Among his foes in scorn and wrath
> Holding to ancient nobleness,
> The high unconsortable one –
> His love is his companion.
>
> (*CM*, xxi)

In this solitary love-struck wanderer we might hear echoes not only of Wagner's Tristan, but also of his Parsifal; even more perhaps of their predecessors in the troubadour epics of Wolfram von Es-chenbach and Gottfried von Strassburg.[16]

Wolfram's tale is of knights who roam the forests and waste places in search of love and battle-glory. Gottfried's tale, while notably more world-weary, is also set in this milieu of glorious deeds, battle and love typical of the earliest romances. Perhaps it is a weird anticipation of confrontation with these elements his predecessors once confronted that haunts Joyce's lover/troubadour/knight in the last poem of the collection:

> I hear any army charging upon the land
>   And the thunder of the horses plunging,
>   foam about their knees:
> Arrogant, in black armour, behind them
>   stand,
> Disdaining the reins, with fluttering
>   whips, the charioteers.
>
> They cry unto the night their battlename:
>   I moan in sleep when I hear afar their
>   whirling laughter.
> They cleave the gloom of dreams, a blinding
>   flame,
> Clanging, clanging upon the heart as
>   upon an anvil.
>
> They come shaking in triumph their long,
>   green hair:
> They come out of the sea and run
>   shouting by the shore.
> My heart, have you no wisdom thus to
>   despair?
> My love, my love, my love, why have
>   you left me alone?

No doubt the most primary echoes here are of Yeats and his Sidhe of *The Wind among the Reeds*. Still, a number of images conjure motifs from Wagner's works or their sources in Wolfram and Gottfried.[17] And, considering the depth of the young Joyce's interest in Wagner, the debt of *Chamber Music* as a whole to Symons and the *fin-de-siècle* with its Wagnerian atmospheres, the careful yet illusive use of Wagnerian motifs which we are going to discover in more mature works, and the extreme range of associations which Joyce always recognized in every phrase and image and word, it would be foolish to discount the possibility that he was even conscious that he was echoing Wagner and his mediaeval sources. With Joyce it is not a question of specific allusion so much as the aspiration shared with Wagner, and present in *Chamber Music* as in *Finnegans Wake*, to create art of the maximum suggestivity.

STEPHEN DEDALUS, SIEGFRIED AND WOTAN

In *A Portrait of the Artist as a Young Man* Stephen Dedalus is identified with a number of mythical figures: the "old artificer" whose name he bears, and with whom he shares the desires to build mazes and to fly away from his captivity; the fallen angel, Lucifer, with whom he shares the attitude, "I will not serve"; also Jesus, to whom he is linked repeatedly – at the moment of his vision of the "dark-plumaged dove" on Sandymount Strand, and in the dialogues with his John the Baptist (Cranly), to name two prominent occasions.[18] These are the major mythical figures against whom Joyce measures the progress of his artist hero, and they account for most of the allusions in the final section of the novel. But to which of them can we connect the central image of his ringing declaration: "I go to encounter for the millionth time the reality of experience and to forge in *the smithy of my soul* [emphasis added] the uncreated conscience of my race"?[19] In a novel so carefully written that nearly every image recalls some previous allusion, one would expect the penultimate sentence to conjure up rich echoes. But what is the echo in "smithy"? Blisset has found an answer. Some pages earlier Stephen has been hailed across the green with the same birdcall from *Siegfried* that, as we have seen, Moore used to hail Martyn. Immediately thereafter Stephen begins to wonder how he can "breed a race less ignoble" than his own (*P*, 238). Ennobling "thoughts and desires of his race" are within him, fragmented as the pieces of Siegmund's sword, and likewise waiting to be *forged*. With his ashplant, which will be directly identified with the Wälsung sword Nothung in *Ulysses*,[20] Stephen wanders about contemplating his entrance into the world, and wondering what trials he will have to undergo to become the hero he feels that his race requires. As Nothung refers to the sword whose fragments the hero Siegfried must forge, so the smithy refers to the smithy of Mime in which he will forge them on the eve of his heroic entrance into the world.

After forging the sword but before entering the world of men (which he does not do until Act I of *Götterdämmerung*), Siegfried must slay the dragon and Mime, shatter Wotan's spear, and awaken Brünnhilde. Stephen Dedalus does approximately half of this in *Portrait*, and in jumbled order. His vision of woman/muse which takes shape in the Sandymount scene and continues to develop in the last section of the novel (particularly in the scene of poetic awakening: *P*, 217–24) parallels Siegfried's awakening of the ideal woman at the end of *Siegfried* and his lingering with her through the Prologue to *Götterdämmerung*. Stephen's rejection of the Jesuits which immediately precedes the Sandymount scene (*P*, 153–64) parallels Siegfried's final rejection of Mime, which immediately precedes his journey to Brünnhilde's rock. Like Mime, the Jesuits have been surrogate parents who have trained their "son" with the appearance of selflessness when actually they intend him to serve their ends. Like Siegfried, who feels free to kill Mime once he can hear through his lies, Stephen feels free to reject the Jesuits once he can see through their intentions. Like Siegfried, Stephen to become hero must serve no one but himself. He must oppose all external authority whether it be of false parents, real fathers, the Church, Ireland or old gods. But unfortunately for Stephen no synthetic authority figure appears in *Portrait*, no convenient Wotan with spear in hand against whom he might raise his ashplant-sword.

When Stephen finally does raise his sword, in "Circe" in *Ulysses*, two years and a false flight (in which Dedalus has become transformed into the fallen Icarus)[21] have elapsed and he is longer the fresh and fearless hero. The Stephen of *Portrait* entered the world of men prematurely, without having properly tested his sword against the dragon and Wotan's spear. He has as a result developed into a Siegfried-*manqué* – an ironic Siegfried: one who has collected the fragments of his art but has not forged them; one who has been wakened to his "racial" calling after a birdcall but has not understood, as Siegfried understands after the Woodbird's song, where to go next and what to do. Where Siegfried acts, Stephen contemplates. Whereas Siegfried never comprehends that he is of the chosen race of Wotan and what that signifies, Stephen fully understands that he is of the race of artists mythically represented by Dedalus and the god Thoth (*P*, 225) and what being a member of that chosen race signifies. Stephen has been called to art, and that calling is in harmony with the allegory of the *Ring* in a way that links him to Wotan as well as to Siegfried. Like Wotan, Stephen wishes to create the revolutionary work – in this case a new form of art, not a hero –that will destroy and supersede a calcified and decadent tradition. On the other hand, Stephen as the fictional hero created by the artist into whom he will logically develop, i.e. Joyce, is also the product of his own revolutionary creative intention.

In this dual self-contradictory role, Stephen like Wotan is divided against himself. As father/artist/creator he thinks and foresees and has intentions, probably too much for his own good. As hero/new work/creative intention he is the natural enemy of his creator-half, by necessity both more and less than his creator-half's intention – just as Siegfried is both more (when he shatters the spear) and less (when he fails in *Götterdämmerung*) than Wotan's intention of what he ideally should be. In "Circe" we see through Stephen's psychological self-accusations that he is less than his intention of what he should be: that is, he is a failed hero, all-too-human in his fear of his mother's ghost. Thus, when he raises his Nothung against *nothing* but the imagined accusers of his own creation (who *block* him in the figurative sense of a mental block), he is performing the same sort of self-destructive act that Wotan performs by blocking the path of the hero who will not be blocked; while at the same time also performing the same sort of self-liberating act that Wotan via Siegfried is paradoxically performing against his failed self. This psychologically realistic ambiguity by which his self-liberating acts are also acts of self-destruction is the respect in which Stephen is most like Wotan. Joyce no doubt intended to underline the analogy by choosing an *ash*plant to be Stephen's "sword"; for it was by breaking a bough from the sacred *Welt-Esche* tree that the young Wotan had obtained his spear in the first place.

That both Siegfried's sword and Wotan's spear should be contained in Stephen's one ashplant is Joyce's way of pointing out not only that his hero is divided against himself but also that Wagner's two personae, Wotan the creator and Siegfried the creative-intention, are one. Joyce, however, took it all a step further, separating the personae again, and by the end of "Circe" completely reversing the archetypal configuration of the *Ring*, in which the father-figure fails and the young hero triumphs. After his sword-play the drunken young Stephen, now missing his ashplant and harassed by officers of the law, reaches as humiliating a low in his career as Wotan has reached by the end of *Siegfried*. Conversely, the father-figure Bloom, quietly triumphant in his act of charity to Stephen, proceeds onward with goodwill and high hopes, distinctly more like Wagner's hero in this than Stephen, that pessimist/sceptic and Siegfried-*manqué*. To comment on the configurations of the *Ring* in such a way as to have them comment on his own work is Joyce's purpose in making the Wagnerian identifications. Casting his unfledged lower-middle-class Dublin poet as the ultimate Romantic hero provides him with an ironic perspective on both shabby reality of his present and the false grandeurs of the departed age. And the fact that Joyce makes the identifications so slight and subtle

shows that he has learned from the example of Moore and others
how excessive an elaborate system of parallels might become.

EXILES: THREE WAGNERIAN PARALLELS

In Act II of Joyce's only play Robert plunks a few notes of Wolfram's
song to the Evening Star.[22] Like the birdcall in *Portrait*, this signals
an extensive relationship to the Wagnerian work in question:
Robert is a Wolfram to Richard's Tannhäuser and Bertha's
Elisabeth. Robert has always been enamoured of Bertha; she in turn
has always had an affection for Robert, but loves her husband
Richard. Richard, however, in his status as wanderer, moody
intense writer, and controversial critic of his homeland, has been as
troublesome to his good Bertha as Tannhäuser to his good
Elisabeth. Moreover, he has perhaps been unfaithful to her, in
Rome, with a dark, independent Venus-type. Robert has heard
rumours to this effect; and, in pressing his suit on Bertha, he
indicates that his main concern is for her honour and welfare – the
noble Wolfram looking out for Elisabeth's best interests. On the
other hand, in spite of his intentions on his friend's wife, Robert
remains as loyal to Richard as Wolfram does to Tannhäuser – at the
beginning of Act II he offers to cancel his tryst with Bertha if Robert
wishes, and in Act III we hear that he has written a favourable article
about Richard in an Irish paper (a defence of his friend to a hostile
audience analogous to Wolfram's defence of Tannhäuser before the
collected *Minnesänger* and Thuringian nobles). That Robert's
doubts about Richard are as restrained as Wolfram's about
Tannhäuser is apparent in their exchange on the subject of
Richard's alleged unfaithfulness:

> ROBERT (*slightly confused*): You know there were rumours here of
> your life abroad – a wild life. Some persons who knew you or
> met you or heard of you in Rome. Lying rumours.
> RICHARD (*coldly*): Continue.
> ROBERT (*laughs a little harshly*): Even I at times thought of her as a
> victim. (*Smoothly*) And of course, Richard, I felt and knew all
> the time that you were a man of great talent.   (*E*, 94–5)

Robert's doubts and rumours from which they have come may in
fact be idle: Richard may well have had no affair at all, only

recurring fantasies of unfaithfulness. In any case, Richard has taken on the role of the guilty Tannhäuser to his wife's chaste Elisabeth: "She has spoken always of her innocence, as I have spoken always of my guilt" (*E*, 98). And, in an attempt to make her less innocent and himself less guilty, he has actually encouraged her to an act of unfaithfulness with Robert. To express this ambiguous position in Tannhäuserian terms, Richard wants to make Bertha into an unpredictable Venus as well as a chaste Elisabeth. So much is evident in the finale of the play when he says, "It is not in darkness of belief that I desire you. But in restless living wounding doubt" (*E*, 162). Richard wants Bertha to become a paradox: a faithless penitent, a Kundry, an improbable synthesis of Venus and Elisabeth – which, after all, is the only satisfactory match for any Tannhäuser type.

In the Notes at the end of the play Joyce compares Richard to the invisible mover, Wotan. This might tip us off to the parallels to *Die Walküre* which come in Act II. Robert plays an ironic Siegmund to Bertha's reluctant Sieglinde, while Richard plays both the immanent Wotan and the absent husband, Hunding. The arguments that Robert uses to try to win Bertha are that passion is the only legitimate law, not marriage; and that for them to make love will release Richard from the "law" that "all his life he has sought to deliver himself" (*E*, 125). Such arguments cannot help but put one in mind of those Act II, scene i, of Wagner's drama, in which Wotan contends that love is the only legitimate law, Fricka insists that marriage must be honoured, and Wotan is ultimately left with nothing but a desperate wish to be released from all law. With these considerations hovering in the background, Robert and Bertha carry on with their tryst in terms distinctly suggestive of Wagner's Act I, scene iii. In that scene a sudden gust of wind blows open the door of Hunding's hut, startling Sieglinde, letting in the radiant moonlight of a spring night, and moving Siegmund to sing his lovely Spring Song (or, as Joyce would have it, to "offer his girl a box of chocolates"). In like manner a sudden gust of wind bursts through the porch door on Robert and Bertha, startling the latter, setting the lamps flickering, and moving the former to a brief attempt at a sort of Spring Song himself:

ROBERT . . . (*He points toward the porch*) Listen!
BERTHA (*in alarm*) What?
ROBERT The rain falling. Summer rain on the earth. Night rain.

The darkness and warmth and flood of passion. Tonight the
earth is loved – loved and possessed. Her lover's arms around
her; and she is silent.   (*E*, 125)

Robert echoes Siegmund's personification of the earth as a woman
being made love to by an exuberant spirit of nature. Beyond that his
comments are but an ironic shadow of Wagner's Spring Song,
especially considering that it is summer not spring, and raining not
moonlit. Robert himself is little more than an all-too-human ghost
of Siegmund. For where that hero after finishing his song sees
Nothung shining in the glimmering light, draws it forth, and forces the
moment to its crisis, Robert after finishing his "song" merely fails to
convince Bertha that there is "nothing" to be startled by in the
flickering lamplight and lets the tryst come to its bathetic close (*E*,
126).

   Also in the Notes Joyce compares the situation of his play to that
of *Tristan*. This relationship is most apparent in Acts I and III
(though Act II, as can be seen, is in its way an ironic *Liebesnacht*). In
Act I Robert tries to play Tristan to Bertha's Isolde. They kiss; then:

ROBERT (*sighs*) My life is finished – over.
BERTHA O don't speak like that now, Robert.
ROBERT Over, over. I want to end it and have done with it.
BERTHA (*concerned but lightly*) You silly fellow!
ROBERT (*presses her to him*) To end it all – death. To fall from a
    great high cliff, down, right down into the sea.
BERTHA Please, Robert . . .
ROBERT Listening to music and in the arms of the woman I love –
    the sea, music and death.   (*E*, 45–6)

". . . the sea, music and death" – Joyce could not have made the
Tristan resonance more clearly. The effect of the kiss on Robert is
like that of the kiss on Tristan and Isolde after they have drunk the
love-potion; and one might even regard Robert's vision of falling
from a "great high cliff" as a Joycean fantasy of the hallucinating
Tristan tumbling off the ramparts of his Breton castle down to his
death on the shore of the vast empty sea, having lost his footing
while trying to spy Isolde's ship on the horizon.[23] Clearly Robert
doth protest too much. Bertha, of course, is sceptical, "lightly"
contemptuous of his performance. She is not eager to play Isolde,
not to Robert's Tristan at any rate – only to Richard's. This she does
ultimately in the finale of the play:

RICHARD I am wounded, Bertha.

BERTHA . . . In what way are you wounded?

RICHARD . . . I have a deep, deep wound of doubt in my soul.

BERTHA (*motionless*) Doubt of me?

RICHARD Yes.

BERTHA I am yours. (*In a whisper*) If I died this moment, I am yours.

RICHARD(*still gazing at her and speaking as if to an absent person*) I have wounded my soul for you – a deep wound of doubt which can never be healed. . . . To hold you by no bonds, even of love, to be united with you in body and soul in utter nakedness – for this I longed. And now I am tired for a while, Bertha. My wound tires me.

(*He stretches himself out wearily along the lounge. Bertha holds his hand, still speaking very softly.*)

BERTHA Forget me, Dick. Forget me and love me again as you did the first time. I want my lover. To meet him, to go to him, to give myself to him. You, Dick. O, my strange wild lover, come back to me again! (*She closes her eyes.*)   (*E,* 161–2)

Needless to say, the "wound" is a version of the Tristan love-wound, the wound–fatigue parallel to the Tristan/Amfortas world-weariness, and the stretching out upon the lounge reminiscent of the collapse of Tristan/Amfortas onto the death-litter.[24] The posture and attitude of Bertha finally is like that of Elisabeth, Isolde and Kundry. She is lover, worshipper and penitent; and her final closing of the eyes is suggestive of the grateful release into death that comes for all three of these heroines of Wagner's (and for Senta and Brünnhilde in slightly different ways as well). Joyce may have intended all of this to be drily ironic; if so, he succeeded in being so subtle that one can hardly tell. And it might be argued with justification that in a direct and unplayful way Joyce reveals here his own Romantic, Wagnerian and futile yearning for an all-embracing, world-eclipsing, *Tristan*-like love. From this point of view *Exiles* ends by seeming as "ninetyish" a work as *Chamber Music*.

ULYSSES AND MYTHIC ASSOCIATION

Beyond the Stephen/Siegfried identifications which carry over from *Portrait* the number of allusions to Wagner in *Ulysses* is small. There is a parallel suggested to *The Flying Dutchman*. In "Calypso" Bloom thinks, "His back is like that Norwegian captain's" (*U*, 61). In "Circe" he at one point interjects: "These flying Dutchmen or lying Dutchmen . . ." (*U*, 479). There may be similar asides in other places as well; and the pertinence of Wagner's early opera to Bloom's progress is clear enough. Like Ulysses, the Dutchman is a sea-faring wanderer looking for woman and home. Like the mourning Bloom, he is traditionally clad in black. Like Bloom, he is also the archetype of the Wandering Jew. The Dutchman is, however, unlike Bloom in one crucial respect: where his years of wandering have made him so suspicious that he mistrusts Senta and brings on tragedy in the end, Bloom's day of wandering – in spite of all the buffetings and disappointments – has left him trusting of his fellows and accepting of Molly's actual unfaithfulness. Bloom does not react to the spectacle of his wife with Boylan in the manner of Vanderdecken to the chance encounter of his betrothed with Eric. Bloom is Wagner's hero with the devils of paranoia, self-pity and despair substantially exorcized.

Even more than in *Portrait* the allusions to Wagner in *Ulysses* are so subtle and subterranean that they only make sense when considered by a process of logical free association. An example rises out of the musical phrase "Heigho" which rings out from the bells of St George's Church at the end of "Calypso" in a sort of invocation or warning preparatory to the events of Bloom's day. Specificially this phrase puts Bloom in mind of "poor Dignam", to whose funeral he thereupon sets off. But why "Heigho"? In Act II of *Götterdämmerung* Hagen repeats this phrase several times as a sort of warning and invocation preparatory to the return of Siegfried, Gunther and Brünnhilde, and the unfolding of the plot which will lead to Siegfried's death and funeral. Could it be that Joyce is announcing an association between Dignam's funeral and the events surrounding Siegfried's death? If so, a number of interesting questions are raised as Bloom proceeds in "Hades" to the funeral. (1) Is there a parallel to be drawn between Bloom's father's difficult relationship with his wife and his ultimate suicide (*U*, 96–7), and Wotan's problems with his wife and his ultimate self-destruction? (2) Is there a Wagnerian resonance to be found in Martin Cunningham's statement "That will be a great race tomorrow in Germany" (*U*, 97)? (3) Do the phrases "Who'll read the book? I, said the rook" (*U*, 103) and "A bird sat tamely perched on a poplar branch" (*U*, 113) allude to the ravens that Wotan sends to observe the death and funeral of Siegfried? (4) Does Bloom's thought that "His head might come up some day above ground in a landslip with his hand pointing" (*U*, 108) allude to the admonitory rising of the dead Siegfried's hand? These questions might seem to lead beyond the bounds of good sense; but then the effect of the unexplained "Heighos" is to lead to speculations about the connections to *Götterdämmerung*, sensible or not. And it seems likely, given Joyce's penchant for relating the mundane event with Shakespeare, Homer, primal myths, or whatever else may have struck him as germane, that he would fill this "paltry funeral" which has such a prominent place in his twentieth-century epic with teasing reminders of that grand funeral scene of the epic artwork of the preceding century.

Such possibilities suggest themselves because of Joyce's subtlety in making mythic associations, not simply out of excessive reader's zeal. One might imagine oneself to be veering into some sort of academic lunacy upon hearing echoes of *Parsifal* in the motifs of saviours, racial orders, mountaintop declamations, boys' shrill voices and woman's sin-bringing that fill the "Aeolus" chapter which follows "Hades" (as *Parsifal* follows *Götterdämmerung*).[25] Still, it would be wrong to assume that such echoes did not cross Joyce's mind. Indeed, Campbell regards the whole of *Ulysses* as a version of the mediaeval *Parzival*, which is also an epic of growth-through-experience with two heroes, the younger Parzival, whom Campbell sees in Stephen, and the older Gawan, whom Campbell sees in Bloom (who, like Gawan to Parzival, is exactly sixteen years Stephen's senior).[26] This theory, far from hurtling the reader beyond the bounds of good sense, only makes the experience of *Ulysses* that much richer. In the end, however, it should be said that the Wagner work which bears the closest spiritual affinity to *Ulysses* is *Meistersinger*, the one drama in which the *Meister* came down from his ideal realm of myth to treat the reality of petty burghers. Wagner treated this with such unusual sympathy that Chamberlain was to call it a tribute to the "Purely Human", and its hero, like Bloom, a symbol of the capacity for "greatness of soul" inherent in the common man.[27]

FINNEGAN: THE WORLD-HISTORIC EPIC

As one might expect, Wagnerian allusions resound and rebound throughout Joyce's last work. We are alerted to the most important of these in the second sentence of the book, which begins, "Sir Tristram, violer d'amores, fr'over the short sea, had passencore rearrived from North Armorica on this side of the scraggy isthmus of Europe Minor to wielderfight his penisolate war . . . " Music, the sea-journey, battle, sex and isolation – the outstanding motifs of the Tristan legend are blithely raised and teased in this sentence just as they are in the last chapter of the second book. This begins with the call " – Three quarks for Muster Mark!" and proceeds with a "scribble-dehobbled" *Tristan* for seventeen pages. Joyce-scholars have analysed this chapter more adequately than we can here. Suffice it to say that this version of *Tristan* follows Blisset's three rules of the *Finnegan* method: (1) whatever it is, make it sound Irish; (2) take it down and lay it low; (3) make it funny.[28] Thus Wagner's final fate at Joyce's hands is to be stood on his head and genially mocked. The tragic mood of the Wagnerian drama has vanished. In its place we find a barely comprehensible dream on a subject which for Joyce as for Wagner was a consistent favourite: adultery. This dream takes place in the mind of Humphrey Chimpden Earwicker, a reincarnation of Finn MacCool, who himself, as the cuckolded husband of Grainne, was a previous incarnation of King Marke of *Tristan* fame.[29]

So much for "Muster Mark". As to Earwicker, he is a version of the *All-Vater* inasmuch as he "Haveth Childers Everywhere", and thus of Wagner's Wotan.[30] Wotan/Odin is in fact one of his Nordic ancestors according to Dounia Christiani in her article. "H. C. Earwicker, the Ostman".[31] Moreover, the Danish root of his name, *evige* meaning "eternal one", combined with the German root, *Erwacher* meaning "awakener", suggests the "eternal awakener" of the *Ring*, the hero Siegfried. The name Earwicker also suggests "earwig"; and indeed Earwicker has an *alter ego* of "Persse O'Reilly", which name, transformed into its French root *perce-oreille*, means "earwig". This leads to the question, why *earwig*? One possibility that has not been raised elsewhere is that Joyce was inspired by Nietzsche's ironic observation that "There is as little prospect of man attaining a higher order as there is for the ant and the earwig to enter into kingship with God and eternity at the end of their career on earth".[32] This seems to be making exactly the point that Joyce appears to be making: that is, ant = earwig = man = higher order = God = eternity, and *da capo* in the *eternally recurring Ring*-like cycles of evolution and history.

This brings us to the main point about Wagner and *Finnegans*

Wake, which is that *Finnegan* is a world-historic epic on the scale and even the pattern of the *Ring*. Using Vico, Joyce constructs a tetralogy which, like Wagner's tetralogy, shows human history to develop through four distinct stages: theocracy or the age of gods (*Finnegans Wake* Book One/*Rheingold*); aristocracy or the age of heroes (Book Two/*Walküre*); democracy or the age of men (Book Three/*Siegfried*); and chaos/*ricorso* (Book Four/*Götterämmerung*). As Blisset points out, "riverrun" at the beginning of *Finnegan* and the flowing out of Anna Liffey at the end parallel the Rhine motifs which begin and end the *Ring*.[33] Moreover, the loving monologue of Anna Livia which closes *Finnegan*, like the loving monologue of Erda/*Urmutter* Molly which closes *Ulysses*, creates an atmosphere of sleep, peace and transcendence into the Eternal Feminine which parallels the effects of the loving monologues of Brünnhilde and Isolde in the finales of the *Ring* and *Tristan*. The fact that Joyce's major works flow out into this blending with the Eternal Feminine of Mother Nature demonstrates amply how much the Celtic artist of the early twentieth century ultimately shared in the pantheistic Nature Mysticism of the German Romantic.

> Das Ewig=Weibliche
> Zieht uns hinan.[34]

* * *

CIRCLE AND *LEITMOTIV*

Finnegans Wake also demonstrates how much Joyce ultimately shared in the Symbolist ambition, growing out of Wagnerism, to write "The Book", that "Grand-Oeuvre de la Suggestion", Mallarmé's ideal;[35] which brings us to the second phase of our discussion, Joyce's relation to Wagner in style and ideas. *Finnegan* ends with "a breath, a nothing, the article 'the' "[36] and thus circles back to its beginning sentence. Molly Bloom's soliloquy ends with "the most positive word in the human language",[37] *Yes*, and thus circles back to the word with which it began. Leopold Bloom's voyage through Dublin ends at the jingling wife-filled bed from which it started. *Portrait* ends with an invocation of a father's blessing for a youth beginning a journey, while it began with a baby-tale journey and an image of a father through glass. *Dubliners* ends with a visit to the home of two sisters in which memories of the dead are awakened, while it began with a visit to the home of two sisters in which a dead man's memory is ascendant. In all of Joyce's works, end and beginning meet, forming a circle. Thus the circle, whether as the circular experience of a Dublin day or the metaphysical cycles of Vico, is the emblem of the structure of Joyce's art.

Rheingold begins with the motifs of the Rhine. Four dramas later *The Ring* cycle ends with the overwashing of those same Rhine motifs. End returns to beginning. As river flows back to sea and sea-water evaporates to create clouds and clouds burst into rain to feed the sources of rivers again, so a new *Ring* cycle may begin. This is the significance of "ring" above and beyond its Nibelungen context: it is the emblem of Wagner's art. It appears as the sacred circle of Grail Knights in *Parsifal*; it reappears a half-century later as the central working idea for Wieland Wagner's restagings of his grandfather's entire *oeuvre*. *Circle* and *ring*. They are generically the same. Their common property is *continuity*. Both Wagner and Joyce aspired to create works that were continuous, "endless". Both aspired to create epics of their culture in their age which could simultaneously transcend historical time and place to suggest all culture in all ages. Both formed their art so that typical dramatic events might be transformed into vortices through which the audience might be whirled back towards those archetypal "earliest picture dreamings".

This effect, the evocation of the racial unconsciousness ("the uncreated conscience of my race"), was Joyce's objective as much as it was Wagner's and he worked towards it through similar techniques. Wagner broke historical fixity by harmonizing emotional and mythic associations, and by use of leitmotivs. Many critics have talked about Joyce's use of leitmotiv. Joyce himself is said to have coined the term *idée-mère* to express the same concept;[38] and it is accepted as commonplace that the concept was as fundamental to his method as it was to that of contemporaries like Mann and Pound. Novels such as *Ulysses* and *Finnegan*, and poems like the *Cantos* which has much in common with them, are finally best understood as musical equations of the conflicting, transforming, dissolving, reconfiguring images and phrases and ideas, the leitmotivs, that are repeated throughout. To illustrate we might take the example of "Throwaway" from *Ulysses*, which enters the fabric of the novel near the beginning when Bloom offhandedly gives his newspaper to Bantam Lyons, saying as he does: "You can keep it. I was going to *throw* it *away*" (*U*, 86; emphasis added).

As Lyons is an avid horse-better, he mistakes Bloom's comment for a tip on the *dark-horse*, Throwaway, who is running in the afternoon's *race* at Ascot. As Bloom is a member of the Jewish *race*, he is an outsider in Dublin; as he is wearing mourning black, he is also conspicuously *dark*. Thus as "Throwaway", "dark horse", "rank outsider", and related phrases crop up throughout the day, we realize that they refer not only to the horse but to Bloom as well. By the time we reach Kiernan's pub in the later afternoon, the news is out that Throwaway has won at Ascot against all odds; and, because of the "tip" to Bantam Lyons, the Citizen and other denizens of the pub assume that Bloom has bet on the dark-horse and is about to collect a sizable purse. Normally suspicious of Bloom because of his race, the pub-denizens are now particularly hostile; and the Citizen reminds the Jew in blatant terms that he is an outsider in Ireland. In the argument about *race* which follows, Bloom *wins* a moral victory against all odds. He remains *in the dark* of course about how he has been identified with Throwaway's freak win. And later that night, when he and Stephen are sitting in the cab-shelter, he happens to glance at the race-results in the newspaper and offhandedly comments to himself on the phenomenon of betting on horses: "Guesswork it reduced itself to eventually" (*U*, 648).[39]

The leitmotiv, Throwaway and the race and so forth, operates with characteristic Joycean punning and irony to suggest several of the novel's most important existential themes: (1) the difficulty of communicating between one individual and another (Bloom and Lyons); (2) the outsider status of the individual in modern urban society (Bloom the alien at Kiernan's); (3) the uncertainty of sure things and the ineffable divine "guesswork" that for Joyce, as for Schopenhauer and Nietzsche, was the ruling principle of events. In one way the motif communicates directly to the characters: every time the pub-denizens think about that outsider winning the race it suggests something they envy, luck's purse, and someone they dislike, the Jew. In another way the motif communicates only to the audience: Bloom will never know the unfortunate influence Throwaway has had on his day, and the other characters may never learn that their particular hostility has been based on a simple communications mistake. These two functions are primary ways in which Wagner's leitmotivs operate as well: (1) to evoke responses from characters that reveal the fundamental flaws in their psychology;

(2) to communicate to the audience a pattern governing events that the individual characters themselves cannot comprehend.[40]

MUSICAL PROSE

The most sophisticated function of the Wagnerian leitmotiv is, as we have said, to lead the audience back towards the deepest, earliest, and least discursive inklings of the meaning of all things: thus, through the vortex of motifs that make up the funeral music of Siegfried, we are led back to the Rhine Journey, the awakening of Brünnhilde, the events of the young hero's life, and his prehistory, all the way to what Thomas Mann identifies as our primal "picture dreamings". Thus, through a similar and equally sophisticated conflation of motifs at the moment in *Portrait* before Stephen awakes to write his poem "Are You Not Weary of Ardent Ways?", we are led back via a vision of a female who is at once his muse, a girl he admired as an adolescent, the prostitute he visited as a student, the Virgin Mary, whose sodality once led, and all women; thence via more shadowy remembrances of his young life, and images of the Christian myths in which he has been drenched, all the way to the glimmers of equally archetypal "picture dreamings":

> Towards dawn he awoke. O what sweet music! His soul was all dewy wet. Over his limbs in sleep pale cool waves of light had passed. He lay still, as if his soul lay amid cool waters, conscious of faint sweet music. His mind was waking slowly to a tremulous morning knowledge, a morning inspiration. A spirit filled him, pure as the purest water, sweet as dew, moving as music. But how faintly it was inbreathed, how passionlessly, as if the seraphim themselves were breathing upon him! His soul was waking slowly, fearing to wake wholly. It was that windless hour of dawn when madness wakes and strange plants open to the light and the moth flies forth silently. (*P*, 217)

Like the descending chromatics of the unfolding chords of Wagner's prelude to *Lohengrin*, Stephen's mind begins to waken "tremulously", "slowly". Like the A held quavering and then so lightly dropped by the violins, a "spirit" begins to enter his consciousness. Like notes, images are stated, half-changed, recapitulated: "dewy wet" in the third sentence, "cool waves" in the fourth sentence, "cool waters" in the fifth sentence, "purest water" and "dew" again in the seventh, "inbreathed" and "breathing" in the eighth, "windless" in the ninth. As the pure spirit of Lohengrin is conceived in the Wagnerian/Freudian feminine of the trembling violins, so this "spirit" of Stephen's is conceived in the Joycean feminine of the "cool waters" of his soul.[41] Slowly down the chromatic falls of the prelude Wagner's spirit descends, gently, the hero to save disordered, maddened Brabant. Slowly, as if on the breath of seraphim, the Joycean spirit descends: descends from a divine sphere above towards a sphere on a more human plane, where madness awaits. Thus Wagner draws us down through picture dreamings, through the twilit archetypal dawn of the race. Thus Joyce draws us down through images that are equally primal/sensual: dawn, water, light, breath, wind, madness, strange plants opening, the moth. Music attends, and Wagner draws us from dreamings towards introduction of the mythic hero who will make flesh the vision of a saviour that has been conceived in the virgin womb of Elsa's innocent mind. Music attends, and Joyce draws us from dream towards myth: "In the virgin womb of the imagination the word was made flesh. Gabriel the Seraph had come to the virgin's chamber" (*p*, 218).

Throughout this passage music is important as a concept as well as a word. Indeed, the passage is an outstanding example of Wagnerian prose, comparable to Mann's description in *Buddenbrooks* of Hanno's improvisation after he has seen *Lohengrin* for the first time;[42] or to Moore's imitation of the spirit of the prelude to *Lohengrin* in a passage in *The Lake*, or Baudelaire's transformation of the same prelude into a prose reverie in *Richard Wagner et "Tannhäuser" à Paris*. After such passages the men of the 1890s might have expected their readers to slip into the sort of beatific contemplations that Dorian Gray sinks into after reading from the book that Lord Henry has given him. But within a few pages of this passage the Modernist Joyce leads his readers back out into the sordid reality of lower-middle-class Dublin and the not-so-beautiful facts of Stephen's life. And after *Portrait* Joyce would create no more of these beautiful illusions, these prose imitations of Wagner that were the hallmark of a previous age. He would, however, remain as devoted to writing musical prose as Wilde or Moore ever was. More so, we might say, considering such experiments as the "Sirens" chapter of *Ulysses*. This chapter contains, by Joyce's statement, a fugue and a quintet like the one in *Meistersinger*. The opening eighty-odd lines, moreover, contain every motif to be developed within the body of the chapter, thus serving as a Wagnerian prelude.[43]

To the first-time reader this "prelude" appears as a collection of phrases ("Jingle jingle jaunted jingling", "tap tap tap", "bronze by gold", and so forth) which are acoustically stimulating but otherwise obscure. If the reader is not hopelessly confused and put off (which, as Blisset says, is most often the case), he might note that some phrases are repeated in modifications and new associations analogous to key changes or chord adjustments. He might go so far as to realize that the sounds are meant to represent the ear-piercing cries of the Sirens as they lure Ulysses towards his rock, in this case Bloom to the Ormond bar. Even so, the reader will not understand until he has finished the chapter that these sounds all refer, in basically the same chronological order, to the events and themes dealt with throughout. Thus "Jingle jingle jaunted jingling" refers to Bloom's jingling bed at 7, Eccles Street, and to his wife's afternoon tryst with Blazes Boylan, ostensibly to arrange for a concert tour but actually for sex. "Bronze by gold" refers to the fixtures of the bar, and to the colour of the barmaids' hair. "Sonnez la cloche" and "thigh smack" refer to the fact that one of the barmaids raises her skirt and snaps her garter at the stroke of the hour to try to entice Boylan to stay in the bar rather than to keep his appointment with Mrs Bloom. And so on and so forth.

The Classical overture was generally a decoration that was added to the opera afterwards and had little or no specific thematic relationship to the whole. The Romantic prelude as Wagner conceived it was a collection of leitmotivs that would become identifiable as the action unfolded and their associations to characters and events were made. In this sense Wagner's preludes were précis of a sort to what was to follow. Joyce's prelude in "Sirens" functions as such. But Joyce in fact was employing the form with an absolutist zeal that actually exceeded that of his predecessor; for not even in his most comprehensive preludes, to *The Flying Dutchman* and *Die Meistersinger*, did Wagner attempt chronologically to foreshadow *all* the events that were to follow. Small wonder that, by the time he had finished composing "Sirens", Joyce had worn out his appreciation for the "artifices" and "tricks" of his most favourite art. The appreciation was to return, however. *Finnegans Wake*, expanding on some of the techniques used in "Sirens", was to take the idea of "musical prose" to a new and unexpected extreme; which may well have constituted the final

Dämmerung of that Wagnerian aspiration shared by literary stylists since the time of Baudelaire.

JOYCE *CONTRA* WAGNER

"There is no help for it, we must first be Wagnerites!" So the renegade Nietzsche had written in his preface to *The Case of Wagner*.[44] So the case of James Joyce amply demonstrates; for Joyce's art, and the concerns embodied in it, almost always stands in some relation to Wagner's – often a relation of exaggeration, reversal or repudiation. We have seen exaggeration in Joyce's experiments at music, reversal in his deflation of the heroic, repudiation in his travesties of tragic grandeurs. But always there is some relation. Mann wrote that Wagner's particular genius lay in his ability to weave together myth and psychology.[45] The same has often been said about Joyce. And, as we have seen, Joyce derived his mythic method from Wagner among others, and his most important psychological technique (the interior monologue) from Wagner both directly and through such literary stepfathers as Moore, Dujardin and Mallarmé. Having said as much, we should also note that Joyce was no less adamant than Stephen Dedalus about being his own "father", and that the great mythic/psychological accomplishment of *Ulysses* was first of all the logical offspring of his self-contemplation of the artist as a young man, which in turn had been the logical offspring of his Naturalistic character-studies in *Dubliners*.

The temperament that exploded the interior monologue of *Ulysses* into the comic/anarchic multilogue of *Finnegans Wake* was not, finally, a Wagnerian temperament. As he matured, Joyce moved further and further from the point of view of the preceding century. The "ninetyish" melancholy of *Chamber Music* and Zolaesque mundanity of *Dubliners* gave way to willing acceptance of the divine comedy of all things by the time of *Ulysses*. The Schopenhauerian pessimism that marked Wagner's mature works at least as much as youthful death-yearning had marked his early ones could only be viewed as ludicrous amid the helter-skelter of "Circe" and *Finnegan*. This perhaps is the most significant point here. Unlike those precursors of *fin-de-siècle* who shared Wagner's growing repugnance at the facts of modern life, Joyce had an insatiable hunger to find out the most minute and vulgar details of that life, with all the veils of Romance pulled aside; and, having found them, to accept them for what they were – natural, "purely human", no less joyous than horrifying, no less comic than tragic, no less "good" than "evil". Joyce ultimately arrived at that ambivalent/ironical Modernist point of view that Mann also achieved, Nietzsche had aspired to, Wagner had glimpsed on the horizon but recoiled from. So much can be seen in Joyce's position *vis-à-vis* Wagner on the subjects of nationalism and the Jew.

Both men were critics of their homelands when young, both became exiles, both spent years lamenting their outsider status. But Wagner (whose exile, it should be said, was political and involuntary, unlike Joyce's) never accepted his foreigner status and in the end returned to his homeland, there to produce the great art of the new German *Reich* and become an outspoken nationalist, at times even jingoist. Joyce, on the other hand, "beat out his exile" and in the end came to see himself as a citizen of Europe, one whose art celebrated his nation's weaknesses as well as its beauties, and did not propose to be typical of the nascent Irish Free State. Both men recognized the new position of the Jew in Europe, identified with the Wandering Jew in their careers, and depicted Jewish prototypes in their art. But Wagner saw the Jew as an agent-of-decay as well as a tragic victim, a Klingsor as well as a Dutchman, and indulged in the "Judaism in Music" kind of outbursts, which obscured the deep Semitic sympathies in his life and art to the end. Joyce, on the other hand, saw the Jew as the type of the modern Everyman, a latter-day Quixote rather than tragic victim, and drew him into his fictional family as *primus inter pares* beside the melancholy young poet, the artist/hero-*manqué*, the Tannhäuserian husband, the morally paralysed Dubliners, and all the others.[46]

The difference between Wagner and Joyce on these points has much to do with the changing attitudes towards *alienation* during the psychology-ridden decades under discussion. The nineteenth-century Wagner was shocked by the fact of his rootlessness and regarded the establishment of alien Jews in positions of wealth and influence, while the native European himself had to wander and struggle, as too great an irony to accept. The twentieth-century Joyce by contrast accepted his rootlessness as an unavoidable destiny and regarded the ability of the Jew to survive, and survive with humanity amid so much alienation and prejudice, as a model for how to carry on. Wagner concentrated on the big Jew, whose status he saw as symptomatic of changes that would gradually destroy ancient European values; and he struck a semi-traditionalist posture anticipating Modernists such as T. S. Eliot, who would prove less accepting of twentieth-century alienation than Joyce was. Joyce concentrated on the lower-middle-class Jew whose struggles he saw as symptomatic of the condition of all Europeans in future; and he struck such ironical balance in depicting Bloom that readers such as Ezra Pound, whose rage at the "Usura" of international financiers would lead to outbursts reminiscent of Wagner's, did not mistake what was intended as art for pro- or anti-Semitic propaganda.

Because of such considerations, Wagner finally did not quite fit into that highly civilized ambivalent persona that Goethe had indentified as proper to the artist. Joyce, on the other hand, always remained true to his youthful precept that the artist must hold himself above and beyond events, like God "paring his fingernails". From this point of view we might characterize the major difference between the two by saying that, while for Wagner art sometimes meant politics, for Joyce art always meant art and art alone. That "heroic vitalist" Wagner, who would become an apologist for Fabianism via Shaw, or the inspirer of Nazism via Chamberlain, had little to do with Joyce. A more congenial Wagner was the Romantic who believed in the "panacea" of Love: the *agape* of *Parsifal* which reappears in Bloom, the *eros* of *Tristan* which hovers behind *Exiles*, the primal Love in the Rhine motifs at the end of the *Ring* which resonates in the waters of Anna Liffey as she flows back to the sea. This Wagner had something to do with Joyce. But the Wagner who had the most in common of all was that art-for-art's-sake figure of semi-divine stature who was "accustomed to dealing with symbols and elevating monstrances" and "ended by feeling like a brother of priests; indeed, like a priest himself".[47]

STEPHEN AND NIETZSCHEAN HUBRIS

The artist as priest; the artist as God standing above and beyond "paring his fingernails";[48] the artist as builder of labyrinths and spiderwebs of metaphor; the artist as magician and word-musician creating a divine night-music; the artist as sorcerer exploiting the potentials of magic, madness, hallucination and dream; the artist as obscurantist concealing all the props to make his illusions seem real; the artist as megalomaniac – Joyce was all these things. To this extent, he was the same type of artist as Nietzsche had derided in *The Case of Wagner*. On the other hand Joyce, was remarkably like the new type of artist that Nietzsche had called for in the three "Voltairean/Mediterranean"[49] books he wrote immediately after the break with Wagner: *Human, All-too-Human* (1878), *The Dawn of Day* (1881) and *The Joyful Wisdom* (1882)[50]. This is not so apparent from the characters Joyce identifies directly with Nietzscheanism: Mr Duffy of the story "A Painful Case" has a copy of *The Gay Science* on his bookshelf, but, far from being the joyful solitary that that book celebrates, is an alienated recluse; and Buck Mulligan, who spouts phrases from *Zarathustra* in the course of the *Ulysses* day, has more of the pomp than the wisdom of Nietzsche's most parodiable persona. On the other hand, Joyce's great heroes, though not directly identified with Nietzscheanism themselves, embody a considerable number of Nietzschean motifs.

Consider Stephen Dedalus. In the course of his development in *Portrait*, he becomes a religious iconoclast in good Nietzschean fashion. Specifically, he rejects performing his "easter duty" as his mother requests (*P*, 239), dramatizing Nietzsche's precepts that "duty [is] interference against power" and that "a mother asking a son to do his duty diminishes his growing individual power" (*DD*, 112). In choosing to reject religion, family, and homeland in order to forge his artistic sword, Stephen recognizes that he may be making a mistake; but he braces himself by declaring, "I am not afraid to make a mistake, even a . . . lifelong mistake, and perhaps as long as eternity too" (*P*, 247), echoing Nietzsche's precept that "To be noble – that might then mean, perhaps, to be capable of follies" (*JW*, 57). Stephen's resolve to become an artist is affirmed at the moment when his confusion after breaking with the Jesuits leads him down to the edge of the sea, there to have a sudden Dantesque vision of a girl (*P*, 171), dramatizing Nietzsche's psychological observation that, "When a man is in the midst of *his* hubbub, in the midst of the breakers of his plots and plans, he there sees perhaps calm, enchanting beings glide past him, for whose happiness and retirement he longs–*they are women*" (*JW*, 99).

Shortly after, Stephen begins to define a theory of art based on rejection of the "ardent ways" of the late nineteenth century and attention to the realities of the mundane world, even its offal and urine-smells, putting into practice Nietzsche's admonition to sweep away "false grandeur" and re-create the world as no more or less "disharmonic" than it is (*DD*, 12). Stephen goes on to outline three standards of beauty – *integritas, consonantia* and *claritas* (*P*, 212) – which would have been wholly acceptable to Nietzsche, just as the three standards of beauty Nietzsche outlines in *Dawn of Day* – happiness, individuality and realism (*DD*, 315) – would be wholly acceptable to the mature Joyce. Finally, at the end of *Portrait* Stephen, fascinated with the free flight of birds,[51] yet not aware of his own destiny as an Icarus, resolves to fly away; and in this we might hear echoes not only of the association of the artist with the free-flying bird in the early English Romanticism of Shelley (and the association of the artist with Icarus throughout French Romanticism[52]), but also the association of the "fearless one" and artist-soul with birds and Icarus and indeed all things that fly which recurs like a leitmotiv throughout Nietzsche's works,[53] notably in the "Songs of Prince Free-as-a-Bird" which end *The Joyful Wisdom*:

> Oh marvel! there he flies
> Cleaving the sky with wings unmoved – what force
>   Impels him, bids him rise,
> What curb restrains him? Where's his goal, his course?
>
>   (*JW*, 363)

Stephen/Joyce left Ireland in 1902 feeling that all his teachers and predecessors had come to a standstill. His mind remained full of the native Yeastsian dream of the Land-beyond-the-Western-Wave that he would put to use later in "The Dead" and ultimately in *Finnegans Wake*. But his initial flight to find spiritual fathers and artistic brethren, proving immature as it would, partook of the very hubris that Nietzsche had so marvellously summed up in the transcendental closing piece of *The Dawn of Day*, "We Aeronauts of the Intellect":

> All those daring birds that soar far and ever farther into space, will somewhere or other be certain to find themselves unable to continue their flight, and they will perch on a mast or some narrow ledge – and will be grateful even for this miserable accommodation! But who could conclude from this that there was not an endless free space stretching far in front of them, and that they had flown as far as they possibly could? In the end, however, all our great teachers and predecessors have come to a standstill, and it is by no means in the noblest or most grateful attitude that their weariness has brought them to a pause: the same thing will happen to you and me! but what does this matter

to either of us? *Other birds will fly farther!* Our minds and hopes vie with them far out and on high; they rise far above our heads and our failures, and from this height they look far into the distant horizon and see hundreds of birds much more powerful than we are, striving whither we ourselves have also striven, and where all is sea, sea, and nothing but sea!

And where, then, are we aiming at? Do we wish to cross the sea? Whither does this overpowering passion urge us, this passion which we value more highly than any other delight? Why do we fly precisely in this direction, where all the suns of humanity have hitherto set? Is it possible that people may one day say of us that we also steered westward, hoping to reach India – but that it was our fate to be wrecked on the infinite? Or, my brethren? or –? (*DD*, 394–5)

Stephen Dedalus of *Portrait* flew to Paris with little inkling that, in the quest that Dante and Wolfram's Parzival and so many others had made before him, he would fail to go all the way to glimpse the divine ineffable in the rose of Paradise or in the stone of the Grail.[54] Thus Stephen of *Ulysses* is the returned bird, the fallen Icarus, the failed "aeronaut" of Nietzsche's prediction. Stephen of *Ulysses* is locked in the "nightmare" of history from which he wishes he could awake (*U*, 34), bound to what Nietzsche had described as the "burden" and "disease" and "fiction" of history, and muttering to himself equivalents of the Nietzschean cry: "If ye could forget your origin, your past, your preparatory schooling!" (*JW*, 95–6). Stephen cannot. His mind is too awake. His eye for his own failure, for his guilt, for history and all learning is too keen for his own good. The gloomy wanderer of the "Telemachiad" and the intellectual creature of "Scylla and Charbydis" and "Circe" is proof of one half of the Nietzschean precept that "The duller the eye so much the further does good extend! . . . Hence the gloominess and grief (allied to bad conscience) of great thinkers" (*JW*, 88). Thus Stephen Dedalus, the "great thinker", gives way to the dull and good Bloom, the proof of the other half of the precept.

ULYSSES AS NIETZSCHEAN IDEAL

Bloom is the practical, honest, cheerful man that Nietzsche lauded (*DD*, 277, 392). He is what Nietzsche called the great man who "intercedes in favour of unassuming things" (*DD*, 316). He is the

fool, the Sternian hero, whom Nietzsche considered to be the best
subject for great art (*JW*, 146).[55] He is the hero who sits in the
stench of his excrement ("Calypso") and glories in the quality of his
fart ("Sirens"), demonstrating Nietzsche's precept that things of
bad odour are part of the heroic (*DD*, 314). He is the exemplar of
bad taste, the crooner of Italian arias, the fantasizer of Spanish
romances – all things that Nietzsche had approved as healthy and
life-fulfilling (*JW*, 108–9). He is a walking compendium of bits of
crankish dogma of the new religion of Science, which, as Nietzsche
had predicted (*JW*, 166), has succeeded that of the Church (to
which Stephen, by contrast, remains imaginatively tied). He is the
embodiment of Nietzsche's observations that the goodnatured man
is most likely to come from a race that has lived in fear (*DD*, 268),
and that the natural actor and artist-type will most likely be a lower-
class man who has an "inner longing to play a role" and a "surplus
capacity for adaptations of every kind" (*JW*, 318–19).

Bloom shares Nietzsche's opinion that there is no more sacred
state than that of pregnancy, and in "Circe" he lives out the fantasy
of being a mother that Nietzsche regarded as typical of the artist-
type (*DD*, 383–4; *JW*, 105). He is the tolerant critic who, like
Nietzsche, is offended at "him who succumbs to the passion of the
belly" as we see in "Lestrygonians", but who "understands the
allurement which here plays tyrant" (*JW*, 38), as we know by the
relish with which he eats his kidney at the beginning of "Calypso".
He is the "man who loves like a woman [and] becomes thereby a
slave" (*JW*, 322), as we can see in "Calypso" and "Circe". Finally,
he is a full embodiment of Nietzsche's advice that a character must
be made attractive through his weaknesses as well as his strengths
(*JW*, 223); also of Nietzsche's opinion that "The great problems all
demand *great love*, and it is only the strong, well-rounded, secure
spirits, those who have a solid basis, that are qualified for them"
(*JW*, 280). Bloom's well-roundedness is self-evident; his "great
love", in spite of all the parody (*U*, 333), is demonstrated in
"Cyclops" and in his charity to the drunken Stephen; and, if Joyce
offers any character who is "qualified" for taking on "the great
problems", it surely can only be Bloom.

Bloom's interior monologue at the centre of *Ulysses* demonstrates
Nietzsche's image of the individual as the centre of the concentric
circles of the universe equipped with "an unceasingly revolving
machine in his head, which still works, even under the most
unfavourable circumstances" (*JW*, 42; *DD*, 122). As we have seen

in the matter of Throwaway, Bloom's position is governed by accident (Bantam Lyons's mistake), coincidence (meeting Stephen at the crucial moment when Stephen needs help), and divine "guesswork" or what Nietzsche had characterized as "the roll of the dice" by some invisible power (*DD*, 134–8). Accepting this "guesswork" as he does, Bloom is a more sensible man in Nietzsche's terms than Stephen, whose persistence in intellectualizing events into terms of "cause and effect" proves ultimately futile. *Ulysses* itself is the grand example of Nietzsche's opinions that reality is the richest area of aesthetic inquiry (*DD*, 51); that reality itself is a symbol (*DD*, 39–40); that Homer is the most glorious of epic-makers, Ulysses the greatest of heroes, and a journey to the Underworld an essential feature of any great tale (*DD*, 201, 282, 390; *JW*, 276, 334, 351);[56] and that to say "Yea" to Life, as Molly Bloom does for the book as a whole in her last word, is finally the most fundamental mark of "noble morality" (*JW*, 213).

* * *

CONCLUSION

The early twentieth-century artist lived in the shadow of Nietzsche as Nietzsche had lived in the shadow of Wagner. This was true of Mann and Hesse, of D'Annunzio, of Gide and of D. H. Lawrence, as we shall see; and it was true of James Joyce. The aesthetic and philosophical spirit of Joyce was the spirit of Nietzsche in his middle works. The great themes of Joyce were what Eric Bentley has identified as the leitmotivs of these works: the free spirit, the good European, we homeless ones, and we immoralists.[57] The accomplishment of Joyce was much like what Nietzsche had been calling for: a new, joyful, realistic yet classical European art, based on the foundations of a partially repudiated Wagner and German Romanticism with its dialecticism,[58] its pantheism, its Goethean joy, its Schopenhauerian pessimism, its ultimate Love, and its transcendentalism. And *Ulysses* and *Finnegans Wake* may well have been the most appropriate answers to that strangely Mallarméan ideal which Nietzsche seems to have been fishing for when he asked the question, "Of what account is a book that never carries us away beyond all books?" (*JW*, 205).

Vis-à-vis Wagner, Joyce stood in the classic relation that Nietzsche had first represented: the artist/thinker observing a colossal father-figure that he could admire and imitate, had to repudiate, but could never finally ignore. The difference between Joyce and Nietzsche in this respect is that Joyce stood at a further remove from Wagner; and in this sense Joyce might be characterized as more of a grandson than a son, more of a Siegfried than Siegmund to Wagner's all-shadowing Wotan. Joyce indeed identified his artist hero with Siegfried, as Moore before him had identified himself with Siegmund. And, as Moore had played father to the young Joyce's Irish Siegfried-*manqué*, so Nietzsche in a different way stood in relation to the mature Joyce's more triumphant pan-European persona. Moore, Wilde, Symons, Yeats – all these Wagnerians of an intermediate generation were in a sense Siegmunds to Joyce's literary Siegfried; and *primus inter pares* among them in the realm of ideas was the contemporary Nietzsche, that short-lived but absolutely indispensable link between the godly grandeur of Wagner's vision and the mortal vulgarity of the great Modernist's.

Both Wagner and Joyce saw human history as a succession of ages: from gods, to heroes, to men, to chaos and back again. So too we might see the genealogy of this period in European art as a succession from the age of Wagner/Romanticism and gods, to that of Nietzsche/Decadence and heroes, to that of Joyce/Modernism and men, and then chaos/*ricorso*.

9 Lawrence

The number of productions of Wagner in London increased steadily between the 1890s and the beginning of the First World War. In 1903 two complete *Ring* cycles were staged at Covent Garden, and twenty-nine of the season's seventy-seven performances were of Wagner. In 1908 a complete English *Ring* was staged for the first time. In 1913 three *Ring* cycles were given. In 1914 the Grand Opera Syndicate mounted a German season referred to as "The Parsifal Season" because the first production in England of Wagner's last work, complete with the original scenery and costumes from Bayreuth, was performed fourteen times in a period of five weeks. During the War, Covent Garden was closed. When it reopened in 1919 no German or Austrian works were included in the "international" repetoire. Wagner did not return to Covent Garden until the 1920–1 season, when the Carl Rosa Company produced *Tannhäuser*, *Lohengrin*, and a *Ring* minus *Götterdämmerung*. A complete *Ring*, along with new productions of *Meistersinger* and *Parsifal*, had to wait until the following season; by which time Wagner and German opera in general had been restored to their normal standing in England.[1] This is not to say that the vogue for Wagner of the pre-War years had returned. On the contrary, the first wave of English Wagnerism had clearly broken. The War was a major factor in this – all things German had taken a propaganda beating. But the primary factors were undoubtedly temporal and aesthetic: Wagner was no longer the revolutionary artist of the epoch, and his artworks were no longer "of the future" so much as of the past.

The aesthetic war against Wagner, or Modernist counter-revolution against the Wagnerian revolution, was well under way by the time of the "battle" of *Le Sacre du printemps* in Paris in 1913. By the time that Wyndham Lewis and Ezra Pound published *Blast!* in 1914, the English front against Wagnerism in literature had certainly opened; and by 1920 the idea of using Wagner's myth and method in the overt manner of Symons or Moore was no more *avant-*

garde than the use of leitmotiv in music, or the chromatic innovations of *Tristan*. During the pre-War years and right up to the 1920s, however, "ninetyish" Wagnerisms continued to appear in English novels. These included works of E. F. Benson, Charles Morgan, Sturge Moore, Arnold Bennett, Virginia Woolf, E. M. Forster and D. H. Lawrence.[2] In most cases the Wagnerism was little more than a matter of cultural reference: the fact that Mrs Dalloway heard *Parsifal* at Bayreuth, for instance, which Virginia Woolf notes in *The Voyage Out* (1915).[3] In a few, however, it was a matter of more extensive Wagnerian configurations. Thus Forster may have patterned his *Room with a View* (1908) on the Christian *versus* pagan dialectic of *Parsifal*: "The novel's protagonists owe their mythic status to the author's availing himself of the structure of oppositions of Wagner's work", according to W. J. Lucas[4] – Lucy bears echoes of Kundry, Mrs Bartlett and Mr Beebe of Klingsor, old Mr Emerson of Titurel, and so forth.

Such instances of Wagnerism followed in the path worn by the social Wagnerism of *Dorian Gray* or the structural Wagnerism of *Evelyn Innes*. They are not of sufficient depth, innovation, or importance to merit more than our passing mention. The one English novelist of the period who appears to have had a more subtle and far-reaching, if often unobvious, relation to Wagner was D. H. Lawrence. This may be owing in part to Lawrence's extensive exposure to things German. This exposure we shall discuss before examining the relevance of Wagner to Lawrence's novels, prose style, plays and philosophy. Several works on Lawrence have touched on matters we shall take up. But the best work on the relationship to Wagner is again offered by Blisset, this time in his article "D. H. Lawrence, D'Annunzio, and Wagner".[5]

BACKGROUND AND GERMAN IDEAS

Young Lawrence studied German and French in school, eloped with the German wife of his French professor, and had a facility if not fluency in both languages. Of French writers he read Baudelaire and Verlaine at an early age, Flaubert, Zola and Proust by middle life; of Germans, Goethe, Schopenhauer and Nietzsche in his twenties, Jacob Boehme and perhaps Rudolf Steiner in his early thirties; of Italians, Leopardi at an early age and D'Annunzio in his twenties; of the English, such Wagnerians as Shaw, Moore and Ernest Newman by his early twenties. Clearly the young Lawrence was extremely well read.[6] Ford Madox Ford, novelist and son of Wagner-critic Franz Hueffer, was "astonished" at the breadth of Lawrence's knowledge, specifically of "Nietzsche and Wagner and Leopardi and Flaubert and Karl Marx";[7] and, when Lawrence fell ill in 1912 and had to give up teaching, Ford sent him *The Oxford Book of German Verse from the Twelfth to the Twentieth Century* and *The Minnesingers* by Jethro Bithell to review for his *English Review*.[8] Lawrence's reviews of these volumes demonstrate his familiarity since childhood with various mediaeval Wagnerian sources, and his sharing of the contemporary interest in the troubadour era. This sharing was with not only the young Joyce, but also the young poet and Provençal translator Ezra Pound, to whom Ford introduced him. Lawrence's reaction to Pound foreshadowed his mature reaction to his Modernist contemporaries: after spending the night in the American's Kensington flat because it had become too late to catch the train back to Croydon, Lawrence wrote that he liked Pound and had much in common with him, but that Pound's muse was "Beauty" whereas his own was "Life".[9]

The distinction was crucial. Lawrence would become an "heroic vitalist", in a loose tradition which included the Wagner of *Siegfried*, Nietzsche and Shaw.[10] Pound, on the other hand, along with other notables of "The Pound Era" like Eliot and Joyce, would carry on in that essentially "art for art's sake" tradition that derived from the Wagner of *Parsifal*, the Symbolists, and the English of the 1890s. Increasingly Lawrence was to distinguish himself from this tradition. In 1913, for instance, he wrote a review for Katherine Mansfield's *Blue Review* in which he repudiated "art for art's sake" as it related to the novels of Thomas Mann.[11] Mann lived for art and nothing else, Lawrence contended; the fact that he reserved no part of himself for life, as Goethe had, left him "diseased" and his art diseased as a result. "Thomas Mann seems to me the last sick sufferer from the complaint of Flaubert", Lawrence concluded. Was he conscious of how he was echoing Nietzsche's comparison of another great German artist to the French novelist ("Hatred of Life [became] dominant in [Wagner] as in Flaubert"[12])? Whether he was or not, it was by this "contra-Wagner" standard that Lawrence dismissed two classics of late Romantic literature, *Madame Bovary* and *Death in Venice*, with the same swift assurance that he would later dismiss two classics of Modernist literature, *Ulysses* and *À la recherche du temps perdu*:[13] "*Madame Bovary* seems dead to me. . . . Thomas

Mann is old – and we are young. Germany does not feel very young to me."

He had just eloped with Frieda and travelled to Germany for the first time. He was writing a story, "The Prussian Officer", and letters home indicating an immediate awareness/wariness of all things German. His reactions were not unlike those which his friend Katherine Mansfield had recorded in her first book, *In a German Pension* (1911). After the War broke out, Mansfield repudiated the anti-German bias of these early stories; and, by the time he was using Mansfield as the model for the more "German" of his Brangwen sisters, Lawrence was undergoing a change in reaction to things German as well. His initial wariness was giving way to the fascination and absorption in German ideas evident from *Women in Love* through the so-called "Dark Period". The War and the British government's harassment because of Frieda's German origins may have given some encouragement to this; also Lawrence's probable discovery of Chamberlain's *Foundations of the Nineteenth Century* during the period.[14] In any case, by 1918 Lawrence was describing the "Great Teutonic Race" in sympathetic terms reminiscent of those of Wagner's son-in-law. *Movements in European History*, a textbook commissioned by the Oxford University Press and published in 1921, lauds the value ancient German tribes put on strength, solitude, taciturnity, instinctiveness and war. It characterizes the race as superior to both the "innumerable hordes of dark, wild, horse-riding Asiatics" who periodically swept across the Continent from the East, and the over-civilized Romans whose empire they had destroyed.[15]

This fascination for the glory of the primitive Germans, mixed with that wariness for the "disease" and "brutality" that renewed itself each time he went back to contemporary Germany,[16] became leitmotivs of Lawrence's attitude for the remainder of his life. So much we can see in the prophetic "Letter from Germany" which he wrote in 1924:

All Germany reads *Beasts, Men and Gods* with a kind of fascination. . . .

The ancient spirit of pre-historic Germany, coming back at the end of history. . . .

These queer gangs of *Young Socialists*, youths and girls, with their non-materialistic professions, their half-mystic assertions, they strike one as strange. Something primitive, like loose, roving gangs of broken scattered tribes. . . .

And it looks as if the years were wheeling swiftly backwards, no more onwards. Like a spring that is broken, and whirls swiftly back, so time seems to be whirling with a mysterious swiftness to a sort of death. Whirling to the ghost of the old Middle Ages of Germany, then to the Roman days, then to the days of the silent forest and the dangerous, lurking barbarians.

Something about the Germanic races is unalterable. White-skinned, elemental, and dangerous. Our civilization has come from the fusion of the dark-eyes with the blue. The meeting and mixing and mingling of the two races has been the joy of our ages. And the Celt has been there, alien, but necessary as some chemical reagent to the fusion. So the civilization of Europe rose up. So these cathedrals and these thoughts.

But now the Celt is the disintegrating agent. And the Latin and southern races are falling out of association with the northern races, the northern Germanic impulse is recoiling toward Tartary, the destructive vortex of Tartary.

It is a fate. . . .

At the same time, we have brought it about ourselves – by a Ruhr occupation, by an English nullity, and by the German false will. . . .[17]

Though he felt it to be dying through "false will" and "nullity", Lawrence retained the Nietzschean affinity for the blue-eyed Germanic type, including the Franks and Visigoth Spaniards who had been responsible for the Gothic cathedrals and other glories of the Middle Ages. The Latin races struck him as civilized but effete, as he would depict Rico to be in *St Mawr* (1925). The Tartar, Hun or Russian, seemed a consistently destructive force in Europe. The Jews, whom he discussed at length in *Movements* and in *Apocalpyse* (1932), were admirable for their racial integrity but pernicious in their "jealous" monotheism, and their lust for a day of judgement in which they would be shown for once and for all to be the "chosen people" – a lust they passed on to the early Christians who wrote the Book of Revelations, thus shifting the emphasis of Christianity from the positive example of Christ's love to the negative fear of ultimate damnation.[18] Race was as paramount a concern for Lawrence as it was for contemporary Germans. While he never proposed a "master race" programme like that of the Nazis (if he had a favourite race it would appear to be the American Indian[19]), he was equally obsessed with racial purity. This, along with his later visions of an elite brotherhood based on blood-and-strength and of an all-destroying-all-renewing apocalypse, links Lawrence to those who, following the racist/Germanic/apocalyptic visions of the later Wagner, sought to establish Aryan supremacy through a latter-day order of Teutonic knights; and, failing that, to bring on a *Götterdämmerung* of "scorched earth" by which over-civilized Europe would be rendered a "waste land".

Lawrence's marriage to Frieda, travels in Germany, and exposure to the glut of proto-fascist ideas current in Europe after the War might explain this sympathy with the most ominous strain of post-Wagnerism. Personal experience led to his major lack of sympathy with that German Romantic ideal of Love for which Wagner had provided the transcendent expression. As early as 1909 he had written home from London, "I went to Wagner's *Tristan and Isolde* last night, and was very disappointed. . . . *Tristan* is long, feeble, a bit hysterical, without grip or force. I was frankly sick of it."[20] In 1913 after eloping to the Continent with Frieda he elaborated,

> I don't think the *real* tragedy is in dying, or in the perversity of affairs, like the woman one loves being the wife of another man – like the last act of *Tristan*. I think the real tragedy is in the inner war which is waged between people who love each other.[21]

Lawrence was ever sensitive to the similarity of the configuration of Lawrence/Frieda/Weekly to that of Tristan/Isolde/King Marke, and sought to distinguish himself from it. As we shall see in his novels, he despised the idea of smothering himself in "love-death". After his own version of the great adultery story was condemned as obscene, he wrote in "Pornography and Obscenity" (1928) that Wagner's *Tristan* was a far better example of true obscenity, being one of those nineteenth-century works that "wallowed in sex, but despised it".[22] Like Shaw, Lawrence felt hostile to the Love "panacea" and warned against the *Liebesnacht* type of experience:

> For the lovers who shoot themselves in the night, in the horrible suicide of love, they are driven mad by the poisoned arrows of Artemis; the moon is against them; the moon is fiercely against them. And oh, if the moon is against you, oh beware of the bitter night, especially the night of intoxication.[23]

Like Shaw, Lawrence was in sympathy with the *Siegfried* idea of breaking down sentimental old orders and creating a new vitalism. But, unlike Shaw, he recognized the greatness of *Götterdämmerung* as a model of how romantic love was doomed in all-too-human modern life.[24] And, unlike Shaw, he shared in that growing twentieth-century desire to find some new type of Love which, if not precisely the ideal Schopenhauerian sympathy by which Parsifal becomes one with the suffering Amfortas, had much in common with the overarching vision of some mystical love-bond between men that Wagner had achieved in his last work.

THE EARLY NOVELS

Lawrence's second novel, *The Trespasser* (1912), was his only full-blown Wagnerian outing. Whether as a result of the sexual frustrations of "the Croydon years", his bouts of illness, or the nature of his company and reading, he put aside his previously expressed distaste for *Tristan* and set about transforming some notes of Helen Corke's into a novel of passionate love, adultery, mental anguish and death. *The Saga of Siegmund* was the working-title of this experiment; Siegmund was the name of its musician hero, and *Die Walküre*, along with *Tristan*, the major source for its extensive allusions. These allusions, as Blisset remarks, create "a sort of super-saturation of Wagnerism, the feeling of exaltation and of fatigue that is a long continuing state of the souls of those possessed by the wizard of Bayreuth".[25] Blisset suggests that Lawrence was working on the model of D'Annunzio. Zuckerman and others have suggested that *The Trespasser* was an ill-conceived attempt at an *Evelyn Innes*.[26] Certainly Lawrence had read D'Annunzio and Moore by this time; and the "oppressive" and "embarrassing" Wagnerian style, which is arguably his major contribution to Corke's notes, may well have been inspired by them. From the first Lawrence himself felt that there was something strange about the work ("I keep on writing, almost mechanically");[27] and, when Ford returned the manuscript with the comment "it is execrably bad art, being all variations on a theme",[28] Lawrence put it away for a month and nursed grave doubts. "At the bottom of my heart I don't like the work", he wrote; "I hate it for its fluid, luscious quality"[29] – in other words, for exactly the quality that recalled D'Annunzio and Moore, commonly regarded as Wagnerian at the time.

In the novels which followed, Lawrence created a style more

typically his own; still, Wagnerian concerns and elements can be detected in them. *Sons and Lovers* (1913) was free of such Wagnerian bric-à-brac as marked its predecessor, but unconsciously Wagnerian in the overall respect that Joyce's contemporary *Bildungsroman* was consciously so. The self-education and liberation of the modern artist hero had been anticipated archetypally by the youthful development of the Romantic hero in *Siegfried*; and, like *Portrait* for Joyce, *Sons and Lovers* for Lawrence represented the "forging of the sword". In the next novel, *The Rainbow* (1915), overt Wagnerian motifs reappeared; but, unlike in *The Trespasser*, they were woven into Lawrence's own system so subtly as to be virtually invisible. The motif of the rainbow itself probably came from *Rheingold*, a work Lawrence knew well enough to perform in a "do-it-yourself" version with Frieda and some Buddhist friends.[30] Ursula's vision of the rainbow in the finale of the book was probably likewise inspired by the vision of Valhalla towards which the gods proceed over their rainbow-bridge in the finale of Wagner's drama. As with Wagner's music, this is interspersed with reminiscences of Nibelungs, promise of Wälsung-like heroes in the future, and high hopes for a New Age and Order:

> And the rainbow stood on the earth. She knew that the sordid people who crept hard-scaled and separate on the face of the world's corruption were living still, that the rainbow was arched in their blood and would quiver to life in their spirit, that they would cast off their horny covering of disintegration, that new, clean, naked bodies would issue to a new germination, to a new growth, rising to the light and the wind and the clean rain of heaven. She saw in the rainbow the earth's new architecture, the old, brittle corruption of houses and factories swept away, the world built up in the living fabric of Truth, fitting to the over-arching heaven.[31]

Utopian and sincere as that of Wagner's Wotan, this vision was just as doomed; and in his next novel, *Women in Love* (1920), Lawrence presented a personal version of the last drama of Wagner's cycle. As in *Götterdämmerung*, we see a blonde and manly high-born hero die through his ill-fated passion for a woman named Gudrun and the plottings of his beloved with a gnomic agent-of-evil, Loerke as Hagen.[32] Also as in *Götterdämmerung*, there are four principals who appear in the configuration of two amorous couples, and two of these four are also siblings. In more general resonances of the Nordic

Götterdämmerung-myth, Lawrence may well have been going further than Wagner's drama, as F. R. Leavis has indicated:

> Taking the hint of the name Gudrun we can't help seeing in Loerke a suggestion of Loki. For in calling this sister Gudrun Lawrence can't have been unmindful of the destructive part played by Gudrun in the saga of the Nibelungs. And that in imagining the snow-death, with its symbolic significance, Lawrence was consciously, as well as profoundly, affected by his knowledge of northern mythology (in which we know him to have been intensely interested) is beyond doubt – northern mythology with its vision of the end of life in the cold of the dreadful final winter that heralds the last battle of the Gods. Birkin tells Gerald that Loerke is a 'gnawing little negation at the roots of life'. We have the clear presence of Niohögg, the evil power who gnaws at the roots of Yggdrasil, the tree of life. 'Loerke' blends the suggestion of 'Loki' with that of the evil 'lurker'.[33]

In Gerald Crich we might see a version of Wotan, for Gerald is the exemplar of a Germanic "master race" which has become filled with "nullity" and "false will" and longs for "das Ende". At the same time Gerald is a modern Siegfried in his capacity of Nietzschean man-of-action, ruthless "industrial magnate", and representative of the New Order. Thus, as in *Götterdämmerung*, we find in Gerald's death two mythic tragedies intertwined: the passing of the god and the passing of the hero.

The symbolic significance of Gerald's death by snow, like that of the near-death by snow of Mann's hero in the contemporary *Magic Mountain*, is that north European man of whatever order is drawing towards the edge of racial suicide. The idea was not unusual for a novel of the War period. What makes Lawrence's treatment so different from that of a "sick sufferer" such as Mann is the fatalistic, even optimistic ambivalence. While regretting Gerald's death, Lawrence's *alter ego* Birkin regards the passing of the old masters and new materialists of Europe as inevitable; indeed, essential if his neo-Rousseauesque and Edenic utopian vision is to be realized.[34] In the chapter entitled "An Island" Birkin describes a world where everyone and everything would be swept away, save Mother Nature with her flowers and rabbits popping their heads up out of the long grasses – a Lawrentian version of Wagner's vision at the end of *Götterdämmerung*, in which everyone and everything is swept away save the Rhinemaidens, who now can go back to frolicking around their gold, and Mother Erda, who is now free to sleep her sleep of Life with no importunate Wotan to disturb her. The "sick sufferer" Mann regarded the spectre of a real *Götterdämmerung* as fearful and worked to prevent it. Lawrence, on the other hand, in spite of his vocal pacificism during the War found the idea of an apocalypse fascinating throughout his career and encouraged it even in posthumous works – for instance, *The Virgin and the Gypsy* (1930), which ends with a sensational Rhine-like flood.

What hope is left for man after such an apocalypse? At the end of *The Virgin and the Gypsy* it is the sexual love of the two of the title. At the end of *Götterdämmerung* it is a memory of the love of Siegfried and Brünnhilde and an intimation of some new love, to be developed by Parsifal and his Order. At the end of *Women in Love* it is the love of Birkin and Ursula and an intimation of the love Birkin wishes to have with a male, the *Blutbrüderschaft* which he lost in Gerald's death but still regards as essential for the building of his utopian world. Birkin's love for Ursula has stood in contrast to Gerald's passion for Gudrun, that type of Wagnerian mistake that had already led the hero of *The Trespasser* to his doom. Since then Lawrence has conceived of a better type of love. On the *Liebesnacht* in the chapter entitled "Moony" he has Birkin smash the still image of the moon on the pond in symbolic rejection of Wagnerian romanticizing. Birkin's love with Ursula must be a matter of "singleness-in-union" – the sort of mutually respectful non-dependent relationship that seems to be dawning for Siegfried and Brünnhilde as they take leave of each other at Daybreak in *Götterdämmerung*, a relationship in which the man goes forth to discover while the woman waits and watches and supports and follows. Having established via Birkin this provisional definition of the proper type of love between a man and a woman, Lawrence could turn to the other question, the Parsifalian one of how a man loves another man. Thus the spokesmen of his next three novels – *Aaron's Rod* (1921), *Kangaroo* (1923) and *The Plumed Serpent* (1926) – seek in various forms the ideal brotherhood.

WAGNERIAN ACCOMPLISHMENTS

The Plumed Serpent, end-point of this quest, was Lawrence's *Parsifal*. This is not to say that Kate was meant as a Kundry or Huitzilopochtli as a Wagnerian paraclete, rather that the novel as a whole was a kind of "sacred festival play" in which Lawrence could merge his Nietzscheanism, his primitivism, and his characteristic ideas about blood, race, the sun, and sensory spirituality with remnants of the Non-conformist Christianity on which he had been brought up – its hymns, its revolutionary and apocalyptic impulses, and its yearning for a chaste/warrior leader like the Jesus of the Book of Revelation.[35] The result was a mystical and quasi-musical representation of the type of new order he wished to see develop in the future. But in the end, as with Somers and the Australian nationalist movement which he had projected in *Kangaroo*, Lawrence makes his narrator reject the new order of the plumed serpent and return to England. At base Lawrence's deeply individualistic nature remained resistant to the idea of self-renunciation in favour of a primitive elite, which Lawrence the public man had taken to preaching. Thus, while offering a quasi-Parsifalian and proto-fascist brotherhood based on blood and spiritual discipline as the model for rule of groups of men, Lawrence like his spokesmen continued on in quest for his own singleness – in union and ultimately in increasing solitude – until finally, like the creator of *Zarathustra* or "the man who died", he "passes beyond our sight".

Of Lawrence's accomplishment in the novels as a group we might conclude by observing that, while he developed in a manner typically his own after the Wagnerian excesses of *The Trespasser*, he continued to sound Wagnerian themes to such an extent as to suggest that Wagner may have remained an important subliminal influence – perhaps even providing inspiration for an overall artistic plan. By the end Lawrence had written a complete *Ring*, albeit in jumbled order and with only two of the four pieces consciously linked: *The Trespasser* as *Die Walküre*, *Sons and Lovers* as *Siegfried*, *The Rainbow* as *Rheingold*, and *Women in Love* as *Götterdämmerung*. He had also written his *Parsifal* in *The Plumed Serpent* after two false starts. And all along, like Wagner, he had produced self-explanatory theoretical works to go alongside his major creative efforts: the Hardy studies of the *Rainbow* period; the European history of the *Women in Love*; the American literature of *The Plumed Serpent*; and *Apocalypse* of the period of his Jesus-tale, *The Man Who Died* (published posthumously in 1931), which corresponds with Wagner's plans for a final work based on the sketch "Jesus of Nazareth". Lawrence's one great Wagnerian nemesis, *Tristan*, remained, it seems, *the* Wagnerian work he wished to match or better. He postponed the subject throughout the "Dark Period" and, when he finally returned to it, wrote three versions before he was satisfied that he had achieved his objective. *Lady Chatterley's Lover* (1928) alludes to *Tristan* no more than *Sons and Lovers* alludes to *Siegfried*. But the overall configurations and developments are parallel; and it seems likely that, to some conscious degree, Lawrence conceived his novel as the modern replacement for a typical Romantic love-story, which he considered mistaken and "obscene".

Throughout his works Lawrence made use of rhythms and patterns of repetition that were chromatic and building, like the music of *Tristan*. Indeed, many passages in Lawrence seem more Wagnerian than the conscious imitations of Wagner-experiences in Moore and Mann, or the application of the "tricks" of Wagner's technique in Joyce. Perhaps this was unintentional. Whether or not it was, Lawrence evidently shared Wagner's instinct for that effect which Nietzsche loved and loathed: the ebb and flow of the great sea of Life's "unending melody", in which it was so easy to lose one's footing. Consider virtually any passage in which Lawrence dwells on "the brooding presences of nature". The stylistic method of these is less to define than to evoke. Sometimes it is possible to lose sight of just what the language is referring to. As one critic has stated, Lawrence's words tend to become "will without idea" – or, to put it in a phrase which would no doubt have annoyed Lawrence considering his aversion to "art for art's sake", word-patterns for their own sake rather than for that of their explicable content.[36] Vague and repetitive and chromatic, Lawrence's prose at these times seems to aspire to the hypnotic rather than the intelligible: to the awakening of slumbering passions and erotic impulses, the communication of a sensation of tumescence of will – of thrusting into some dark new sensual/spiritual realm.

The high-water mark of this Lawrentian style comes in the long mystical passages of song and ritual-description in *The Plumed Serpent*. In these the desire to produce an effect clearly reducible to the rational meanings of words was no more the point than in the music of *Parsifal*. For Lawrence, like Wagner, was trying to evoke a vision –

> Beyond the white of whiteness,
> Beyond the blackness of black,
> Beyond the spoken day,
> Beyond the unspoken passion of night

– which did not exist in concrete terms –

> The light which is fed from two vessels
> From the black oil and the white
> Shines at the gate

– but was ineffable –

> A gate to the innermost place
> Where the Breath and the Fountains commingle,
> Where the dead are living, and the living
> are dead

– one might even say Symbolist –

> The deeps that life cannot fathom,
> The Source and the End, of which we know
> Only that it is, and its life is our life,
>   and our death

– only to be intuited, not to be thought or seen –

> All men cover their eyes
> Before the unseen
> All men be lost in silence,
> Within the noiseless[37]

– not even to be heard so much as felt, felt in the viscera and with the spirit, as one was meant to *feel* the music of *Tristan* or *Parsifal*. Such passages were, in a word, obscure: obscure in the manner which Hugh Kenner has insightfully analysed in talking of Eliot's incantatory repetitions in *The Hollow Men*, say, or the *Four Quartets*.[38]

This kind of obscurity is different from that to be found in the work of Modernists such as Pound and Joyce, Kenner argues. The obscurity of the *Cantos* results from the deletion of narrative situation in the interests of emphasizing the concrete image in all its psychological realism, thus can be dispelled by merely reconstructing the deleted situation. Likewise, the obscurity of the prelude to "Sirens", as we have seen, results from the removal of key words from their proper contexts and thus can be dispelled by referring on to those contexts. The obscurity of the *Four Quartets* however cannot be dispelled in such a manner; for an oxymoron such as

> What might have been and what has been
> Point to one end, which is always present[39]

is finally a metaphysical perception that has no concrete situation or removed context to which to be re-attached. We find a similar difficulty in the hymns and ritual-descriptions of *The Plumed Serpent*, and the repeated invocations of stars and jaguars and eagles and snakes, and the Eliotic oxymorons such as

> All men cover their eyes
> Before the unseen.

Such things can finally only be understood by what symbolic associations, spiritual revelations and emotional feelings they provoke in the reader. In this respect we might say that Lawrence's songs, like Eliot's "quartets", aspired to the condition of music, the non-discursive artform, in a more Wagnerian, *Tristan*-like manner than the *Cantos* or *Ulysses*; for the status of the latter works as literary music depends on comparison of their highly calculated, discursive, and ultimately explicable patterns to sequences of strictly identifiable motifs in, say, *Rheingold*, the work in which Wagner applied his theory of leitmotiv most systematically.

PLAYS: WAGNERIAN CONFIGURATIONS AND EFFECTS

In his first play, *A Collier's Friday Night* (1909), Lawrence presented for the first and last time a hero in the guise of a *fin-de-siècle* aesthete. Ernest remarks on the fact that Swinburne has just died,[40] talks about Impressionist and Pre-Raphaelite painting (*P*, 524), and reads to his girlfriend from *Les Fleurs du mal*, of which he says enviously,

> That's what they can do in France. It's so heavy and full and voluptuous: like oranges falling and rolling a little way along a dark-blue carpet; like twilight outside when the lamp's lighted; you get a sense of rich, heavy things, as if you smelt them, and felt them about you in the dusk. (*P*, 501–2)

This young working-class would-be Baudelaire claims to be afflicted with *ennui* (*P*, 505) and sees his role in life as that of a casuist: someone to *épater le bourgeois* of his provincial environment. He also exhibits a budding misogyny. This we see first in his reaction to a tough working-class girl who teases him about his sex life at college: "Vous m'agacez les nerfs", he says to her; "Il faut aller au diable!" (*P*, 505). Later, in reaction to his mother's scolding he snaps, "You talk *just* like a woman!" (*P*, 524). Clearly *A Collier's Friday Night* was the work of that young provincial who so impressed Ford with the scope of his studied modernism. In another "ninetyish"/Wagnerian touch we are told that Ernest likes to eat at a vegetarian restaurant called "The Savoy" (*P*, 485). This may indicate a connection to Shaw; but the young Lawrence had yet to make his Shavian discovery that he was not suited to playing the Decadent aesthete, thus to repudiate the French-oriented art-for-art's-sake type and declare faith in his own version of the "Life Force".

Lawrence's next four plays, all written in 1912, reflect the experience of romance and elopement with Frieda. In them we can see development of his characteristic ideas on race and love, and Wagnerian elements stand behind them as with the novels of the same period. *The Merry-Go-Round* demonstrates the anti-German bias that Lawrence shared with Mansfield and other compatriots before the War, and puts to rest any illusions that he was always pro-German at heart. The German baron and baroness of the play are imperious aristocrats-*manqué*, absurd puritans (*P*, 421), gross materialists (*P*, 429), cowards in spite of their martial airs (*P*, 428) – indeed, possessors of few redeeming qualities whatever. *The Fight for Barbara*, set in Italy, suggests the influence of D'Annunzio, and is filled with such overdone Wagnerisms as the deserted husband's complaint to his wife that she is "twisting [a] spear" into his "secret wound" (*P*, 295). The atmosphere is as *"chargé"* as that of *The Trespasser*; the subject again is adultery and elopment, and the configuration that of Tristan/Isolde/King Marke. *The Daughter-in-Law*, a more considered and satisfying play, shows Lawrence as he is beginning to recoil from that *Tristan*-like type of love. The mother-in-law, as Lawrence's mouthpiece, warns her daughter-in-law, "When a woman builds her life on men, either husbands or sons, she builds on summat as sooner or later brings the house down crash on her head" (*P*, 265). The daughter-in-law is about to unbuild her marriage when her husband returns from a mine-strike slightly wounded, thus with a conventional claim to the wounded hero's treatment. The daughter-in-law is not liberated enough to deny this to him; as a result, the play ends with her supporting him reclined in her arms – a *Tristan*-like posture no doubt meant ironically to dramatize the mother-in-law's contention that all men want after all is to be able to smother themselves in women.

The Married Man, which Lawrence revised in 1926, contains an ironic parallel to *Lohengrin*. The hero fancies himself to be God's gift to women, and the heroine is a liberated woman named Elsa whose manner of hailing her "hero" is to call, "Knabe, Knabe, wo bist du?" (*P*, 197). In her version of the Forbidden Question, this Elsa asks her hero why he does not act in her presence in the manner that he would in the presence of his male friends. "I want the real you," she tells him, "not your fiction" (*P*, 198). If the message of Wagner's opera is that the only way to have a happy marriage is to have faith in the face of withheld information, the message of Lawrence's play would seem to be that the only way to have a happy marriage is to give the impulse to unfaithfulness free rein and talk about it openly.

The Widowing of Mrs Holroyd (1914) continues to bear marks of the working-out of the relationship with Frieda, and has strong echoes of Act I of *Die Walküre*. An unhappily married woman is approached by an outsider who professes his love to her, and his desire to take her away from her unhappiness. During a tryst by a glimmering hearth while the gruff drunken husband is upstairs asleep, the woman tells a Sieglinde-like story of how she has been an orphan since the age of six; how she "belonged to nowhere, and nobody cared"; how she only got married "to get out of [her] place" (*P*, 41–2). Her outsider/lover offers to stay the night to protect her from the potential violence of the drunken husband. When she hesitates, he takes up the line of Siegfried in *Götterdämmerung* or Tristan in the mediaeval legend: "There will be the drawn sword between us", he says (*P*, 36). She assents; he stays; they determine to elope, using the £120 the woman's uncle once left her should she need it one day (the uncle as a Wotan? the money as the Nothung by which the lovers can cut their way to freedom?) Their plan is ruined, however, by the sudden mysterious death of the husband in a mine-shaft accident. The woman takes this event as a judgement of fate against her; and the play ends with her weeping penitently over her dead husband's body.

Touch and Go (1920) is a dramatic sequel to *Women in Love* with Gerald Crich resurrected as Gerald Barlow, Gudrun transformed into Anabel, Birkin into Oliver, and so forth. As in *Women in Love*,

Nietzschean terms are generously applied: the play opens with a union-leader haranguing the miners against being "slaves" (*P*, 325), and the action turns on a conflict between representatives of "slave" and "master" morality – that is, between the miners and the owner, Gerald, who refers to the union-leaders as "anti-Christs" and is himself compared to Christ (*P*, 363). All this "neo-Nietzschean clatter" could be averted, according to Oliver in the climactic scene, "if the people for one minute pulled themselves up and conquered their mania for money and machine excitement" (*P*, 350) – a Lawrentian explanation of the problems of the world reminiscent of Wagner's reduction of the problems of the *Ring*-universe to greed for gold and Nibelungen "industrialism", and not unlike Pound's contemporary blaming of the problems of the twentieth century on "Usura". *Touch and Go* also provides another statement of the mature Lawrentian attitudes on love and solitude. The spokesman in this case is the mad Mrs Barlow, who says on the occasion when Gerald informs her of his intention to marry Anabel:

> MRS BARLOW [*to Anabel*]: . . . Learn your place, and keep it. Keep away from him, if you are going to be a wife to him. Don't go too near. And don't let him come too near. Beat him off if he tries. Keep a solitude in your heart even when you love him best. Keep it. If you lose it, you lose everything.
>
> GERALD: But that isn't love, Mother . . . .
>
> MRS BARLOW: . . . What do you know of love, you ninny? You only know the feeding-bottle. It's what you want, all of you – to be brought up by hand, and mew about love. Ah, God! – Ah, God! – that you should none of you know the only thing which would make you worth having.
>
> GERALD: I don't believe in your only thing, Mother. But what is it?
>
> MRS BARLOW: What you haven't got – the power to be alone.
>
> GERALD: Sort of megalomania, you mean?
>
> MRS BARLOW: What? Megalomania? What is your *love* but a megalomania, flowing over everybody, and everything like spilt water? I hate you, you softy! I would *beat* you. . . .
> (*P*, 355–6)

Here Mrs Barlow not only prophesies Gerald's self-destruction through Tristan-like love and Wotan-like semi-blindness, but also echoes in her image of the feeding-bottle Brünnhilde's words to the sorrowing Gibichungs after Siegfried's death:

> You are children
> Whining to your mother
> About the milk you have spilled![41]

Beyond Brünnhilde's words, the image of Love's megalomania flowing over everybody like spilt water recalls the overflowing of the Rhine and the Love motifs which end Wagner's drama; and Mrs Barlow's point is that, until Gerald and his all-too-human kind learn the Nietzschean lessons that Siegfried unlearned in *Götterdämmerung*, i.e. to have "the power to be alone" and the ability to "keep a solitude in your heart", they will never achieve more in their lives than petty human versions of the self-destruction that comes for the world-weary heroes of *Tristan* and the *Ring*.

Lawrence's last complete play, *David* (1926), was his only one built directly on myth. The myth in this case was Hebrew, but many of the configurations might have just as easily been derived from Wagner;[42] and the play makes it clear that by this stage of his career Lawrence was moving towards a technique of multiple mythic allusion like that which had characterized the recently published *Ulysses*, and was making the old Wagnerian style of strict overt allusion which had produced *Evelyn Innes* and *The Trespasser* obsolete once and for all. Though many of the scenes in *David* suggest specific scenes from Wagner and opera in general,[43] Lawrence intended direct allusions no more than Shaw did in those scenes of his plays in which a character performs in a manner reminscent of, say, Wotan. What Lawrence was clearly intending, however, was to create the sort of dramatic *effect* that such scenes had achieved for Wagner or Verdi; and, as these composers had achieved their effects through music, Lawrence attempted a type of music as well. The best demonstration of this comes in scene ix. This opens with Saul's daughters, Michal and Merab, leading their maidens in chants in expectation of the imminent return of David and Saul from their triumph over the Philistines:

MAIDENS: Lu-lu-a-li-lu-lu-lu! Lu-lu-lu-li-a-li-lu-lu! A-li-lu-lu-lu-a-li-lu! Lu-al-li-lu! Lu-al-li-lu-a!
MERAB: Out of Judah Saul comes in!
MICHAL: David slew the Philistine.
MERAB AND HER MAIDENS: Out of Judah Saul comes in!

MICHAL AND HER MAIDENS: David slew the Philistine.

MAIDENS (*repeat several times*): A-li-lu-lu! A li-lu-lu!Lu! lu! lu! lu! li!
      lu! lu! a! li! lu! lu! lu! lu!   (P, 108–9)

The obvious intention of this passage is to evoke a musical and
liturgical atmosphere. It has more in common with choruses from
Handel's *Saul* or Verdi's *Aïda* or Gertrude Stein's contemporary
Four Saints in Three Acts, which was later made into an opera by
Virgil Thompson, than with passages in any conventional play. The
fact that it was written in the same period as *The Plumed Serpent*
should help explain what Lawrence was after with this musical
effect-making: *David* might also be seen as an attempt at a "sacred
festival play".

NIETZSCHE AND LAWRENCE

Where we can see a number of Nietzsche's aesthetic principles being
worked out in Joyce, we can see much of his social and psychological
philosophy being worked out in Lawrence. Where we can hear
echoes of Nietzsche's middle works in Joyce, we can hear those of his
later works in Lawrence.[44] Where we can see the contra-Wagner
Nietzsche in Joyce, we can see on the whole a more pro-Wagner
Nietzsche in Lawrence – a Nietzsche who was expanding on that
German Romantic tradition he shared with Wagner, rather than
recoiling from it. Lawrence was the first to distinguish his thought
from Nietzsche's, and critics have been splitting hairs on the subject
ever since. Like the English wartime propagandists, Lawrence
attacked the Nietzschean idea of *Wille zur Macht*, and in *Women in
Love* he associated it with the coercive and pathological sides of
Hermione, Gerald and Gudrun.[45] The effect of this was to suggest a
far greater divergence from Nietzsche than actually existed. In the
first place Lawrence was surely overemphasizing the destructive
aspect of Nietzsche's concept and mixing it with his own notion of a
German "false will", much in the way he had overemphasized the
morbid subjects of Mann's novels and ignored their anti-morbid
irony in order to fit them into his notion of Germany as old and
diseased. In the second place Lawrence himself had an emphatic
belief in *Wille zur Macht*, amply demonstrated in his spokesman
Birkin, who, if less physically violent, is more intellectually wilful
and destructive than any of the other characters in *Women in Love*.

In his discussion of Lawrence and German ideas Ronald Gray
has argued that in *Women in Love* Birkin and Ursula were meant to
represent English ideas and end up full of promise, while Gerald and
Gudrun to represent Nietzschean/German ideas and end up full of
death and destruction.[46] Gray suggests that the pattern demonstrates Lawrence's rejection of German ideas as a whole. This
has some merit: we have seen that Lawrence did reject such
characteristically German Romantic ideas as love-death. On the
other hand, it tends to obscure Gray's own overarching assumption:
that, for an English writer, Lawrence was unusually preoccupied
with German ideas, Nietzsche's in particular. German Romantic
philosophy was in the first place dialectical and, as Gray points out,
Lawrence was almost always dialectical.[47] In the second place, it
was Nature Mystic or neo-Rousseauesque and, as many critics have
pointed out, Lawrence was first and foremost a Naturist and all his
mysticism stemmed from the fact.[48] In the third place, it was anti-
material, anti-industrial and anti-progress in the Western bourgeois
sense (the Rhinegold is beautiful and good in its natural state, but
the source of exploitative capitalism, industrial rape and general
ruthlessness as the object of man's greed) and, as we have seen in
Women in Love and *Touch and Go*, Lawrence was equally anti-
materialist, anti-industrialist and anti-progress – unless and until
progress came to mean a reawakening to primal and sensual values.

As to ideas which Lawrence shared more specifically with the
pro-Wagner Nietzsche, we might summarize several important
ones.

1. The will-to-power idea, discussed above.
2. The belief in the necessity of solitude for development of the
   individual and the heroic, dramatized by Nietzsche in
   Zarathustra's retreat to the mountaintop; by Wagner in
   Siegfried's wanderings in the forest and Parsifal's wanderings in
   the waste land; and by Lawrence in every character from Birkin
   to Jesus (*The Man Who Died*) who turns from society to seek his
   singleness.
3. The respect for animal consciousness, symbolized by Nietzsche
   in Zarathustra's lion and eagle; by Wagner in Grane, the
   Woodbird and the swan; and by Lawrence in many places, but
   notably in St Mawr.[49]
4. The belief that the Dionysian consciousness must be brought
   back into Western life, articulated by Nietzsche in *The Birth of*

Tragedy and dramatized in *Zarathustra*; expressed by Wagner in *Oper und Drama* and in Siegfried; and dramatized by Lawrence in his Count Dionys in "The Ladybird" (1923) and his celebrations of the phallic cult of Quetzalcoatl in *The Plumed Serpent*.[50]

5. The desire to break the old European morality and move beyond good and evil, enunciated by Nietzsche thus: "As clothes dress the body, morals dress the man. As European man is not brave enough to go naked, so he is not amoral enough: For the body to be beautiful naked, man must accept his animality, his 'evil'."[51] Siegfried in his scant bearskin was surely the most naked hero on the European stage of Wagner's day; Lawrence delighted in stripping his men to the waist, and finally down to the buff.

6. The belief in Life its amorality and cruelty, demonstrated by Nietzsche in his statement that one has to kill that which is dying, be cruel to that which is weak, and impious to that which is old;[52] by Wagner in his Siegfried, who kills Mime with one swift and unsympathetic thrust of Nothung; by Lawrence in his characters in *Women in Love*, who watch weak old Mr Crich die with surprising lack of sympathy, and his Huitzilopochtli, who kills four plotting peons with a swift unsympathetic thrust of a dagger[58] – an act we are asked to regard as somehow noble and clean.

7. The obsession with health, demonstrated by Nietzsche in his statement that "He whose soul longs to experience the whole range of hitherto recognized values and desirabilities ... requires one thing above all for that purpose, *great healthiness*";[54] by Wagner in his personal life as described by Mann in "The Sufferings and Greatness of Richard Wagner", and demonstrated in his art by the fact that Klingsor has been excluded from the Grail Order on the basis of uncleanness, sexual and otherwise; and by Lawrence in numerous instances, such as his attack on Mann as "sick suffering".

8. The fascination for an ideal of male brotherhood, indicated by Nietzsche in the "O my brothers!" refrain of *Zarathustra*; by Wagner in the *Blutbrüderschaft* of *Götterdämmerung* and the Order of *Parsifal*; by Lawrence in detailed contemplation of the subject in every novel from *Women in Love* to *The Plumed Serpent*.

9. The belief that the artist is at his best in details, which is not so much a shared philosophical idea as a perception of Nietzsche's

about Wagner which has been echoed by critics about Lawrence, i.e. that Wagner was a great artist when a "miniaturist", according to Nietzsche, and a great deceiver when a histrio-and man-of-the-theatre;[55] likewise that Lawrence was demonstrating his true genius, according to Ronald Gray, when pausing to describe a flower in *Sons and Lovers* or an old chair in a market in *Women in Love* (also, Gray adds, his un-Germanness as an artist).[56]

10. The preference for Italy to the North as a place to live and create, a preference of course true of many other northern European artists of the time, but worth mentioning here in order to point out that Nietzsche, Wagner and Lawrence all had a "Mediterranean" side which coexisted with the Germanic values with which they are more usually identified. Nietzsche sang paeans to Italy and rejected Wagner as "Northern", but no less than Nietzsche Wagner loved to "go south in the winter". All three went to Italy for their health. Nietzsche broke down there, Wagner died there, and Lawrence died in nearby Vence. All three spent most of their lives in opposition to the religion of the South, but all three returned to the Christ-myth in their final works.

As a footnote to these many philosophical sympathies, we might also note the remarkable similarity between Nietzsche and Lawrence in the course of their lives. Both had a health crisis at the age of twenty-six which took them out of the teaching profession for ever. Both had an intellectual crisis at about the age of thirty-two which led them to break with their spiritual fatherlands – Nietzsche's the shock of what happened to his Wagner-dream at the first Bayreuth festival, Lawrence's to his status in England as a result of the suppression of his books and the war. Both thereupon set out as nomads and wrote their most characteristic and philosophical works. Both at about the age of forty created their most pagan, Dionysian and godlike personae, Zarathustra and Quetzalcoatl. Both at around the age of forty-four wrote their personal versions of the Christ-myth. Both "passed beyond our sight" in their forty-fifth year as a result of diseases that had taken hold of their bodies twenty years before, syphilis and tuberculosis respectively. Finally, beyond what we have already discussed, both left a legacy of the following overarching metapolitical ideas: (1) that Western democracy was wrong; (2) that history was cyclical; (3) that an apocalyptic death and phoenix-like[57] rebirth of man was imminent; (4) that a new religious/political system was going to rise up; (5) that the pre-eminent need of Western man was for a new type of leader.

HEROIC VITALISM

These ideas were Wagnerian, particularly the last. Nietzsche had contended that the fundamental theme of all Wagner's works was the search for salvation;[58] and at least three of Wagner's heroes – Lohengrin, Siegfried and Parsifal – were self-proclaimed experiments in a new type of saviour/leader. Nietzsche's advice to his own disciples had been that "The sense of all your efforts here on earth . . . [is] that the Great Man should be able to appear and dwell among you again";[59] and Lawrence, whose spokesman Birkin is described with only partial facetiousness as "*salvator mundi*", was clearly seeking throughout his mature works for what was male, what was great in maleness, and what constituted the great male leader. That this theme should have been so powerful in all three, and should have grown in importance during the course of their careers, is a testament not only to their similarity as thinkers, but also to the fact that the theme was a major concern to the entire era under discussion. This concern only increased as Romanticism decayed into Modernism. Leopold Bloom, after all, was the result of the quest for the Great Man as well, different from Wagner's and Nietzsche's and Lawrence's ideals as he may appear. *The Waste Land*, as we shall see, was in one sense a dramatization of the quest itself; and the fact that the Great Man does not appear in the poem, but can only be divined through signs and symbols strewn about, only heightens our awareness of how much the age saw itself as being in need of such a leader.

Mussolini, of course, was one attempt at such a leader, Hitler another; and the charges of complicity in the bringing-on of fascism which have been laid at the doorstep of various figures we are discussing are justified inasmuch as they were looking and waiting for someone like Hitler, if not for the Nazi anti-Christ himself.[60] At the end of his textbook on European history Lawrence had written,

> We must never forget that mankind lives by a twofold motive: the motive of peace and increase, and the motive of contest and martial triumph. As soon as the appetite for martial adventure and triumph in conflict is satisfied, the appetite for peace and

increase manifests itself, and vice versa. It seems a law of life. Therefore a great united Europe of productive working-people, all materially equal, will never be able to continue and remain firm unless it unites also round one chosen figure, some hero who can lead a great war, as well as administer a wide peace. It all depends on the will of the people. But the will of the people must concentrate in one figure, who is also supreme over the will of the people. He must be chosen, but at the same time responsible to God alone. Here is a problem of which a stormy future will have to evolve the solution.[61]

This is the attitude of the heroic vitalist. In it the Western liberal finds the alien notions that war is as noble or nobler than peace; that it is natural, even imperative at times, to seek a Caesar; and that somehow these things are matters of historical and evolutionary inevitability. Eric Bentley in his wartime book *The Cult of the Superman* traces the progress of these ideas through Carlyle, Wagner, Nietzsche, Shaw, Spengler, Stefan George and Lawrence, and places them all in a single tradition opposed to the Western liberal tradition in the following ways:

Western liberalism	*Heroic vitalism*
Regularity and uniformity	Change and difference
Smoothness and gradualness	Uneven leaps
Rectilinear progression	Recurring cycles
Equality	Inequality
Perfectibility of man	History of rise and fall
Fraternity	A noble, solitary end
Contemplation	Action
Politics	War
Unity	Duality
Loving *vs* hard-hearted	Bold *vs* cowardly
Humble *vs* arrogant	Noble *vs* vulgar
Man of truth	Man of fact
Common-sense	Magic
	Destiny[62]

Peter Viereck in his *Metapolitics*, which reviews the intellectual origins of Nazism and concludes that Wagner was the single most important source for the ideas of Hitler and Rosenberg,[63] presents a breakdown similar to Bentley's:

Western (Mediterranean) tradition	New German paganism
Law	Life
Form	Content
Static	Dynamic
Classicism	Romanticism
Politics	Metapolitics
Internationalism	Racism
Liberal capitalism	National Socialism
Pacifism	Militarism
Freedom	Tribal Führer
Individualism	Totalitarianism
Atomism	Organic *Volk*
Reason	Force
Gold	Blood
Christ	Wotan
The Westerner	The Nordic
Civilization	*Kultur*[64]

Such lists provide, though with less irony and qualification, the sort of dialectical oppositions in the European personality that Mann had posed in his Settembrini *versus* Naphtha, and his Zeitblom *versus* Leverkuhn. Like Mann's opposed pairs, they may be useful in measuring the extent to which the artists we are discussing belonged to one camp or the other as the West split apart in the twentieth century. And, while we have noted that he too had a "Mediterranean" side, it is plain that Lawrence stood generally in opposition to the Western liberal tradition as defined – much as Wagner, Nietzsche and others had before him. Lawrence never ultimately bore the relationship to an English Hitler that D'Annunzio bore to Mussolini;[65] but it would be wrong not to admit that he too was that type of artist whose ideas and style anticipated the dictators.

CONCLUSION

Having said so much, we should make the qualification that a genealogy of particular ideas does not necessarily constitute a pervasive relationship. Lawrence can be placed in an ideological tradition with Wagner. So too, we have indicated, can Yeats. But are these traditions necessarily the same? Yeats, for instance, can be placed in a Symbolist tradition with Wagner; but can Lawrence? Symons can be placed in a Decadent tradition with Wagner, but can Lawrence? Joyce can be placed in an aesthetic tradition with Wagner, but can Lawrence be placed in the same one? Such questions indicate the tentative value of proposing traditions altogether. And, when we come to perhaps the most intriguing question about Lawrence's relationship to Wagner, i.e. whether he should be placed in the same racialist/heroic-vitalist tradition that led from Bayreuth to Hitler to the Holocaust, we must answer only with qualification – perhaps. Perhaps via Nietzsche. Perhaps in Count Dionys, that central-European ex-soldier whose war-wounds and mystical speculations have led to a vision of a new European order with a strongman at top, we might discover Lawrence's most Wagnerian and sympathetic anticipation of Hitler.[66] On the other hand, Dionys is no Aryan Siegfried; he is a dark little Slav – a type, in short, that Hitler quite likely would have sent to death.

Like Shaw, Lawrence seemed to find as he became acclaimed as an artist that he should devote himself more and more to political and philosophical prophecy. Thus it is tempting to see his relationship to Wagner as primarily one of sympathy in these areas. When all is said and done, however, Wagner and Lawrence merit our attention for their art, not for ideas that in other hands led on to destruction; and similarities in their art surely constitute the area of relationship of which we should take most notice. Like it or not, Lawrence's lifelong focus on sensuality forces comparison to *Tristan*, whose configuration was a major motif of his career. Acknowledged influence or not, Wagner in his focus on apocalypse and messiah was the major artist-precursor of Lawrence's later works. Opposed to "art for art's sake" though he may have been, Lawrence in his incantatory repetitions and musical effects often partook of the very rhythmic fog and narcotic style which Nietzsche had no derided in Wagner's "art of decadence". The mature Lawrence would doubtless have challenged any contention that he aspired to Wagerian ideals or achievements. For most of his adult life he appears to have regarded Wagner as boring, obscene, or simply unspeakable. Still, for his use of Wagnerian themes and configurations, his evocative prose with its musical effects, and his *oeuvre* of such curiously Wagnerian scope, Lawrence must be considered one of the most intrinsically Wagnerian writers of the twentieth century.

10 *The Waste Land*

The octogenarian "miglior fabbro" of *The Waste Land* was walking with his mistress one day by the Giardini Publici in Venice. Coming on a plinth decorated with pelicans in bas-relief, they had the following conversation:

> "Ezra!" (the American voice of Miss Rudge,
> custodian of the oracle). "Why is Wagner's bust here?"
> (In slow remote tones) "He died here."
> "Ezra! What on earth do young pelicans tearing
> at the old bird's entrails have to do with Wagner?"
> (A short pause. The Imperial moment:) "Toujours
> les tripes."[1]

The image provides a near-perfect summation of the public attitude of the Modernists towards the nineteenth-century *Meister*: an old bird, full of tripe, unappetizing yet nourishing, perhaps even necessary sustenance to the scavenging artists of subsequent generations. The dismissive yet grudgingly respectful tone was typical; so too the playful and arrogant obscurity. On the subject of Wagner few Modernists were willing to be vocal – elsewhere in Pound's career of pronouncements there was sepulchral silence. In Pound's case this was no doubt the result of an honest distaste for Romantic music: his preferences were for the Classical and the Modern, Vivaldi and Anthiel. In T. S. Eliot's case a similar silence, leaving unexplained the major allusions and similarities to Wagner in *The Waste Land*, seems to have concealed a latent taste for the "magician of Bayreuth". Eliot's one published comment about Wagner, in "A Dialogue on Dramatic Poetry" (1928), stated that, while he considered Wagner to be "pernicious", he cherished the memory of the Wagner-experience.[2] Years later in conversation with another Modernist who had fed surreptitiously off "the old bird" – that is, with Stravinsky – Eliot confessed to having had a passion for Wagner in his youth.[3]

Eliot's lifelong silence otherwise can be explained by two things: (1) Wagner was out of fashion among Western intellectuals for most of Eliot's mature career; (2) any admission to passion for Romantic art would have been in conflict with his celebrated admonitions against "extreme emotionalism",[4] and his espousal of Classical values and Anglo-Catholic morality. Unfortunately this silence has prevented us from knowing when, where, and with whom Eliot's early Wagner experience(s) might have taken place. Moreover, it has contributed to the general avoidance of discussion of Wagner's place in *The Waste Land*, in spite of the fact that Wagner's works are alluded to more prominently and frequently in the poem than those of any other single artist. This critical avoidance has not been absolute. In *The Invisible Poet: T. S. Eliot*, Hugh Kenner remarked on the importance of Wagner to Eliot's style: "The opulent Wagnerian pathos, with its harmonic rather than linear development and its trick of entrancing the attention with *leitmotifs*, is never unrelated to the methods of *The Waste Land*." He remarked further on Eliot's use of the Grail motif: "Wagner, more than Frazer or Miss Weston, presides over the introduction into *The Waste Land* of the Grail motif." Kenner went on to conclude that, no less than Baudelaire, Wagner represented for Eliot the conspicuous model for the decadent European worldview he was trying to evoke.[5] Another critic, Stephen Spender, seemed on the verge of pioneering new territory when he remarked that he had come to suspect that the libretti of the *Ring* and perhaps *Parsifal* were the important models in Eliot's mind as he composed, a possibility that Eliot in conversation had once given him reason to believe.[6] Spender unfortunately did not expand on this in his subsequent book on Eliot. Thus we are left after sixty years of criticism on *The Waste Land* with but one obscure study on the relationship of Wagner to the poem, *Wagner, the King, and "The Waste Land"* by Herbert Knust,[7] a book which makes several unusual and provocative observations that we shall take up later in this chapter.

Given the lack of information on Eliot's Wagner-experience and of criticism on Wagner's place in *The Waste Land*, this chapter will be somewhat free-ranging. The overall goal is to show how Wagner relates to the poem, and how the poem might be seen as a synthesis and logical endpoint to a Wagnerian tradition, roughly the one outlined in the preceding chapters. The specific goal is to suggest how the poem might be read as a version of *Parsifal*, with which it shares the Grail-legend framework. In doing this we hope to

indicate similarities and differences of worldview between an artist
of 1882 and an artist working in essentially the same tradition in
1922 – in other words, roughly the period covered in this study. *The
Waste Land* lends itself to such a reading for three reasons: (1) its
Grail-legend framework suggests a connection with the previous
age, in which Grail works experienced such widespread vogue; (2)
its major focus is on the psychosis of a sensibility whose essentially
Romantic expectations are in conflict with the realities of the post-
war modern world; and (3) if we are to take the word of a recent
book on Eliot's early life, the legendary Parzival was the major
secular figure who, along with such religious figures as St Augustine
and Lazarus and Ezekiel, formed "the model of manhood by which
[Eliot] measured himself".[8] We shall proceed towards indications
of this Parsifal reading through discussions of the relationships to the
poem of the *fin-de-siècle* artist, German thought and contemporary
Zeitgeist, and Wagner and his life and works.

*   *   *

THE FRENCH PRECURSOR

In a now-celebrated statement, Eliot once described *The Waste Land*
as a personal "grouse against life".[9] This it may have been. But,
even accepting the poem as a very personal "grouse" set down in
feverish spasms of automatic writing, we recognize that it has a
significance extending beyond Eliot's own painful situation. The
atmosphere is full of the art and artists that were crowding Eliot's
mind at the time. These included: the French of the *fin-de-siècle*; the
seventeenth-century dramatists, Dante, and others whom he had
discussed in *The Sacred Wood* (1920); Joyce, whom he had recently
recognized as having discovered "the modern method";[10] Pound,
who had recently bidden a bitter farewell to London in a poem
about a poet-*manqué* adrift in a sea of Romantic refuse;[11] *et cetera.*
The resonances of these others encourage us to see the poem as a
vortex through which the spirit of the age and its artists run; from
which perspective we might interpret its Wagnerian allusions as a
function not only of Eliot's own latent Wagner-passion, but also of
the Wagnerism of those artists who peopled his mind as he wrote.
Prime among these are the French. Their influence on Eliot dated

from his reading of Symons' *Symbolist Movement* in 1908.[12] It has long been accepted as a chief factor in his development, and its presence in *The Waste Land* is clear. We might go so far as to say that a synthetic French precursor, or "artist-father", stands behind the poem. We can sketch in his features by looking at the figures Eliot quotes.

Baudelaire. Eliot's direct allusions ("Unreal City" in l. 60, "Hypocrite lecteur" in l. 76, and so forth) are visible manifestations of the pervasive influence of the poet whom Wilde had described as a modern Dante;[13] nor is it by chance that the allusions announcing his presence in the poem come in a stanza recalling a canto of the *Inferno*. Several overall motifs are typical of Baudelaire: the setting, which alternates between sumptuous *salon* and decadent street; the imagery, which alternates between the magnificent and the macabre; the point of view, which alternates between fascination and horror. Indeed, *The Waste Land* is a Baudelairean poem in the very respects which Eliot would attribute to that genre in his introduction to Isherwood's translation of *Journaux intimes* (1930): it is a city poem; it has the atmosphere of nostalgia and waiting ("the *poésie des departs*, the *poésie des salles d'attente*"); it is a pathology and the disease of the patient is Baudelaire's disease of accidie; it focuses on modern urban sexual relations and demonstrates the attitude which Eliot praised in Baudelaire – "that to conceive of the sexual act as evil is more dignified, less boring, than to think of it as the natural, 'life-giving', cheery automatism of the modern world".[14] The speaker of *The Waste Land* recalls, both in tone and behaviour, Baudelaire the urban wanderer and *voyant*: that "strange sad brother" who had so appealed to "students of Arthur Symons' generation".[15] More specifically perhaps, he recalls Baudelaire of the last years: a sorry figure, catatonic and without passion except with regard to Wagner's music and Impressionist art; silent finally and able to utter only the words of Christian penitence, "Sacre Nǫm", as he grew paralysed with syphilis and approached the horror of an end brought on by a previous sexual indulgence – "the awful daring of a moment's surrender" – which no amount of subsequent prudence, hard work, or penitence could retract.

Verlaine. The direct quotation is the last line of "Parsifal". Knust speculates that that sonnet may refer specifically to Ludwig II of Bavaria, whose sexual problems and personal connection with

Parsifal were well-known among the Parisian *cognoscenti* of the age (Knust points to the fact that Verlaine placed the sonnet directly after the one entitled "Á Louis II de Bavière" in *Amour*[16]). More generally, as we have seen, "Parsifal" reflected the conflict between sexual indulgence and Christian purity which dominated the life of the Decadent *prince des poètes* – indeed, the volume in which it appeared was published just after the death of Lucien Létinois, Verlaine's young lover; from which time, as Harold Nicolson tells us, "We can trace [Verlaine's] decline toward complete moral and mental breakdown."[17] Possibly Eliot was consciously echoing this breakdown in the disturbed situation of his speaker. In any case, by quoting a line which so beautifully harmonizes the divergent impulses to the flesh and the spirit which Verlaine could not harmonize in his life, Eliot underlined two themes common to the typical Decadent: (1) the gap between the ideal aesthetic vision and the vulgar reality of modern life (Verlaine's sublime line is placed amid a vignette about "apeneck" Sweeney, a decadent Jacobean "prick song", and the unsavoury invitation of Mr Eugenides); and (2) the folly of alternately giving way to sexual temptation and then renouncing it, by which Verlaine ultimately lost both the mortal flesh for which he lusted, and the will to Christian discipline through which he might otherwise have attained the comfort of the Holy Spirit.

Laforgue. Though he is never quoted directly, Laforgue's importance to *The Waste Land* seems substantial. We can see this in the handling of male/female encounters, particularly in "A Game of Chess". The non-responsive speaker might recall Lord Pierrot of the "Complainte" that Symons had quoted in *The Symbolist Movement*; the *grande dame* might recall the Empress Augusta whom Laforgue had described in *En Allemagne* as suffering from "l'alterable mauvaise humeur de nerfs", and as given to speaking in a "sibylline" tone;[18] the scene as a whole might recall Laforgue's evocations of the *ennui* of Augusta's court, or his fantasy-representation of endless evenings in the chambers of the doomed aristocracy of Europe in "Lohengrin, fils de Parsifal". Laforgue's "gently agitated melancholy mingled with urbane irony",[19] which Eliot had first imitated in "Prufrock", is echoed with new hollowness and horror in the tone of the speaker of *The Waste Land*. And, as in the case of Baudelaire, one is tempted to think of the French poet's early breakdown and to hear echoes of that frail yet stoic trepidation which, mixed with reminiscences of bits of Wagnerian music and popular song, marked his final style; also of the fascination for that new "religion", mixing German Romantic philosophy with Eastern mysticism in the *Tristan*-like fashion, which encouraged the world-weary young aesthete to yearn for transcendence into the great unconscious Beyond. As Warren Ramsey says, "Laforgue lost one faith [Christianity] only to acquire another, aesthetic Buddhism; and, whatever the merits of the latter, it left him even more open than before to vague but powerfully felt attitudes of resignation."[20]

Gérard du Nerval is the one other French poet directly quoted. The line, from *El Desdichado*, refers to a dispossessed prince; and dispossession, as we shall see when we come to Knust's discussion of Marie Larisch and Ludwig II, is an underlying theme of *The Waste Land*. As a wanderer and *voyant* and pre-Symbolist, Nerval was another apt figure to allude to in a work which was synthesizing such motifs; further, as a "mad" poet who ultimately hanged himself, Nerval may have a more particular relevance to the motif of madness and the mysterious choice of the "Hanged Man" card from the Tarot pack (l. 55).

Beyond Nerval there may be other French figures who have equally suggestive relationships to the poem: Mallarmé, Rimbaud and Corbière, for instance. But in the interests of brevity we shall rest our case on those actually quoted and Laforgue.[21] From them we can fill in the salient features of the synthetic type behind the poem: he is a dispossessed bourgeois tied to a literary tradition but adrift in the physical world; an aesthete attracted to Wagner; a *voyant* preoccupied with modern sex and its futility; a fallen Christian who is attracted to the idea of renunciation, but has a disease of the will which prevents him from developing religious discipline; an unhealthy and incompletely matured man susceptible to catatonic silence, breakdown, madness and early death. He is, in short, a type whose fate a successor might well have had reason to fear. And in this sense *The Waste Land* may have constituted, among other things, Eliot's cryptic warning to himself to avoid the fate of this precursor to whom he felt such an affinity.

THE "NINETYISH" ENGLISH

While *The Waste Land* makes direct allusions to the French, it also echoes the English of the 1890s with their preoccupations with the

French, Wagner, and the Tannhäuserian conflict between sex and spirituality. The most prominent allusions to English works are to dramas of the seventeenth century; but this may well support rather than negate the argument that Eliot was primarily concerned with the *fin-de-siècle*. The dramas alluded to come from the period preceding the Puritan upheaval and Civil War, and might suggest a historical analogy to Eliot's own epoch, in which *fin-de-siècle* decadence had preceded the upheaval of European civil war. Moreover, as Eliot and critics of his school were wont to point out, the Baudelairean type of the contemporary period had been prefigured by the decadent type of the Jacobean.[22] Almost all the English of the 1890s we have discussed styled themselves as Decadents after the Baudelaire fashion. Eliot himself had entered the field of criticism of seventeenth-century drama through the studies of two of these English Baudelaireans, Symons and Swinburne. And, though he had recently objected to the critical method of both as "emotional" and "impressionistic",[23] it is not unreasonable to assume that he continued to associate seventeenth-century drama with them as he alluded to it in *The Waste Land*.

The pervasive *fin-de-siècle* atmosphere of the poem echoes not only figures such as Conrad and James, whom we know influenced Eliot, but also the Wagnerians we have discussed. Consider the cases of Wilde and Moore. Both *Dorian Gray* and *Evelyn Innes*, for instance, are focused on the theme of indulgence *versus* renunciation which is central to *The Waste Land*. Both, moreover, contain incidental motifs which are relevant to its Wagnerism. Like the Wilde of *De Profundis*, Dorian Gray after his years of indulgence is a sick sufferer of accidie; and his remark, "I wish it were *fin-du-globe*. . . . Life is such a great disappointment",[24] anticipates the sentiment Eliot's seeker acts out when he sits down by the waters and imagines a *Götterdämmerung*-like "burning burning". At that moment in Eliot's poem the Thames takes on characteristics of Wagner's Rhine – much as it also does at that moment in Moore's novel when Evelyn Innes, lunching with one of her old Valkyrie sisters at the Savoy, is tempted to return to Bayreuth to sing *Götterdämmerung* again.[25] Such parallels, though no doubt accidental, point to a sympathy between Eliot's poem and the works of these two precursors which becomes even more evident if we consider the poetry each had written as a young man come to sophisticated London in search of literary fortune.

Much of Eliot's imagery, ivory and hyacinths and violet and so forth, recalls Wilde's in his *Poems* or Moore's in *Flowers of Passion*. So, too, does the atmosphere of "A Game of Chess" and its *femme fatale*, reminiscent as she is of some "cruel" caricature by Aubrey Beardsley. The ghostly religious atmosphere of the beginning of "What the Thunder Said" recalls that of Moore's playlet "Ginevra", with its decadent setting and its mysterious mixture of music and nuns' chants. Eliot's Hyacinth girl who returns with her hair wet from a tryst in a garden recalls, perhaps, Moore's "Bernice":

> With linkèd hands we went
> Unto the lake of fountain born,
> And bathed unwatched amid the flowers.
> She was a vision of voluptuousness,
> And o'er the waters streamed her wondrous hair.[26]

The type of the doomed Ophelia into which the Hyacinth girl merges at the end of "A Game of Chess" might likewise recall another of Moore's most Pre-Raphaelite passages, this from "Annie" in *Flowers of Passion*:

> I throw
> Into the stream below
> The flowers I refuse,
> As men throw the love they use.
> Some how it happeneth
> They weave a fairy wreath,
> The basil and mignonette,
> The rose and the violet,
> The graceful eglantine
> With the scented jessamine,
> And hundred other buds,
> Entwine within the floods.[27]

In addition to such general atmospheric echoes we might specifically recall the Moore of *Confessions* in Eliot's quotation of the last line of Verlaine's "Parsifal"; for Moore, as we have seen, had been the first in English to quote that sonnet, singling out the last line for particular praise. And we might think of the Wilde of *The Ballad of Reading Gaol* in Eliot's choice of the "Hanged Man" card; for Wilde's poem was the swansong of a broken Decadent, focusing on the fate of a hanged convict and dramatizing the necessity of the turn to "the cross".

THE CASE OF SYMONS

But of all English figures who may have relevance to *The Waste Land*, the case of Arthur Symons presents the most intriguing questions. It was in Margate in Kent, where Symons had struggled to regain his sanity and subsequently made his home, that Eliot went for the "rest-cure" during which he began to make a form out of the nerve-wracking recollections of music and verse which were crowding his overwrought mind; and we might ask whether Eliot recalled that Symons had found himself in a similar position in Venice a dozen years before, only could not forge coherence out of similar gluts of sound and image in his own mind, and thus went mad. We might ask further, in relation to this, what of Symons's "charming"[28] poetry Eliot might have known and recalled, consciously or not, as he wrote. Did he, for instance, recall, as he conceived Mme Sosotris, Symons's "Tarot Cards", written a matter of days before his breakdown?

> The Tarot cards that rule our fates
> Slip through her hands like shaken sands;
> Her charmed sight upon them waits,
> She holds the future in her hands;
> Her fingers can unlatch the gates
> That open on forbidden lands.
>
> Rise up from the accursed pool,
> Lest the grass wither where you lie;
> Fold up the Tarot cards that rule
> Our Fates, and put your witchcraft by:
> Only a madman or a fool
> Would will to know his hour to die.[29]

Did Eliot recall Symons's lifelong fascination with the persona of Tristan as he alluded to Wagner's music drama, or Symons's free imitations of "Parsifal" as he alluded to Verlaine's sonnet? Did he remember Symons's most ambitious Decadent poem, "Mundi Victima"; and, if so, did he recall such lines as I have italicized below as he conceived the mute procession to the Grail Chapel in "What the Thunder Said", or the sounds of wind over the nervous

repartee of "A Game of Chess", or such nostalgic cadences as "O
City city, I can sometimes hear . . ."?

> O subtle voices, luring from the dream
> The dreamer, till love's very vision seem
> The unruffled air that phantom feet have crossed
> *In mute march of that processional host*
> Whose passing is the passing *of the wind*;
> *Avenging voices*, hurrying *behind*
> The souls that have escaped, and yet look back
> Reluctantly along the flaming track;
> *O mighty voices* of the world, *I have heard*
> Between our heart-beats your reiterate word
> And I have felt our heart-beats slackening[30]

Had he read Symons's most recent poetry – for instance, "Mad
Song", with its Decadent contempt for orthodox respectability and
the "passing fashion" of the Modern?

> They say that I am mad.
> I worship the Abhorred
> And O the ways I had
> Of banishing the Lord!
>
> I hate the passing fashion
> But not the moving crowds;
> If Satan gives me passion
> I wander with the clouds. . . .[31]

Had he read Symons's most recent critical work, the overwrought
study on Baudelaire, with its preoccupations with Wagner and the
"dark Venus" and pagan sexual rites?

To this last question we can answer that, because of his
concurrent interest in Baudelaire, Eliot probably knew of Symons's
study; and, though rejecting it for its "impressionistic" method, he
might well have recalled its point of view in the pathetic
Baudelaireanism of his poem. A factor here is that Symons
dedicated his study to John Quinn, the American patron who had
been helping him for some years and who had recently become
aware of Eliot's work through Pound. Quinn was to play an
influential role in the American publication of *The Waste Land*;[32]
and the general fact of his relationship to Symons during a period

when Eliot himself was in need of a patron is one practical reason why Eliot should have continued to pay attention to the work of the once-celebrated Decadent, though perhaps with some feelings of professional jealousy. Putting this aside, we cannot say much in specific about Eliot's knowledge of Symons's breakdown or his recall of Symons's poetry. Certainly he had read Symons's criticism when preparing *The Sacred Wood*, for he acknowledged a debt to Symons's ground-work on the seventeenth century, much as he was later to acknowledge his debt to *The Symbolist Movement* for his introduction to the French *fin-de-siècle*. But these brief acknowledgements are not couched in terms of reverence; and it seems likely that the older English poet and critic was one precursor from whom Eliot wanted to distance himself completely.

This, combined with the paucity of information about Eliot's reading and personal thoughts during composition of *The Waste Land*, forces us to speculate that: (1) Eliot had Symons in mind as he wrote, but was not eager to acknowledge the fact, for reasons similar to those which led him to conceal his youthful Wagner-passion; (2) Eliot's own mental state during composition left him unaware of the extent to which he was echoing the tone, interests, and style of Symons; or (3) Eliot did not have Symons in mind at all, and any echo of Symons in the poem was purely accidental. This last seems improbable. For, whatever thoughts of Symons may have crossed Eliot's mind, these facts remain: (1) *The Waste Land* is preoccupied with the theme of sexual indulgence, which obsessed Symons; (2) it is built on references to artists and works in which Symons was extremely well versed; (3) it is a "mad" poem and Symons was the conspicuous "mad" poet of the day; (4) it is the apotheosis of the Imagist poem and Symons was *the* Imagist poet in English long before such a term existed. Pound, the coiner of the term *Imagisme*, was to recall Symons and his "Modern Beauty" in a poignant passage of his great "mad" poem, *The Pisan Cantos*:

> 'I am the torch' wrote Arthur 'she saith'
> in the moon barge βροδοδακτνος ‘Ηως
> with the veil of faint cloud before her
> κυθπρα δεινα as the leaf borne in the current
> pale eyes as if without fire[33]

Pound would not miss the relevance to his own situation of Symons's "memory and desire" for the departed aesthetic age:

and with Symons remembering Verlaine at the Tabarin
  or Hennrique, Flaubert
Nothing but death, said Turgenev (Tiresias)
  is irreparable[34]

Given that "il miglior fabbro" would have recognized the connection of Symons with his own "mad" fragments, it seems unlikely
that he would have missed it in relation to the manuscript which
"mad Tiresias" Eliot presented to him in Paris twenty-three years
before; or that cryptic, tight-lipped Mr Eliot should have been
unaware of it himself.

With his chief mentor and aesthetic-sympathizer having written
Mauberley and departed for Paris, Eliot might have looked around to
find with a sort of horror only the strange out-of-time figure of
Arthur Symons representing the two traditions most important to
him: the poetic tradition which had bloomed out of the French of
the *fin-de-siècle*, and the critical tradition leading back from these
French to the seventeenth century and back further to Dante and
the troubadours. It would have been virtually impossible for Eliot
not to have recognized that the tradition which he had entered in
The Sacred Wood, and was pursuing through *The Waste Land*, was
largely the same one that Symons had entered years before; or that
Symons had become lost in the quest, permanently deflected into
Wagnerian preoccupations with decadence and sensual
indulgence, and rendered as pathetic a figure as the wounded
Amfortas – his mind "burning burning" with alternately glorious
and painful memories. *The Waste Land* is a poem about Symons's
type of psychosis. In terms of the Parzival analogy, Eliot's relation to
Symons, and the synthetic precursor that Symons most fully
typifies, is like that of Parzival to the wounded fisher-king. And
Eliot's act in *The Waste Land* – to embark on the same quest,
experience the same psychosis, and draw perilously near to the same
sort of breakdown – is to pursue the symbolical path that ends by
asking the crucial question that the aspiring hero of any new
generation must ask the broken survivor of a preceding "tragic"
one: "What ails thee, Uncle?"[35] According to the legend, the mere
asking of the question heals the fisher-king's wound and restores the
ancient order to the land.

* * *

Eliot originally came to Europe to study philosophy in Germany. He was prevented from staying in Germany by the War and forced to return to England, where he finished his thesis on F. H. Bradley and began to eke out a living as a poet and reviewer. He did not return to Germany after the War nor continue with various thesis-related studies, such as Sanskrit, which might have led towards that vaguely Eastern spiritual endpoint typical of much German thought of the era. Origins of *The Waste Land* may be traced to this early period as a student in Europe. Like Pound's *Mauberley*, with which it has much in common, the poem may on one level be taken as an autobiographical account of the young American's intellectual progress from the time of coming to Europe to that of composition. As such, it constitutes a summation of that phase of Eliot's career in which things German were of the most interest.[36] As Spender has pointed out, *The Waste Land* is the most German of Eliot's poems.[37] It is underpinned by the German Romantic philosophy he had studied as a student – the Hegel which he read during a critical period in Paris on his first trip to Europe in 1911;[38] the Schopenhauer which he was familiar with by that time, and, through his study of Laforgue perhaps, Hartmann and Schelling as well. More weirdly, the poem captures the mood of contemporary Germany, which had fallen further from pre-War heights than any other Western culture; and of the German petty bourgeois artist-*manqué* who had grown up with vaguely Wagnerian ideas of racial purity and destiny and heroism, but now found himself adrift in a tawdry existence between "barroom bohemia" and "the businessman's club",[39] and so would go on to support the rise of the National Socialist hero. These things we shall consider briefly in this section before moving on to the poem's specific Wagnerism.

NIETZSCHE, HEROIC VITALISM, ELIOT *VERSUS* LAWRENCE

That Eliot read Nietzsche in the Levy edition seems likely. In any case, by the War he had sufficiently digested the German "impressionist" philosopher to strike a distinctive attitude in a review of Abraham Wolf's *The Philosophy of Nietzsche* for the *International Journal of Ethics*, in which the current debate on whether to blame Nietzsche for the War was raging.[40] Nietzsche's philosophy "evaporates" when stripped of it's author's "demagogic" literary gift, Eliot contended; moreover, it had a potential for influence over the unschooled mass-mind which was probably undesirable. Eliot's attitude here reveals elements of academic snobbery, also of the partisanship which was shortly to move him to attempt to join the American army in order to fight the Germans;[41] and it seems entirely logical that a critic who was within a decade to declare his principles to be Anglo-Catholic and royalist could have little sympathy with the German vitalist whose attitude towards English "moralists" was of this kind:

> There is little to be learned from those historians of morality (especially Englishmen): they themselves are usually, quite unsuspiciously, under the influence of a definite morality, and act unwittingly as its armour-bearers and followers – perhaps still repeating sincerely the popular superstition of Christian Europe, that the characteristic of moral action consists in abnegation, self-denial, self-sacrifice, or in fellow-feeling and fellow-suffering. . . . The coming generation could easily face the terrible alternative: "Either do away with your venerations or – with yourselves."[42]

The Waste Land depicts a Europe which had taken a lurch in the direction of Nietzsche's prophecy. The surrender to the "neo-Nietzschean clatter" of war and anti-Christian morality is in large part what the poem suggests that "an age of prudence" would not be able to retract. And Nietzsche himself, with his miserable end in syphilis and madness, fits neatly along with Baudelaire and the rest into the scheme of the *fin-de-siècle* artist/thinker type at the point of breakdown.

In general Eliot's poem of decadence presents a picture of cultural sickness much the same as that presented in Nietzsche's philosophy of decadence. It is only the indicated cures that are different; and this pattern of similar diagnosis yet different prescription is typical of Eliot's position on the many concerns he shared with heroic vitalists of the day. So much is apparent if we compare him to Lawrence, whose concerns with love-death, *Götterdämmerung*, and the sudden unleashing of chaos from the East are strikingly similar to the pre-eminent German issues of *The Waste Land*. For Eliot's evocation of "hooded hordes" swarming across the Polish plain there is Lawrence's prediction about "Tartary" in "Letter from Germany"; for Eliot's picture of the decadence and death-

wishing of the Western capitalist/industrialist order there is
Lawrence's characterization of the Crich family in *Women in Love*;
for Eliot's apparent expectation of an imminent apocalypse there
are Lawrence's concurrent "prophecies" of the same. On the other
hand, where Lawrence like Nietzsche saw such prospects as
inevitable and even welcome, Eliot like Mann regarded them as
cause for concern and alarm. Eliot's response was conservative
where Lawrence's was radical. Eliot was like the Wagner of *Parsifal*
who wanted to revitalize the old sacred tradition, where Lawrence
was like the Wagner of *Siegfried* who wanted to destroy the corrupt
old order root and branch. Eliot was like the contemporary German
who wished to preserve the old Prussian Protestant values and
rallied around Hindenburg, where Lawrence was like the militant
"Young Socialists" and Nietzschean *Wandervögel*, who were fascinated by the prospect of a ruthless new leader. Eliot, in, sum wanted
to shore up the post-War ruins of Europe and restore what
traditional values could be salvaged, while Lawrence pursued the
millennial apocalypse with anarchic glee:

> Why limit a man to a Christian brotherhood? I myself, I could
> belong to the sweetest Christian-brotherhood one day, and ride
> after Attila with a raw beefsteak for my saddle-cloth, to see the
> red cock crow in flame, over all Christendom, the next.[43]

Thus in these two contemporary writers in English we can see a
division like the one that was opening in post-Wagnerian Germany
and Europe. On the one side is the man of God and tradition, who
was appalled by the spectacle of revolutionary chaos and wanted re-
establishment of an old moral order; on the other, the self-confessed
anti-Christ who could thrill to the Nietzschean ideas of a cathartic
blood-letting and a new age of "transvalued" values. To Eliot this
Lawrence seemed "sick, diabolic, sensualist in the worst sense",[44]
while to Lawrence this Eliot must have seemed yet another "sick
sufferer from the complaint of Flaubert". Yet, in spite of such a
severe divergence in response, the two were virtually identical in
their diagnoses of the chaotic state of European civilization,
German preoccupations, and even ultimate visions of some mystical
moment of serenity as the alternative. In an unpublished poem on
the "blaue Blümen" of German Romanticism written at the end of
his life, Lawrence would say:

> There is nothing to save . . .
> But a tiny core of stillness in the heart
> like the eye of a violet.[45]

Here we find imagery, an idea, and a mood which, besides partaking heavily of the German tradition, have much in common with the spirit of *The Waste Land* – even more so with that of the *Four Quartets*.

EASTERN AND WESTERN MYSTICISM: ELIOT'S SYNTHESIS

"Stillness in the heart" – heart of what? Lawrence sought mystical transcendence in his personal version of the heart of darkness, in the "blood-knowledge" he identified with the dark and ostensibly primitive races of the American South-West. Eliot's speaker, on the other hand, seeks mystical transcendence in "the heart of light", a realm not only of *Tristan*-like Romanticism but also no doubt of the wisdom of the East, with which the young Eliot had become familiar through his studies of the *Bhagavadgita* and *Upanishads*.[46] According to Spender, Eliot was seriously considering becoming a Buddhist at the time he wrote *The Waste Land*.[47] But, while he may have entertained the general Schopenhauerian attraction to the knowledge of the East, he demonstrated in the poem a general wariness of all that came from the East, a wariness not unlike that which Wagner had dramatized in his Young Squires' reaction to Kundry. The hooded hordes, the Smyrna merchant, Mme Sosotris with her "bad cold" and her suggestions of the type of Mme Blavatsky, who had made such an impression on the generation of the 1890s by her importation of alleged spiritual secrets of the East – Eliot's treatment of such elements suggests the view that one analyst has ascribed to Lawrence: "L'Inde et l'Asie centrale, chère aux Blavatski et aux Besant, prophétesses si influentes sur la mentalité anglo-saxonne, étaient regardées . . . comme un foyer de forces destructives."[48] From this perspective, the seriousness of Eliot's alleged consideration of Buddhism must come into question; also the sincerity of his apparent celebration of Indian principles of behaviour at the very end of *The Waste Land*. Do they constitute principles in which he had seriously come to believe? Or are they on the other hand a subtly ironic characterization of the sort of quasi-

Buddhistic "words to live by" that Theosophists, Wagnerian mystics, and other souls hungry for spiritual comfort but belonging to a culture and era which had succumbed to the Nietzschean folly of abandoning Christianity might see fit to incant to themselves, mantra-like, in moments of crisis? This brings us to the crucial question of what system of belief the poem actually leads to: is it Buddhist, Christian, simply nihilist in the despairing post-War manner, or some combination?

The conventional view that the poem leads to a Christian "moral" gains support from the choice of landscape. As Laforgue had observed in the last year of his life

> Qu'où songe à la nature, mère et berceau du Germain pur, vraie terre de Védas du Nord, c'est la forêt panthéiste – comme le désert est monothéiste, selon le mot Renan – la forêt sacrée du theories nationales de Wagner; où la grande voix mélodique de la forêt est faite de symphonies à mille voix des arbres et des choses et les domine.[49]

The Wagnerian forest, which as the "forêt des symboles" had inspired the poetry of such decadent Christians as Baudelaire and Mallarmé, leads in general to a brand of Nature Mysticism which synthesizes ancient German pagan pantheism with the new Schopenhauerian Western Buddhism. But the desert, which along with vanished gardens and waste seas and decayed cities and dry rocky mountains formed the typical locus of Eliot's poetry, is the natural landscape of Theistic Mysticism and birthplace of the One God. Considering as much, we might hear in the authoritarian voice of the thunder at the end of Eliot's poem not just the Indian rainmaker, but also the angry Yahweh who sent the Flood to Noah's decadent world: the same God who turned the skies black and sent the storms down at that moment on Good Friday when his Son was crucified. This interpretation harmonizes with the following pair of rare comforting passages, which might bring to mind Jesus gathering his first disciples from among the fishermen of Galilee:

> O City city, I can sometimes hear
> Beside a public bar in Lower Thames Street,
> The pleasant whining of a mandoline
> And a clatter and a chatter from within
> Where fishmen lounge at noon: where the walls

of Magnus Martyr hold
Inexplicable splendour of Ionian white and gold.

(ll. 259–65)

And:

The boat responded
Gaily, to the hand expert with sail and oar
The sea was calm, your heart would have responded
Gaily, when invited, beating obedient
To controlling hands.

(ll. 418–22)

This evidence supports the conventional view at least so far as to say that *The Waste Land* implies a Christian moral, though through such a veil of Eastern motifs that Eliot's intentions at the time of composition must remain in considerable doubt.

In the end this blending of Eastern and Western mysticism suggests indecision. Only after *The Waste Land* did Eliot move to his clear espousal of Christian orthodoxy. In this his progress contrasts with that of Wagner, whose blending of Eastern and Western mysticism in *Parsifal* represented the goal and endpoint of a life's work; and whose scenarios on Christian and Buddhist subjects still under consideration when he died, "Jesus of Nazareth" and "The Victors", were conceived to continue such a blending. In general, Wagner, the German Romantic, pressed towards dialectical synthesis in his thought, as did others in his tradition from Goethe to Mann. Eliot, on the other hand, as he became more certain of his status as an Anglican and royalist and anti-Romantic, pressed towards isolation of thesis distinct in its singleness, away from synthetic blendings into the One. In his view of culture Eliot came to preach conservative class-distinction,where Wagner had espoused a vague classless revolutionary brotherhood. In his view of religion Eliot came to believe in the Theistic Mysticism of the single God ever outside of man, where Wagner had taken the Nature Mystic's view that man had the potential to integrate the divine powers of the Universe in the Self. These differences suggest a fundamentally contrasting pattern of intellection. Unlike his Celtic contemporaries, Yeats and Joyce, who like the German Romantics tended towards ultimate synthesis of the One and Nature Mysticism, Eliot came to typify the anti-synthetic impulse common to at least two other Anglo-Saxon Modernists. Lawrence, as we have seen, rejected *Tristan*-like merging and sought "singleness-in-union"; Pound objected to Wagnerian/synaesthetic blending of the arts and called in *Blast!* for reconstruction of the boundaries of the separate arts ("The vorticist will only use the primary pigment in his art", etc.).[50] Eliot likewise rejected the Parsifalian merging of mystical traditions in the end, and celebrated Western Christian tradition in its singleness.

ANTI-SEMITISM, BOURGEOIS *ANGST*, FASCISM

In the main line of discussion of *The Waste Land* it is essential to point out that, whatever hint of a religious resolution may be made, the atmosphere is predominantly one of aimlessness, oppression and futility. In such an atmosphere there may be a tendency to project blame; and, as in the case of contemporary Germany, the most likely target for blame appears to be the Jew. *The Waste Land* implies a vague anti-Semitism partaking of that of many of the influential figures behind it. These would include Wagner; Symons, whose prejudice was of a sentimental type common in both France and England at the turn-of-the-century –

> A poor old man, a crossing-sweeper, stands
> Bent on his broom that sweeps a foot of way;
> A fat furred Jew with jewels on his hands
> Passes the crossing-sweeper twice a day[51]

and Pound, whose prejudice took a more typically American and polemical form. The poem's latent anti-Semitism also partakes of less covert statements in earlier Eliot poems. These would include "Gerontion", which at one point Eliot considered placing before *The Waste Land* in the same book:

> My house is a decayed house,
> And the Jew squats on the window-sill, the owner,
> Spawned in some estaminet of Antwerp,
> Blistered in Brussels, patched and peeled in London.[52]

Also "Burbank with a Baedecker: Bleistein with a Cigar", which may provide the original linkage between the decaying influence of the Jew and the mysterious "rat" who is ubiquitous throughout *The Waste Land*:

> The smoky candle end of time
> Declines. On the Rialto once.
>   The rats are underneath the piles.
> The Jew is underneath the lot.[53]

Ironically, what kept *The Waste Land* from being overtly anti-Semitic (and unattractively misogynist as well) was that Pound, otherwise so loud about the perniciousness of Jews, deleted the long passage about the unsavoury Lady Kleinwurm; also such lines as "Full fathom five your Bleistein lies", which tightened the tentative linkage between Bleistein and the Jew and the rat, and possibly the Smyrna merchant and drowned Phoenician sailor as well.[54]

As in the cases of Wagner and Pound, Eliot's anti-Semitism was linked to socio-economic theory and analysis. Spender has suggested that Major Douglas's Social Credit theory may have had some influence on the poem.[55] Eliot's exposure to Social Credit came via Pound, who yoked Douglas's theory to his own historical analysis that a usurious banking system was the primary reason for the decay of Western culture:

> With usura hath no man a house of good stone
> each block cut smooth and well fitting
> that design might cover their face,
> with usura
> hath no man a painted paradise on his church wall
> *harpes et luthes*[56]

Like Wagner, Pound regarded the creative artist as a particular victim of the usurer's evil influence; and Eliot's personal situation seemed to provide an unusually apt illustration of this. The necessity of working for a bank was destroying Eliot's ability to realize his formidable creative gift, Pound averred: having prevented creation, it had led to the breakdown which had forced the rest-cure which had produced, miraculously, the manuscript of *The Waste Land*; a return to working for the bank, however, would most likely cause renewed frustration of the creative gift and further breakdowns, the results of which could not be expected to be so miraculous.[57] Pound was so struck by what he regarded as the danger to Eliot's gift that he tried to set up a fund to free Eliot financially. Eliot resisted Pound's charity; but he could hardly have failed to have shared some of the sense of injustice and resentment Pound was so eager to feel for him. And, though it was not in character for him to vituperate against the System in the manner of his compatriot (a fact which may explain why he was so ready to accept Pound's deletions of the most angry passages in his manuscript), it was in character for him to let resentment be felt in quieter and more subtle ways. This may help explain the atmosphere of futility in the poem, especially in those passages dealing with the City and the "young man carbuncular", recalling as they do the situation in which Eliot himself had existed as a foreign-accounts clerk.

The daily mulling through endless correspondence from German banks relating to accounts held before the War, the checking and rechecking of voluminous regulations set by the Treaty of Versailles with regard to such accounts – Eliot's situation had been characteristic of the petty-bourgeois type of the day.[58] One can easily imagine how the War, the peace, the Germans, the Jewish bankers, the contrast between pre-War order and post-War disorder could have overcrowded the mind of this type, frustrating its vaguely romantic and aesthetic aspirations, luring it to prejudice and resentment, driving it even to a semiconscious wish for a *Götterdämmerung* (which in Eliot's case actually manifested itself in an hallucination of London Bridge collapsing and the City vanishing).[59] One can further imagine how such a type might have comforted itself in vague daydreams of some "good old days" before the War, which of course could never come again; thus gradually and quietly begin to wish for some saviour/leader to come and wipe out such meaningless existence, charge life with new purpose, and raise sights towards some renascent heroic vision. In Eliot's speaker, in short, we might detect the voice and character of a type ready not only to discover Buddha or Christ, but also to acclaim a fascist leader. His aimlessness and *Angst* are those of the pan-European mass of the petty bourgeois which was lamenting the passing of Romantic grandeurs and in a few years would console itself with new nationalist/spiritualist dedications. And the subsequent enthusiasm of Mrs Eliot for the English fascists,[60] of Pound for Mussolini, and of Eliot himself for the programme of the French quasi-fascist Charles Maurras[61] support the suggestions that fascism is one of the directions towards which *The Waste Land* was pointing.

* * *

PURITANISM *VERSUS* EROTICISM

Beyond his indirect importance to the poem through his influence
on artists and ideas which stand behind it, Wagner has a direct
relevance to its theme and content. This we shall discuss briefly
before taking up Knust's arguments. The one piece on Wagner in
The Criterion is a review of a selection of his letters, praising them as a
"refreshing" chronicle of the "neurosis of genius".[62] The review is
anonymous, the style not unlike Eliot's; and, while there is no
evidence who wrote it, Eliot no doubt gave his editorial approval to
it. In any case, it matched his own opinion of Wagner; and its
characterization of the *Meister* as a neurotic genius provides a neat
explanation for why Eliot should have given the German composer
such a prominent place in a poem which, on one level, was a
pathology of the artist-type of the greater Wagnerian epoch. In
Wagner's "extreme emotionalism" Eliot might have perceived an
origin of the neurosis that had subsequently afflicted Baudelaire and
Symons, and which appears to have been afflicting Eliot himself
while he composed the poem. As I. A. Richards, Edmund Wilson
and other early commentators noted, *The Waste Land* demonstrates
a remarkable fear and fascination with eroticism, and distinctly
implies that neurosis must attend them.[63] Eliot's cure for this
neurosis, both in the poem and in his career generally, was in large
part to recoil towards ascetic puritanism.

Though notorious for his *Tristan*-like eroticism, Wagner himself,
as we have seen Shaw contending, had a powerful impulse to
puritanism. Tristan's tragedy itself has a puritan "moral", as do
Tannhäuser's and Siegfried's and in a less obvious way Lohengrin's,
and as does the *Angst* of Amfortas quite clearly. The finale of the
Ring, in which a sinful world is burned and drowned in order to
make way for those innocent daughters of Nature, the
Rhinemaidens, is distinctly puritan. And the finale of Wagner's
oeuvre, in which a fool is crowned king of an elect order of celibates on
account of his successful resistance to seduction by a voluptuous
woman, is puritan to the point of revulsion to many – Nietzsche and
George Moore as we have seen. Thus in *The Waste Land*, while we
might detect an anti-Wagnerian impulse in the recoiling from
Tristan-like eroticism, we might equally see a deeply Wagnerian
impulse in the fact that the puritan message of his *oeuvre* is
reproduced almost point by point. The love-tryst of the Hyacinth
garden leads, like that of *Tristan*, to disaster. The self-indulgent sex

of the "young man carbuncular" episode and the prospect of a civilization at a terminal stage of corruption lead, like the self-interested sexual politics in Gibich-land and the terminal decay of the gods' civilization in *Götterdämmerung*, to a finale of "burning burning". And the principles of conduct set out at the end of the poem – give, sympathize, control – are, like those set out in the example of the puritan paragon at the end of Wagner's last work, the apparently perfect synthesis of Eastern and Western asceticism.

The fundamental similarity between Wagner and Eliot of *The Waste Land* rests on this pervasive puritan impulse. Both men were obsessed with the idea of salvation from decadence, and both emphasized the decadence of their age by concentrating on (1) the tragic futility of sexual indulgence; (2) the rape of Nature by industrial/materialist civilization; and (3) the falling away of Western man from his traditional spiritual values and duties. While Wagner's works and *The Waste Land* thrive on the tension between this puritanism and the opposite impulse to eroticism, here arises the fundamental difference: whereas in Wagner the puritan impulse could never win more than pyrrhic victories, in *The Waste Land* it triumphs almost conclusively. The explanation for this difference lies in the distance between ages and styles: whereas Wagner, working in the twilight of Romantic grandeurs, made music that was erotically so suggestive as inevitably to drown any puritan message, Eliot, working in the heyday of the Modernist reaction, made a form designed precisely to break up the grand old Romantic flow. If Eliot used Wagnerian techniques in *The Waste Land* as Kenner and Knust and others have argued, he used them as Joyce had used them in *Ulysses*, or in a manner analogous to Strauss in his allusive symphonic poems or Stravinsky in *Le Sacre du printemps*:[64] the young birds were adapting the old bird's tricks – leitmotiv, chromatic progression, never-resolved melody and so forth – to produce dissonances counter to those of the old Romantic's erotic song.

THE LEGENDARY FRAMEWORK

Kenner's contention that Wagner "presides over the introduction into *The Waste Land* of the Grail motif" seems all the more accurate when we consider that Jessie Weston, whose *From Ritual to Romance* Eliot cited as his principal source, was herself a devout Wagnerian.

Prior to her publication of *From Ritual to Romance* in 1920, Weston had published voluminous studies on the Parzival and Grail legends, translated Wagner's sources of Wolfram and Gottfried, and written a lengthy book entitled *Legends of the Wagner Drama: Studies in Mythology and Romance.* Her interest in the subjects discussed in *From Ritual to Romance* had originated in her early Wagner-passion; and, as she pointed out in her preface, the particular studies which led to the book had been set off in 1911 at Bayreuth in discussions with one Professor Schroeder.[65] *From Ritual to Romance* was able to provide Eliot with anthropological details and incidental motifs, such as the Tarot cards, which were absent from Wagner's Grail-work. At the same time, Weston's book could not have provided adequate models for such central "characters" as the decadent *femme fatale* and the stabilizing Tiresias, which Wagner's work could in Kundry and Gurnemanz. The mythic sources of the Grail-legend on which Weston focused could not supply that typically *fin-de-siècle* obsession with erotic indulgence *versus* Christian purity which is central to Eliot's poem, while, of course, Wagner's work provided one of the most remarkable dramatizations of it. These things support Knust's observation that, while *From Ritual to Romance* offered a wealth of academic trappings, *Parsifal* alone could have provided Eliot with the subtle and overarching artistic inspiration.

As for other possible sources of the Grail-legend framework, Tennyson and Arnold and the Pre-Raphaelites with their general fascination for Arthurian legend undoubtedly must have crossed Eliot's mind. But the single inclusion of Tennyson's line "O Swallow swallow" in the cut version of the poem as Eliot let it stand surely does not constitute convincing evidence that the English Victorians were a primary source.[66] There is, furthermore, no evidence to suggest how much Eliot might have been inspired by earlier versions of the legend. Had he read Wagner's sources, *Parzival* and *Tristan*, perhaps in Weston's translations? or Chrétien de Troyes in the original Provençal[67] or Marie de France, to whom Pound had pointed in his *Spirit of Romance* (1910) as the first poetic recorder of these ancient Celtic legends? Though we have no sure answers to these questions, we might assume that a man of Eliot's era and erudition would have read something of the mediaeval epics, and that they might have crossed his mind as he composed. Pound's wide knowledge of the subject may have helped from Eliot's general impressions; and in Pound's first critical book, which Eliot later wrote should be read "entire",[68] Eliot might have noted an unusual detail by which we might link the Tristan-allusions of the first section of his poem to the "Game of Chess" which follows. When spirited away from his homeland by sea-faring merchants, Pound wrote, the young Tristan passed his time aboard ship playing a *game of chess*.[69] (This detail from the mediaeval legend had, we might note, already begun its transformation to the Modernist context in Yeats's *Deirdre*, whose lovers occupy themselves while awaiting their inevitable doom by playing a game of chess.)

But to return to the Parzival/Grail legend, which is undoubtedly more central to Eliot's framework than its sibling the Tristan legend, we should note one further relationship – that is, between Wagner's Grail-work and *The Tempest*, to which Eliot also alludes extensively. As W. J. Lucas points out in his essay on Wagner and Forster, "It's not difficult to regard *Parsifal* as occupying a position very similar to that of *The Tempest*. Since both were taken to be last works each could be interpreted as the last message of the dying master."[70] Eliot may have perceived this general similarity. If so, he may also have noted several particular motifs shared by the two works, and relevant to his poem: (1) the passing of power from an old to a young generation of ruler; (2) ritual ceremonies linked to a process of initiation; (3) magic and a magician whose character is not without ambiguity, and whose role has been identified with that of his creator (Klingsor and Prospero);[71] (4) themes of dispossession, ostracism and revenge linked to issues of racial impurity and sexual brutality (Klingsor and Caliban); (5) the presence of an ineffable and ethereal spirit of Good, the objective correlative for which is a delicate music (the songs of Ariel and Wagner's "enfants chantant dans la coupole"). Considering such parallels, Eliot's allusions to *The Tempest* might be seen to reinforce the pervasive importance of *Parsifal* to the poem in an indirect way, much as the allusions to seventeenth-century drama reinforce that of the *fin-de-siècle* and its Decadents.

WAGNER, THE KING, AND "THE WASTE LAND"

Knust begins his argument on the relationship of Wagner and his patron Ludwig II of Bavaria to *The Waste Land* by expanding on G. L. K. Morris's theory that one of Eliot's major sources was *My Past* (1913),[72] a memoir by Marie Larisch, cousin of the Hapsburgs and also of Ludwig. Morris suggested that Eliot took the following motifs from *My Past*:

> Marie herself; her home on the Starnbergersee, her cousins, the archdukes; her going south in winter; her observation that only in the mountains did she feel free; deaths by fire and water, especially the drowning of the "mad" Bavarian King Ludwig in the Starnbergersee; the neurasthenic Empress Elizabeth's dressing room "with its notable combination of magnificence and ennui" as a model for the neurotic rich lady's boudoir in Part II; and a weird scene round a "tumble-down chapter-house at Heilgenkreuz", suggesting the "Chapel Perilous of Part V".
>
> $(K, 3)$

Knust explicates these motifs, adds to them, and sums up what he regards as the pervasive importance of *My Past* as a source of imagery, allusions, and themes by "merely glancing over the index titles:

> Her wonderful hair . . . daughter of sun and fire . . . Daydreams . . . A religious examination . . . How I met Richard Wagner . . . Vienna . . . Munich . . . A Royal Family . . . I visit King Ludwig . . . We are overtaken by a storm . . . The fisherman's widow . . . A strangely fulfilled prediction . . . Flowers . . . A family failing . . . "Goodbye" . . . Marriage without love . . . The pearl fisher . . . jewels . . . pearls . . . The Empress . . . Paris . . . London . . . Queen Victoria . . . Louise . . . Albert . . . Vienna . . . strange moods . . . contempt for life . . . The shadowy third . . . The beginning of the end . . . The real and the ideal . . . The degenerate Hapsburgs . . . Archduke . . . The Archduke Franz Ferdinand . . . Shades of the dead . . . The Mad King of Bavaria . . . The insanity of royal houses . . . A disappointment in love . . . The King's castles . . . The ghosts of the past . . . A hint to "hurry up" . . . "The Sea-gull and The Mountain Eagle" . . . Elizabeth corresponds with the King . . . The winter garden at Munich . . . Under the shadows of the "Himalayas" . . . I see the "Himalayas" . . . King Ludwig's death . . . King Otto – Another mad monarch . . . "All in a garden fair" . . . An animal existence . . . Locked in . . . Dust . . . Water

everywhere . . . "She burns in torment" . . . She will not
listen . . . The weariness of life . . . I review the situation
. . . Am I a pawn in this game? . . . "Beware" . . . A
social downfall . . . "I shall drown myself" . . . Goodbye-for
ever . . . I fear the future . . . The hair of the furies . . . The
bells . . .   (*K*, 63–4)

Neither Morris nor Knust offers proof that Eliot read *My Past*, but
another critic tells us that Eliot actually met Marie Larisch
sometime between 1913 and 1921.[73] The fact that Eliot never
acknowledged the book as he did such academically respectable
sources as *The Golden Bough* and *From Ritual to Romance* does not
discount it as a source. The subtlest influences often come from those
popular books one reads for pleasure and then for the most part
forgets, Eliot once contended; and *My Past* may well have been such
a book for him.

The landscape of *The Waste Land* is "strikingly adaptable to the
actual myth of the Fisher-King", Knust observes (*K*, 3);
furthermore, it suggests the very part of Bavaria in which King
Ludwig spent most of his short life. This is particularly true of the
first section of the poem, in which we see the colonnades of the
Hofgarten in Munich; the waste plain surrounding the city; the lush
mountains to the south where Ludwig built his personal Grail-
castle, Schloss Neuschwanstein; the "mass of red rocks and debris"
behind the castle, which tumbled down when the foundation for the
huge construction was levelled off; the Starnbergersee nearby,
where Ludwig drowned in 1886 and which became "an international resort where, after World War I, an uprooted and
decadent society assembles from all over Europe" (*K*, 8–9). Knust
speculates that Eliot took the customary tour of these sights when he
first travelled through Germany. That would have been in August
of 1911, at the very time when Jessie Weston was at Bayreuth
conversing with Professor Schroeder on subjects which led to the
writing of *From Ritual to Romance*. Knowing this, we might be
tempted to carry Knust's speculation a step further and ask whether
an impressionable young Eliot might not have travelled on from
Ludwig's Munich to Wagner's Bayreuth, "experienced" Wagner in
the midst of *fin-de-siécle* types and members of the doomed European
aristocracy, and perhaps even overheard conversation on ideas that
in further-developed form he would one day read in *From Ritual to
Romance* and use in *The Waste Land*. Unfortunately, the details of

Eliot's 1911 travels are incomplete. But, leaving aside such tantalizing speculations, Knust is no doubt justified in seeing in Eliot's choice to model his waste land on a landscape where Ludwig II's memory had taken on mythical proportions a probable connection between Ludwig and the poem which has not been considered previously.

Ludwig was well-known for qualities that loom large over the poem: world-weariness, psychological torment over questions of sexual indulgence, madness, death by water, and of course the inordinant Wagner-passion. This last led him to such eccentricities as having a suit of swan-armour made for those moments when he felt in a Lohengrin mood, and a swan-drawn boat for those moments when he wished to take respite on his castle-side lake like the world-weary Amfortas. His favourite Wagnerian hero was Tristan, with whose pain he identified; but, throughout his life, his favourite heroic legend was that of Parzival, and he had the walls of his castles decorated with murals depiciting moments from it. Wagner particularly encouraged this latter passion – as Knust tells us: "Once he discovered his young patron's nostalgic propensity, Wagner contributed essentially to the King's romantic fusion of the Grail legend and his own personal history" (*K*, 16). Ludwig's passion in turn encouraged and coloured Wagner's own fascination with the legend; and, throughout the years leading up to the composition of *Parsifal*, Wagner and the King in their correspondence "took turns in identifying themselves respectively with Parzival the redeemer or Amfortas the sufferer, according to the individual occasion of giving and taking" (*K*, 17). This habit of merging identities of heroes with oneself had obvious benefits for Wagner, whose almost Modernist genius for merging identities was matched by a complementary dramatic genius for unmerging and differentiating. But in the case of King Ludwig, where there was no such artistic need or genius, the habit of over-identification could only lead to a permanent confusion of the self with the redeemer, the redeemed, and a range of heroic personae ultimately as empty as his swan-armour –that is, to a version of the psychosis evident in the speaker of *The Waste Land*, whose identity merges with shadows of various heroes and types of a departed age, but whose self can hardly be distinguished.

Ludwig's intimate relationship with Wagner was chronicled in Wagner's poems of homage to his patron. These move Knust to argue:

If Eliot was impressed by Wagner – as Igor Stravinsky relates –
and if he studied Wagner's works closely – of which *The Waste
Land* gives evidence – then he must also have come across
Wagner's poems to Ludwig, which are included along with his
music drama in his collected works.   (*K*, 18–19).

There is no evidence what Eliot may have read of Wagner's *Prose
Works*, but again it seems likely that a man of his era and erudition
might have read something. Thus it should not seem incredible for
Knust to suggest that Eliot may have borrowed the following motifs
from Wagner's Ludwig poems: (1) images of Spring and Easter
repeatedly intertwined with references to Christ, Parsifal and
Ludwig(*K*, 20); (2) reference to the Sibyl, whose death-wishing
matches that of Amfortas and of Ludwig (*K*, 21); (3) an invocation
(in "Wagner's most important Ludwig poem") of Indra "the
thunderer and rainmaker", i.e. the diety who speaks through the
thunder at the end of Eliot's poem (*K*, 25–32). In connection with
this common Indian motif, Knust argues that Wagner more than
Jessie Weston or Sir Hugh Frazer stands behind the blending of
Eastern and Western elements in *The Waste Land*. "Miss Weston has
been given too much credit for the discovery that the Grail legend
goes back to ancient vegetarian cults in Aryan tradition", Knust
says: Wagner had espoused the idea of "an Indo-German unity of
myths" more than a half-century before the appearance of *From
Ritual to Romance*. Moreover, Wagner was the only one of Eliot's
sources to offer "*poetic* models for the artful intwining of myths,
symbols and ideas" (*K*, 23–4).
    These are Knust's main points. If they sometimes depend on
speculation, they nevertheless add up to a strong case for Wagner as
the pre-eminent influence on *The Waste Land*. To this Knust adds
several minor points which may enhance a Wagnerian reading.
(1) Like Eliot's mysterious drowned sailor Ludwig was known as
"handsome and tall" (*K*, 10). (2) The name Phlebas probably
derives from the Greek *phléps*, *phlebós*, one meaning of which is
phallós, a detail reinforcing the sexual "moral" which might be read
into Phlebas's drowning; also a possible acoustic connection to
phoenix, the bird symbolizing death and regeneration, which, along
with the peacock, was the favourite bird-emblem of both Amfortas
and King Ludwig (*K*, 38). (3) The Smyrna merchant bearing a
pocketful of currants (dried-up fertility symbols) to London recalls
the Syrian merchants "who spread the cults relating to the Grail

legend" to the West; and both relate intriguingly to the fact that in 1877 Wagner, carrying the Grail-document of the just-completed libretto of *Parsifal*, came to London on a business trip and, after completing his business, was fêted at a great banquet at the Cannon Street Hotel (*K*, 51). (4) Eliot's Thamesmaiden songs, with their sudden shift into a simple two-stress rhythm, recall Wagner's Rhinemaiden songs:

Bíst du verlíebt	Elízabeth and Léicester
und lüstern nach Mínne?	Béating oárs
Lass' séh'n, du Schöner,	The stérn was fórmed
Wie dú bist zu scháu'n!	A gílded shéll
Pfúi, du háariger,	Réd and góld
höck'riger Géck!	The brísk swéll
Schwárzes, schwíeliges	Ríppled both shóres
Schwéfelgezwérg!	Sóuthwest wínd
Súch' dir en Fríedel	Cárried down stréam
dem du gefállst!	The péal of bélls (*K*, 58)

The poem at this point may recall Wagner in other respects as well. For instance, the names with which Eliot identifies his Thamesmaidens – Richmond/Moorgate/Margate – interconnect in a manner similar to the names of Wagner's Rhinemaidens – Flosshilde/Woglinde/Wellgunde (*K*, 59).

In his conclusion Knust makes much of Eliot's one published comment about Wagner, the passage in "A Dialogue on Dramatic Poetry" which labels the *Meister* of Bayreuth as "pernicious" but confesses to a cherishing of the Wagner-experience:

> This short but characteristic reference gains its full meaning only after we have realized Eliot's previous concern with Wagnerism, tantamount to a "Wagner nostalgia", as Stravinsky recalled it. Eliot's divided opinion, voiced by the two characters [of "A Dialogue"], is symptomatic of the traditional Wagner malady, for it shows that Eliot, too, after initial attraction to Wagner's art, later rails at him as pernicious and yet at the same moment realizes and admits his influence and significance. (*K*, 65–6).

Knust argues that (1) Eliot, like Nietzsche, was using Wagner as a "touchstone of the European malady"; (2) that malady, with its symptoms of aristocratic decay and epidemic death-wishing as described by Marie Larisch and exemplified in Ludwig II, is the primary subject of *The Waste Land*; and (3) Eliot, again like Nietzsche, saw Wagner's art as both anticipating the malady and contributing to it. Knust reminds us that, in Nietzsche's assessment, Wagner's characters, in spite of all their larger-than-life heroics, become mere Parisian Decadent types when transferred from their mythic realms to everyday life – the Isoldes and Kundrys deflate into Madame Bovary, and Parsifal into a naïve prig with a public-school education (*K*, 67–8). It is but one step further for us to recognize that Eliot's "characters" in *The Waste Land* are the same types in later and more ghostly versions – Tristans, Amfortases, Kundrys and Parsifals further deflated; mixed with elements from the Bovarys and Baudelaires, and their English counterparts the Evelyn Inneses and Symonses; and now so reduced by the progress of decay that they are haunted and mocked by their former identities: those "unreal" heroic identities of Wagner's, in which "madmen" such as King Ludwig drowned their all-too-human selves in moments of aesthetic "surrender" typical of the *fin-de-siècle*.

*   *   *

We have suggested the following: (1) that *The Waste Land* is a poem about the relationship of an alienated modern sensibility to a *fin-de-siècle* precursor who has suffered terminal breakdown; (2) that it is set in the context of post-War ideological confusion, and strains after belief amid elements of heroic vitalism, German Romanticism, Christianity, anti-Semitism, fascism and nihilism; (3) that it portrays a neurotic fixation on eroticism and sex, and counters this with a strong latent impulse to puritanism; (4) that it is framed on the Grail parable of quest and initiation, which has roots in the oldest Indo-European myth and ritual; (5) that it dramatizes the fascination for predominantly heretical mysticism typified by this legend and its associated tradition; (6) that it suggests that these things have had a pernicious influence on the recent fate of the West, both in general in the Nietzschean "initiation" of the War, and in particular in such "quests" as those of the Parsifals-*manqués*, Ludwig II and Symons. Our thesis is that: (1) in each of these respects there is direct linkage between Wagner's Grail-work and Eliot's; (2) as the former was an idealistic and hopeful programme for the future age of the latter, the latter is a hyper-realistic and hopeless assessment of the effect of the past age on the former; (3) in theme, texture, character and form, Wagner's work may be intertwined with Eliot's in such a subtle and extensive way as to provide as coherent a reading as this bafflingly ambiguous poem can provide.

Whatever resistance *The Waste Land* makes to a Parsifalian reading may be more a function of its Modernism than a disqualification of the reading. An allegorical framework, anathema in Symbolist dogma, had to be submerged thoroughly if employed at all – we have already seen in the case of Joyce how difficult the Modernist method of universal suggestiveness makes it to determine whether a system of echoes is intended or accidental. Eliot's poem in any case invites a Parsifalian reading not only for the general reasons stated at the beginning of this chapter, or the specific allusions to Wagner (which, as one feels in the cases of the *Tristan* and *Götterdämmerung* quotations, actually distract from the predominantly Parsifalian development), but most of all because of striking similarities in scene and atmosphere – the first part of "A Game of Chess" portrays a *milieu* like that of *Parsifal*'s Act II, for instance, while the first part of "What the Thunder Said" bears an analogous relationship to *Parsifal*'s Act III. In overall form, the poem superficially follows a five-part pattern like that of the original *Fleurs du mal*.[74] But closer analysis suggests an intrinsically three-part pattern of beginning, middle and end like that of Wagner's last drama. Specifically, "Burial of the Dead" presents the problems and personalities like *Parsifal*'s Act I; the middle three sections present the conflicts and climax like Act II; and "What the Thunder Said" presents the ritual return, mystical initiation, and evocation of principles like Act III. Analysis of theme in each of Eliot's sections further supports this suggestion of a three-part form on the *Parsifal* pattern. The beginning section concentrates on evocation of decay, the middle three sections on issues of sex, and the final section on possibilities for regeneration.

The fact that Eliot's middle three sections do not share the remarkable conflation of Wagner's middle act may raise some difficulties for a Parsifalian reading of *The Waste Land*; but the requirements of an epic poem are different from those of a stage-drama, and in any case Eliot's sections are bound together by the same overarching eroticism-*versus*-puritanism dialectic which motivates *Parsifal*'s middle act. "The Fire Sermon" presents in the swift brutal consummation of the young man carbuncular with the secretary an antithesis to the tedious and pathetic non-consummation of the seeker and the *grande dame* in "A Game of Chess"; the raped Thamesmaidens provide more general and vulgar counterpoint to this antithesis by their contrast to the expectant pub-bawds of the end of "A Game of Chess"; and the seeker's Augustinian experience of the purifying fires of conscience, along with the strange sense of peace in "Death by Water", which follows, suggests a solution for the erotic dilemma posed in the troubled preceding scenes – a solution much in the spirit of the finale of Act II of *Parsifal*, in which the hero escapes temptation once and for all, turns Klingsor's decadent domain into ash, and ascends in peace towards the puritan order of Montsalvat. The reader is not asked to accept that Eliot was consistently or consciously imitating Wagner, only to consider whether the overall ambiguity of *The Waste Land* cannot be elucidated by reading it against the background of *Parsifal*, better than by the traditional piecemeal exegesis. He is asked in any case to suspend disbelief until he has had a chance to consider the poem in conjunction with the libretto of *Parsifal*, which Spender has suggested that Eliot knew and possibly consulted; or, better still, in conjunction with a recording of Wagner's "sacred festival play", though bearing in mind that Eliot could not have had benefit of this, only of an impressionistic recall of some experience in an opera house.

PARSIFAL-*MANQUÉ*

If *The Waste Land* is a poem on a *Parsifal* pattern, then why does Eliot introduce us to Wagner by allusions to *Tristan*? The answer may lie in context: the Tristan sequence offered is a brutally swift descent from the sailor's "song of happy love"[75] which opens Wagner's drama, through the dusky memory of a *Liebesnacht* in a hyacinth garden, to the pessimistic news of the shepherd in the final act – "*Oed' und leer das Meer*" (l. 42). Eliot's Tristan, in short, hardly has a chance to present himself as the hero/lover of Wagner's first two acts before being sped into the pose of the broken and death-lusting figure of the third act, whom Wagner has cry out, "Parsifal!" As in Wagner's conception this Tristan dying of his love-wound metamorphoses directly into Amfortas dying of his sex-wound, so in Eliot's scheme the shadowy Tristan might be seen to metamorphose into the shadowy fisher-king hovering behind the action. Whether

Eliot's fisher-king finds personification in the drowned Phoenician sailor, as Knust indicates, is uncertain; but, in any case, Phlebas shares with the Amfortas version of the fisher-king the status of a noble precursor hastened to untimely doom by some combination of his own indulgence and the machinations of a vague lurking force of evil. Moving from this signal similarity, we might regard the admonition to "Fear death by water" (l. 55) by which Eliot's seeker is warned to avoid Phlebas's fate, as playing a role in Eliot's overall scheme analogous to that which the unspoken admonition to avoid Amfortas's fate plays in the progress of Wagner's hero.

The monotonous voice, listless movement and general air of futility which attach to Eliot's seeker alert us from the outset that, as a version of Parsifal, he is *manqué*. Like Wagner's hero, he begins his progress without comprehension of the admonition received or the purpose of his mission. Like Wagner's hero, his initiations are for the most part concentrated into the sexual encounter. Like Wagner's hero, he recoils from seduction by the *grande dame*. Unlike Wagner's hero, Eliot's seeker recoils with no sudden revelation of the point of the admonition of the purpose of his mission. Wagner's hero indicates his revelation by the cry "Amfortas!" Eliot's seeker by contrast merely makes the cryptic remarks, "I think we are in rats' alley/where the dead men lost their bones" (ll. 115–16); and "I remember/Those are pearls that were his eyes" (ll. 134–5). These statements may suggest some subliminal awareness of a Klingsor-like presence of evil (see discussion of Klingsor and rats below) and some remembrance of the admonition to fear the fate of the pearl-eyed precursor; but they hardly constitute the type of decisive revelation which leads Wagner's hero on to combat evil. In fact, like the catatonic shade of Tristan returning from the Hyacinth garden, Eliot's seeker is remarkably inert ("neither living nor dead") and shares with his Wagnerian counterpart at this point little more than a capacity to exasperate his seductress to rage.

In "The Fire Sermon" this inertia and general despair become so unsatisfactory that Eliot abandons identification with his seeker, externalizes him as the young man carbuncular (who exhibits quite the opposite of Parsifalian resistance to his "seduction" by the secretary), and shifts his own narrative "I" into the neutral and safe persona of Tiresias. Tiresias is described as "the old man . . . who can see" – much the status of Gurnemanz in Wagner's scheme. Like Gurnemanz, Tiresias performs the function of holding the audience at a respectable distance from distatsteful proceedings. Like

Gurnemanz, he adds to these latter-day cathartic events the authority of his ancient experience and wisdom. Like Gurnemanz, he can himself in no meaningful way *act*, for his preordained role is to *see*, or at most to show. Tiresias does, however, join Gurnemanz in demonstrating the only credible sympathy for victimized woman: as Gurnemanz defends Kundry against the racial/sexual suspicions of the Young Squires and later offers her shelter and servitude, so Tiresias "suffers all" with the secretary to whom the young man carbuncular offers his perfunctory affections – this because, in his mythic age, he has assumed female as well as male perspective.

KUNDRY AND KLINGSOR

The victimized woman of *The Waste Land* is as many-faced and ambiguous as Wagner's last female. In the first section we see her first as the vague Isolde of the Hyacinth garden, then as the fortune-teller of dubious yet faintly exotic origins, Mme Sosotris. In both of these forms we might recall Kundry of Wagner's first act: first the solicitous bringer of balsam, then the gypsy clairvoyante of vague Arabian origins. As Kundry is transformed in Wagner's second act into the *femme fatale* whose seductions Parsifal must resist, so Eliot's female is transformed into the "stylish vixen" *à la* Cleopatra. Precisely like Kundry, Eliot's vixen *"est une nérvose"*, suggesting the Baudelairean female of the *fin-de-siècle*, or Judith Gautier with her "épilepsie-catalepsie" – the *décadente* as Nietzsche defined the type: alternately innocent, artifical and brutal.[76] The "Venusberg interior" of her *salon* is described by a sentence which "dissipates itself among glowing and smouldering sensations, like a progression of Wagner's".[77] The luxurious *mise-en-scène* might call to mind that chamber at Wahnfried adorned by the lush materials Judith Gautier had sent from Paris to feed the heightened sensual cravings of "the artist of decadence" as he conceived Kundry's act. That act is set in the enclosure of an enchanted castle cluttered by "magical instruments and necromantic apparatus", and overgrown by plants with violet blooms that give off odours, one imagines, as seductive as those of the "strange synthetic perfumes" of Eliot's *grande dame*. There, to suspiciously luxuriant music, the barbarous sorcerer, Klingsor, calls upon Kundry to awaken and, from the innocent self as which she took balsam to Amfortas, change into the vicious self as which she seduced Amfortas, causing his wound in the first place, and now must seduce and likewise betray the approaching Parsifal.

> The change of Philomel, by the barbarous king
> So rudely forced. . . .
>
> (ll. 99–100)

She tries to sleep on. Klingsor insists; she resists. Finally, forced awake and into his presence, she cries out, her rich mezzo-soprano filled with the pain of violation.

> yet there the nightingale
> Filled all the desert with inviolable voice
> And still she cried . . . .
>
> (ll. 100–2)

Horrified at the magic power overcoming her and evil deed she is commanded to perform, she rushes about in *déshabille* and confusion. Swiftly, however, Klingsor's power takes effect. Her hysteria gives way. She begins to calculate preparations and goes off to preen, perfume, cloak herself in erotic allures.

> Under the firelight, under the brush, her hair
> Spread out in fiery points
> Glowed into words, then would be savagely still.
>
> (ll. 108–10)

When she returns for the task of seducing the boy, she appears brutally assured. Yet, beneath words as artificial as her make-up, she is in a brittle state: "My nerves are bad to-night. Yes, bad. Stay with me" (l. 111). She knows that she will suffer Klingsor's wrath if she fails in seduction. Ironically, only by such failure can she liberate herself; but in her present state she can hardly comprehend such a paradox. Thus she grows increasingly harried. She knows that Klingsor, now invisible, is present somewhere, and the knowledge haunts her in the form of fear – her own fear, her own paranoid psychosis – *where is he?* "What is that noise?" (l. 117). She knows that he might appear in his wrath to wound the boy at any moment – *where lurking?* "What is that noise now? What is the wind doing?" (l. 119).

The boy himself, meanwhile, responds little. He is, after all, the guileless fool who, when asked of his origins, could only reply "Das weiss ich nicht" four times in succession. Thus the seductress makes little headway – *why is he so unresponsive?* – even playing on his mother-love – *what is preoccupying him?* – until, finally, on top of her "bad nerves", his guileless foolishness can only seem a form of wilful insolence.

> What are you thinking of? What thinking? What?
> I never know what you are thinking. Think.
>
> (ll. 113–14)

But her attempts are doomed. And, after her seduction fails, Wagner's *grande décadente* fades into a broken and shadowy penitent, and then out of the drama altogether. So too, with many differences yet remarkable atmospheric and psychological similarities, it transpires for Eliot's female. And, shortly after failing to elicit any more than the ambiguously Parsifalian responses we have noted from Eliot's seeker, she likewise fades – first into a pathetic shade of Ophelia, then into the vulgar obverse of herself in the secretary, finally out of Eliot's "drama" altogether.

While Eliot offers no single character as counterpart to Wagner's Klingsor, he suggests the presence of several elements of the evil force Klingsor embodies: degeneracy, black magic, brutality in power, decadence – elements, in short, which Eliot joined Wagner in regarding as responsible for the general decline of the West. Eliot's notable "objective correlative" for these is the *rat*. This first appears in the seeker's cryptic comment: "I think we are in rats' alley/Where the dead men lost their bones" (ll. 115–6). Later it appears as the rat which "crept softly through the vegetation/ Dragging its slimy belly on the bank" (ll. 187–8). Later still it appears as the rat whose foot rattles the "bones cast in a little low dry garret" (l. 194). This rat, as we have pointed out, claims a precursor in the rat of "Burbank with a Baedecker: Bleistein with a Cigar", which was linked with the Jew whose influence has implicitly been a source of Europe's decay; and we are no doubt justified in associating the rat of *The Waste Land* with this attitude that the Jew is a decadent force in Western culture, both as evil landlord ("little low dry garret") and as usurious financier (the pun on *bank*). This is much the same unsympathetic characterization of the Jew that Wagner apparently sought in Klingsor. Klingsor's last appearance in *Parsifal* was as a cowed creature of the shadows, slinking down from the ruins of his enchanted castle. And Eliot's rat's last appearance in *The Waste Land*, if we are justified in assuming that *bat* represents a metamorphosis of *rat*, suggests an analogous, if more uncertain, final solution of the issue:

> And bats with baby faces in the violet light
> Whistled, and beat their wings
> And crawled head downward down a blackened wall
> And upside down in air were towers . . . . (ll. 379–82)

Such indications are no doubt ample to demonstrate the course a Parsifalian reading of Eliot's poem might take. The reader moved to consider further might find rich rewards in the parallels between the first part of "What the Thunder Said" and Act III of Wagner's "sacred festival play". Eliot's landscape here is remarkably similar to that described in Wagner's stage-directions. The procession to the Grail Chapel with that mysterious brown-clad "third" walking beside can hardly help but bring to mind Gurnemanz and Kundry ascending to Montsalvat with the mysterious monk-robed third who later reveals himself to be *der Erlöser*. And such a passage as "Tolling reminiscent bells, that kept the hours/And voices singing out of empty cisterns and exhausted wells" (ll. 383–5) so suggests Wagner's entrance of the bass-voiced knights to the sound of bells, which is musically "reminiscent" of the similar moment in Act I, that one ends by suspecting that Eliot's general and perhaps semiconscious system of echoes is interspersed with actual unacknowledged allusions.

FINALES: *PARSIFAL* VERSUS *THE WASTE LAND*

The finale of *Parsifal* is dramatically satisfying. Amfortas's pain is cured. Kundry's pain is cured, and she is released into the death she has long sought. Parsifal is elevated to the office of fisher-king, in which he will presumably inaugurate a glorious new age for the Order, on the principle of guileless foolishness "through sympathy made wise", and on his proven ability to take on the pain of another – to Love in the Schopenhauerian sense. The Grail Knights sing again in reverent strong voices. The ritual unveiling of the Grail and a quasi-Catholic Mass are performed. A holy and transcendent effect is achieved as the music and voices ascend towards the Chapel dome and beyond. And, after the last strains are played out and the applause begins and the lights come up in the theatre, those afflicted with the Wagner "malady", high in a realm of ideal reverie, suffer sharp sudden pangs of regret that all has been only a dream of art and illusion. Now they must return to the light and artless cacophony of the outer world, infected with nostalgia for that magical aesthetic effect, which allowed a few hours oblivion of the paltry reality and absence of the heroic in the modern existence in which they must live.

The Waste Land captures the *Angst* of the type who loves art to the point of loathing life. From beginning to end the poem dramatizes the tension between the Wagnerian ideal and the Modern reality. It even suggests a tragical hubris in the attempt to cling to the illusory realm of Romantic heroism in an age and a real world where Romanticism, heroism, and the grand illusions of High Art are no longer tenable. But, while the poem suggests this hubris in its hazardous and confusing ways, it does not, like *Parsifal* (or a contemporary work dealing in similar themes such as *Ulysses*), offer a dramatically satisfying solution or counter-force. Futility alone seems to triumph over *The Waste Land*. Some solution may be offered; but, if so, what exactly is it? What has it altered that we can see within the limits of the poem? What futility has it removed? What pain has it cured? We know that something analogous to Amfortas's pain has been felt –

> My friend, blood shaking my heart
> The awful daring of a moment's surrender
> Which an age of prudence can never retract . . . .
> (ll. 402–4)

But have we seen any relief for that pain? Once, perhaps, a chance for escape from such pain seemed at hand –

> I have heard the key
> Turn in the door once and turn once only . . . .
> (ll. 411–12)

But has the chance been taken? Has there been an escape?

> The boat responded
> Gaily, to the hand expert with sail and oar
> The sea was calm, your heart would have responded

Gaily, when invited, beating obedient
To controlling hands . . . .   (ll. 418–22)

Surely the sick suffering, the Amfortas pain, could have been relieved and escaped had the boat actually come and the saviour "invited". But has this in fact occurred? Do the crucial words "would have" not indicate that the chance has come and gone, leaving the sufferer sitting on the bank, abandoned to his impervious sense of futility and pain?

The Grail-work of the Modern era is more *real* perhaps than that of the Romantic, but much less dramatically satisfying. The Modernist refuses to offer a beautiful illusion with conclusive dramatic unity when a devastating war has recently divided his culture, leaving ugliness and wreckage in its wake, and causing expectations for the future to be ominous and uncertain. Thus, in apt reflection of the new age, the last stanza of the poem leaves us certain only that what has occurred and what it signifies are uncertain. The boat that "would have" provided salvation has vanished. The fisher-king sits idly on the shore, his lands in disorder, his mind glutted more than ever with broken images and extraneous framents of the past: "These fragments I have shored against my ruins" (l. 430). These are the most substantial weapons he has to combat the premonition of impending doom – "London bridge is falling down" (l. 426). And our final impression is that the Decadent fascination for escape via breakdown ("Hieronymo's mad againe"), which has been responsible for the moral immobility and thus the triumph of futility throughout the poem, remains essentially intact. Who is this fisher-king then? Is he just the old king, still pained, mad, and waiting as he will presumably wait forever? Or is this the new king, Eliot's Parsifal-*manqué* – that catatonic, manic-depressive seeker – now enthroned? If so, what improvement on the old king? If so, what hope? So we must wonder after the obscure and perhaps ironic benediction of "Shantih shantih shantih" has been sounded, after the illusion has been broken, after we have been released from the claustrophobic confusion of this remarkable artwork to return to a real world which, by an optimistic contemporary like Joyce, might have been transformed into a far more joyous *inferno* than the one through which Eliot's ghoulish persona has conducted us.

*　　*　　*

CONCLUSION

Wagnerian analysis of *The Waste Land* has illuminated several elements behind the poem which have been too much neglected in the great body of criticism: (1) that Eliot as a young man probably experienced a considerable Wagner-passion which he later sought to repress, along with Romantic "emotionalism" in general; (2) that in *The Waste Land* he was both recalling with nostalgia and seeking to distance himself from the thoughts and fates of *fin-de-siècle* precursors of the Wagnerian/Symbolist/Decadent type; (3) that the poem touches on many of the attitudes of the chaotic post-War era which led to the excesses of fascism, specifically fear of *Götterdämmerung* and the hordes of the East, spiritual despair and nihilism, anti-Semitism, petty bourgeois "*Kultur*-philistinism" and resentment; (4) that the Wagnerian tension between eroticism and puritanism is central to the poem, and Wagner's last work on these themes the pre-eminent artistic model for its Grail-legend framework; and (5) that a reading of the poem against *Parsifal* suggests numerous similarities in form and character, and proves the poem's implicit thesis that self-direction and heroism are hardly possible in the Modern "real" world in the manner which self-deceiving Romantic idealists loved to imagine. We might add that, since Eliot's famous Anglo-Catholic solution to the personal and cultural disorder presented in *The Waste Land* is not conclusively enunciated within the bounds of the poem, it might more suitably be described as a drama of disintegration like *Tristan* or the *Ring*, only a prelude to the truly Parsifalian turning Eliot would make by the time of *Ash Wednesday* and the *Four Quartets*. Though discussion of these later works goes beyond the limits of this study, we might nevertheless observe that, in their celebration of "escape from self" into Christian order, they comprise the area of Eliot's deepest sympathy with that Wagner who turned in his last work towards "the depicting of a soul which is characterized by oblivion of itself and an inner compulsion of eternally hearkening to the source flowing in its most sacred depths".[78]

General Conclusion

We have established that, both directly and via the French, Wagner exercized considerable influence over several outstanding writers in English over the next two generations. The influence appears slight at first, in the cases of Swinburne and Wilde, yet is already acknowledged as significant for the future. It reaches a peak in the overt Wagnerism of Shaw, Symons and Moore. It merges almost wholly with the spirit of the age in the case of Yeats. Finally it begins to decay with the Moderns, those whom we have discussed rejecting their early Wagnerism only to return to Wagnerian techniques and motifs in less overt ways in their major works. The influence was pervasive, extending to plot, theme, style, theory, political and philosophical ideas, artistic conduct – indeed, every conceivable aspect of artistic life. It was not, however, always noted as Wagnerian; and many of the writers we have compared to Wagner might well have been surprised or even chagrined by the fact. In concluding, then, we should return to the title and intention of this study and repeat that what we have sought is less an *influence* than a *relationship*, a relationship often less apparent to the writers in question than to the reader who takes Wagner as a measure of the period, something in the manner that others have taken Freud or Jung.

The outstanding theme that has emerged is the conflict between Romanticism, with its emphases on transcendent love and individual self-determination, and Modernism, with its emphases on the "real" world, destruction of old forms, and forging of new order out of their rubble. Modernist rejection of Romanticism was already implicit in the personal crises of the tragic lovers of Wagner's middle works, and renunciations of self in favour of larger social imperatives in his last-realized "heroes", Sachs and Parsifal. Still, passionate grandeurs of music and myth sufficiently triumphed over intellectual scepticism in all Wagner's works as to obscure this anti-Romantic element. Thus, the writers first to feel the influence of the "magician" of Bayreuth were often moved to linger yet longer in the

Romantic twilight; and the English of the "tragic" generation created in *Tristram of Lyonesse, Salomé, Tristan and Iseult* and *The Shadowy Waters* Romantic lovers who travelled to their doom down paths very like those that Wagner's lovers had trod shortly before them. At the same time, growing recognition of the futility (even fatuity) of such Romantic posturing encouraged Decadents such as Wilde and Beardsley to follow Baudelaire, Huysmans and Laforgue in creating characters such as Dorian Gray and the *ancien régime* Tannhäuser, who proceed with something less than Wagnerian heroism towards ends in varying degrees of debauchery. For such pre-Modern types the Romantic precepts of transcendent love and individual self-determination become at least as corrupting as fulfilling. Counter to them stand characters such as Evelyn Innes, and later Leopold Bloom, in whom the Romantic precepts begin to be renounced in favour of more Life-serving concepts of duty and order. Alongside such Parsifalian partial-Romantics appear characters who strike out against Romanticism directly, Modernist opponents to the Tristan *Angst*, Nietzschean exponents of the Siegfried *Wille* such as Shaw's Tanner, Lawrence's Birkin, and (with qualifications) Joyce's Dedalus. In these, the new Modernist "heroism" of destruction, realism and new order begins to be realized. Still, the shadows of Wagnerian grandeur stretched far. And, just as Beardsley's "Siegfried" had to be a knock-kneed narcissist in contrast to Wagner's manly hero, so these Modern literary Siegfrieds in general proved unable to forge their swords or win their Brünnhildes without revealing themselves to be in ideal terms *manqué*.

The Modernist escape from Wagner was, in short, incomplete in the period we have discussed. So much can equally be seen by the developments in aesthetics. The Modernist break-up of old forms had begun with Wagner, the "liberator" of music, who twisted or simply scuttled classical rules in order to make the whole of his art serve a single-minded dramatic effect. The men of the 1890s, following the example of French Symbolist dramatists, experimented in single-minded "musical" drama and produced such Wagnerian works as *Salomé, Tristan and Iseult, The Shadowy Waters* and *Deirdre*. At the same time, following Wagner the "liberator" rather than Wagner the pre-Symbolist, Shaw began to compose his "drama of ideas", the focus of which was equally single-minded but the form quite opposite to that of the tight poetic dramas of his contemporaries. Shaw's chief sympathy with Wagnerian aesthetics lay in aspiration to "unending melody"; which innovation of Wagner's, held absolutely in check by rigid and economic dramatic form, led in such cases as that of *Back to Methuselah* to the excess of "unending drama". Similar aspiration in the case of Moore led to similar excess of "unending narrative", as in *The Brook Kerith*; and in the case of Joyce to what we might term the "infinite narrative" of *Ulysses* and *Finnegans Wake*. Wagner's example, in short, led concurrently to opposed experiments in extreme dramatic concision and epic endlessness; and perhaps only in *The Waste Land* were the two impulses happily synthesized. A related phenomenon is the subscription to some form of the aesthetic precept, enunciated for literature by Baudelaire and Pater and Mallarmé but exemplified most influentially by Wagner, that "all art aspires to the condition of music". This led all those we have discussed to experiment in making musical patterns of their words, adapting such techniques as leitmotiv and chromatic progression, as well as the notorious "unending melody". Such experiments produced not only the formal successes of *Salomé* and *Ulysses* and *The Waste Land*, but also the excesses of *Evelyn Innes* and *The Trespasser* – also of *Finnegans Wake* and perhaps Pound's *Cantos*, which might constitute the final *reductio ad absurdum* of the aspiration to form literature as music. Thus, as in the case of Gertrude Stein in her contemporary experiments in a kind of Cubist prose, we see the Modernists taking the synaesthetist theories of the 1890s to logical limits which become untenable. In this way, partially in spite of themselves, they may well have indicated the necessity of a return to pre-Wagnerian separation of the arts as much or more than the desirability of adapting music to prose.

In theory and philosophy most of the writers we have discussed exhibited a Schopenhauerian desire to recoil from the world into the citadels of High Art, there (1) to cultivate rarefied, obscure, or otherwise anti-Life-ish ideals; (2) to claim brotherhood in some mythic or actual aesthetic elite; (3) to enunciate critical systems designed to justify individual aesthetic practices, and outline a tradition into which such practices might be fitted. These impulses matched those of the Wagner who, as Baudelaire first noted and Yeats later echoed, spent years defining and arranging his theories before embarking on his most characteristic work. In terms of tradition, Swinburne, following Shelley in the indigenous tradition, and Wilde and Joyce and others to lesser degrees joined the Wagner of *Oper und Drama* and the Nietzsche of *The Birth of Tragedy* in praising and imitating Greek models. Yeats and Joyce and Lawrence and others to varying degrees followed Wagner in reviving Celtic and Germanic legends neglected since the twelfth century. And Wilde and Symons and, most dramatically of those we have discussed, Eliot followed Wagner in identifying with the myth of the archetypal seeker of Christian mystic tradition. Definition of tradition was of less consequence to "heroic vitalists" such as Shaw and Lawrence, whose sights were more characteristically directed towards future new orders than past aesthetic grandeurs. Still, Wagner the "social agitator", revolutionary and prophet was a prime precursor in their unspoken tradition, an acknowledged one at least in the case of Shaw. In this connection we might observe that the Modernist conflict with Romantic ideas led in the period under discussion to no more hopeful new ideas than Shaw's Darwinian Life Force, Yeats's mystical "vision", Joyce's all-purpose Viconian cycles, Lawrence's mystical "semi-fascism", and Eliot's archaic and elitist religiosity. Such programmes for a new Western orthodoxy all harked back to the visions of Wagner's later years in some way. And, like the thought of such activist Wagner-disciples as Chamberlain and D'Annunzio and Charles Maurras, they veered in various ways towards sympathy with the pan-European phenomenon of fascism. Where this sympathy was most obvious, as in the cases of Shaw and Yeats and Lawrence and perhaps Eliot, it fell short of that violent and rabidly anti-Semitic strain which rose in part from Bayreuth to dominate central Europe. Still, in no case of those we have discussed do orthodox principles of Western liberalism seem to have been truly championed – though Wilde's remarks on Goethe and freedom of thought and criticism, and Joyce's celebration of Christian charity in his Jewish Ulysses, demonstrate that hopeful impulses towards tolerance and humanity lingered amid the elitist pronouncements more typical of artists of this type.

"That the Great Man should be able to appear and dwell among you again is the sense of all your efforts here on earth", Nietzsche had counselled future disciples, thoughts of Wagner's Siegfried no doubt in his mind. That the dictator/hero whom Wagner had imagined in works from *Lohengrin* to *Parsifal* should have come to dominate Europe at the end of the Romantic era was the logical political consequence of this principle. That the cult of the artist-as-genius should likewise have reached its apogee at this time is a wholly related and equally Wagnerian development. An eccentric, outsider, social agitator, lover, ascetic and voluptuary – the artist as

Wagner conceived and exemplified him was, no less than his creative personae, a hero. In his unique position as *voyant* and prophet, the artist held special rights and claims to the respect of mankind. And, though mankind in its innately philistine jealousy might end by deriding or even martyring him, the artist must ever maintain his personality as a unique work of art in itself, typical of his genius. This Wagnerian concept, grafted by Gaspérini and others onto their indigenous Baudelairean tradition of the artist-as-existential-hero, produced the cults of the artist of the French Decadence. Thence grafted by the English of the 1890s onto their indigenous tradition of the Romantic poet from Shelley to Swinburne, it produced similar postures of the artist-as-genius. Though Wilde with his claims for the artist-as-Christ was most typical of this impulse, it was no less formative in the cases of Shaw with his aspirations to social prophecy, Symons with his demonstrative Romantic *Angst*, Moore with his intentions to "preach personality" to his race, and Yeats who believed that to be a poet one must first look like a poet. Moderns such as Lawrence with his messianism and Joyce with his latter-day dandyism and encouragement of the adulation of the Beaches and Becketts were equally exemplary of the impulse. Even Eliot, busy announcing his "escape from self", cultivated in his very anti-personal pose the idea that to be an artist was to be in some respects specially ordained.

Personality is freed in *Siegfried*, runs to excess in *Götterdämmerung*, then seeks to escape its freedom and be bound to new principles of conduct in *Parsifal*. So, too, the impulse to artistic personality which had been released in the high afternoon of Romanticism ran to excess in the twilight of the Decadence, sought to escape its freedom in the dark breakdown years of early Modernism, then to be bound to new rules and orders in the dawning of the fascist era. Breakdown is the key word here. For it seems that, after Wagner, the artist-type, as if under too great a pressure to assume the grand persona, ended his efforts more often than not in some form of personal breakdown. Nietzsche and Baudelaire in their prophetic ways assured their inevitable demise from syphilis. The French as a group, defining their "tragedy" as that Tannhäuserian one of suspension between sin and the cross, typically ended careers of the former in breakdown at the foot of the latter. Wilde found this, along with the identification with Christ, an equally apt model for his long-foreseen denouement. Symons, trying to live beyond his mortal limitations as a Wagnerian hero, succumbed like Ludwig II to madness as a result. Lawrence, trying to realize in himself the Siegfried will without complementary Parsifalian renunciation, broke down at exactly the same age as Nietzsche. Yeats and Eliot in characteristic ways at various times in their careers veered close to wafting away on some Tristan-like or Parsifalian dream of transcendence, only holding on by strict adherence to systems of belief, heterodox or orthodox, reminiscent of those Wagner had synthesized in his last work. This phenomenon of breakdown reflects the spirit of an age which saw the great developments of the Romantic century, both in art and society, suddenly smashed and replaced by chaos and frantic scrambling after new beliefs. Even Shaw, as we have indicated, exhibits in certain outbursts after the First World War marks of a subtle type of breakdown. And, of all those we have discussed only Joyce and Moore, and perhaps to a lesser degree Swinburne, might be considered free from this pervasive spectre.

Interestingly, these are the writers who exercised the least restraint over the impulse to "unending melody", and have been accused of prolixity and excess as a result. Shall we attempt to draw any lessons from this? Perhaps we should return to a matter too much neglected in this study and consider the formal divergence towards the epic and the dramatic mentioned a few paragraphs ago. Those who pursued "unending melody" moved in the direction of the epic: the depiction of an ever-changing but never-ending stream of existence in which one day's breakdown may contain the germ of another's triumph, and a civilization's apparent decline is of less importance than the eternal flow of life behind all which will inevitably lead to a new civilization's rise. Those on the other hand who pursued the Wagnerian organic absolutism moved in the direction of the dramatic, in which (1) end is implicit in beginning; (2) development is as direct as Salomé's passion; (3) implications are, on a personal level, death and, on a cultural level, a *Götterdämmerung* possibly preparatory to some phoenix-like rebirth but temporally destructive nevertheless. In writers of the first type we see the desire to celebrate on-going life, to look outward, to accept; of the second to freeze life, look inward, deny. In the first thus we see the tendency to longevity, freedom from breakdown, sanity and welcoming of the future; in the second, the quick-burning of the "hard gem-like flame", impulse to self-immolation, genius of imbalance and longing for spirit-realms of the past. In the end the first type loses through its pursuit of the Life-oriented, unending and psychological "real" something of the intensity, completion, and perhaps even moral suggestiveness of the best art; while the second loses through its pursuit of the formally perfect, finished and pathologically typical something of the balance, veracity and humanity of the best lives.

That we should find the latter drawing so much from Wagner should, considering the twentieth-century myths about the Master of Bayreuth, not be surprising; and the troubled dramatic grandeur which he passed along to them has descended to much subsequent art of our century, particularly popular art – German cinema of the inter-war years, *film noir* in general, science fiction and strains of English contemporary rock-music. That we should find the former drawing likewise from Wagner is perhaps more surprising. For it is in less obvious matters of technique that a Promethean figure like Joyce benefited from Wagner; likewise in matters of technique – leitmotif, "monologue intérieur", unresolved melody – that what has been acclaimed as *avant-garde* in post-Modernist art has most carried on elements of "a Wagnerian tradition".

Notes

Books in French published in Paris, books in English published in London, unless otherwise stated.

NOTES TO THE PREFACE

1. See Kurt Reichett, *Richard Wagner und die englische Literatur* (Leipzig, 1912) for discussion of this subject.
2. Baudelaire admitted his ignorance to Wagner on the occasion of presenting him with a copy of *Richard Wagner et "Tannhäuser" à Paris* (1861). See Enid Starkie, *Baudelaire* (1957) p. 493.

NOTES TO CHAPTER ONE: WAGNER AND THE FRENCH

1. "Lohengrin" was first published in *La Presse* (1850). It is collected in *Lorely: souvenirs d'Allemagne* (*Oeuvres*, 1956).
2. Gautier's article appeared in *Le Moniteur universel*. A second article on Wagner appeared in *Le Journal officiel* in 1869.
3. See Maxime Leroy, *Les Premiers amis français de Wagner* (1925) p. 16.
4. According to Bryan Magee, *Aspects of Wagner* (1968) p. 77.
5. *Baudelaire, Wagner et "Tannhäuser" à Paris*, p. 55.
6. Leroy, *Les Premiers amis*, p. 64.
7. Ibid., p. 59.
8. Mendès's article appeared in *Le National*.
9. Catulle Mendès, *Richard Wagner* (1886) p. 278.
10. See Léon Guichard's introduction to his translation of Wagner's *Lettres à Judith Gautier* (1964).
11. Arthur Symons, *The Symbolist Movement in Literature* (1958 edn) p. 23.
12. Arthur Symons, *Charles Baudelaire: a Study* (1920) p. 54.
13. Grange Woolley, *Richard Wagner et le symbolisme français*, p. 14.
14. Paraphrased from *À rebours* by John Munro in his *Arthur Symons* (1969) p. 55.
15. Friedrich Nietzsche, *The Case of Wagner* (*Complete Works*, Levy edn, 1909–11). Lure of Bayreuth, pp. 41–2; Wagnerian fog, pp. 3, 32; unending melody, p. 61; Flaubert, pp. 28, 67; art as religion, p. 18.
16. Woolley, *Wagner et le symbolisme français*, p. 82.
17. The other two sonnets are "A Louis II de Bavière" and "Sang Réel". The three appeared together in *Amour*. See *Oeuvres complètes*, II, pp. 44–7.
18. Verlaine told Edouard Dujardin and George Moore that the poem was autobiographical. See Joanna Richardson, *Verlaine* (1971) p. 197.
19. See Harold Nicolson, *Paul Verlaine* (1921) p. 186: "He disliked all the classification and labelling. . . . He considered it 'German'. . . . He annoyed the Symbolists by calling them the 'cymbalists'. . . . He distressed many by beginning a poem with the words: 'Schopenhauer m'embête un peu/Malgré son épicurisme'."

20. Woolley, *Wagner et le symbolisme français*, p. 83.
21. Edouard Dujardin, "Richard Wagner et les poètes français contemporaines", *Revue de Genève* (1886). Quoted in Woolley, *Wagner et le symbolisme français*, p. 104.
22. Ibid., p. 93.
23. See ibid., pp. 96–117 for detailed discussion of the relationship between the theories of Mallarmé and of Wagner.
24. See Marcel Raymond, *From Baudelaire to Surrealism* (1957) pp. 23–31.
25. As Edmund Wilson points out in *Axel's Castle* (1931) p. 31 and elsewhere.
26. Symons, *The Symbolist Movement*, p. 88.
27. See Katharine Worth, "*Symbolism in Modern English Drama*" (University of London thesis, 1952) pp. 88–107, for discussion of Maeterlinck and his influence.
28. Woolley, *Wagner et le symbolisme français*, p. 76.
29. According to Kenneth Cornell, *The Symbolist Movement* (1951) p. 38.
30. See Warren Ramsey, *Jules Laforgue and the Ironic Inheritance* (1953) p. 69.
31. Edouard Dujardin, *Les Premières poètes du vers-libre* (1922) p. 63.
32. Jules Laforgue, "Lohengrin, fils de Parsifal", in *Moralités légendaires* (1917) pp. 103–34.
33. See Baudelaire, *Wagner et "Tannhäuser" à Paris*, p. 41; also Mendès, *Wagner*, p. 63.
34. Thomas Mann, *The Magic Mountain* (New York 1927 edn) pp. 332–43. As part of this passage is in French, the problem becomes like Laforgue's over the choice between *tu* and *vous*.
35. For discussion of the development of French interest in German Romanticism, see Woolley, *Wagner et le symbolisme français*, pp. 5–25.
36. The phrase is Chamberlain's. He discusses the importance of Schopenhauer to Wagner at length in *Richard Wagner* (1897) pp. 150–62.
37. See Jules Laforgue, *Mélanges posthumes* (1913) p. 11.
38. For discussion of German Romanticism and Laforgue, see Ramsey's *Laforgue and the Ironic Inheritance*, chapters entitled "The World Is My Idea", "The Great Dream" and "Aesthetic Ideas".
39. Laforgue, *Mélanges posthumes*, pp. 137–8.
40. Thomas Mann, "The Sufferings and Greatness of Richard Wagner" in *Freud, Goethe, Wagner* (New York 1942 edn) p. 176.
41. Laforgue, *Mélanges posthumes*, p. 128.
42. See Ramsey, *Laforgue and the Ironic Inheritance*, pp. 93–4. The image of the vast sea in which one eventually loses one's footing is of course Nietzsche's characterization of Wagner's "unending melody" (*Case of Wagner*, p. 61).
43. See W. B. Yeats, *The Wind among the Reeds* (1903), pp. 65–6. "When the country people see the leaves whirling on the road they bless themselves, because they believe the Sidhe to be passing by."
44. See Cornell, *The Symbolist Movement*, p. 183.
45. See Magee, *Aspects of Wagner*, pp. 78–85.

NOTES TO CHAPTER TWO: SWINBURNE

1. In his introduction to the privately printed edition of *Queen Yseult* (1913).
2. J. O. Fuller, *Swinburne: A Critical Biography* (1968) p. 38.

3. See Harold Rosenthal, *Opera at Covent Garden* (1967) pp. 59–69.
4. See Edmund Gosse's introduction to the privately printed edition of *Les Fleurs du mal and Other Studies* (1913). Baudelaire wrote "Un jour, M. Richard Wagner m'a sauté au cou pour me remercier d'une brochure que j'avais faite sur *Tannhäuser*, et m'a dit: 'Je n'aurais jamais cru qu'un littérateur français put comprendre si facilement tant de choses.' N'etant pas exclusivement patriote, j'ai pris de son compliment tout ce qu'il avait de gracieux. . . . Permettez-moi, à mon tour, de vous dire: 'Je n'aurais jamais cru qu'un littérateur anglais pût si bien pénétrer la beauté française, les intentions françaises, et la prosodie française'."
5. Swinburne later read with interest both Baudelaire's study and Gaspérini's *La Nouvelle Allemagne musicale* – see *The Swinburne Letters* (1959) II, p. 38. His inscribed copy of *Wagner et "Tannhäuser" à Paris* was bequeathed to Arthur Symons, for whom, as we shall see, it was to become a sacred possession.
6. Fuller, *Swinburne: A Critical Biography*, p. 82.
7. Hyder's article, "Swinburne's *Laus Veneris* and the Tannhäuser Legend" appears in *PMLA* (1930) p. 1203.
8. An example of Swinburne's creative habits is the case of "Faustine", which, Fuller relates, was conceived and completed on a train journey from Waterloo to Hampton Court – *Swinburne: A Critical Biography*, p. 120.
9. See *"Fleurs du mal" and Other Studies*, p. xiii.
10. "Laus Veneris" can be found in *Swinburne's Collected Poetical Works* (1924) I, pp. 13–26. Further references to *P* plus volume and page number.
11. Swinburne was attacked for it nearly as severely. The publishers were reluctant to publish, because of the lines "Lo, she was thus when her clear limbs enticed/All lips that now grow sad with kissing Christ." A typical reaction was that it was "the work of either a misdirected and most disagreeable youth or of a very silly man". On the basis of *Poems and Ballads* as a whole, Swinburne's first book, the poet was declared "deliberately and impertinently insincere as an artist". See Fuller, *Swinburne: A Critical Biography*, p. 153; and *Swinburne: the Critical Heritage* (1970) p. 33.
12. The terms are Hyder's. *PMLA* (1930) p. 1212.
13. This depends on one's interpretation of the lines "Stained with blood fallen from the feet of God/The feet and hands whereat our souls were priced."
14. Nietzsche, *Case of Wagner*, pp. 71–3.
15. Richard Ellmann, *James Joyce* (New York, 1959) p. 632.
16. Harold Nicolson in his lecture "Swinburne and Baudelaire" (Oxford, 1930) compares the personality and background of these two poets and notes several common characteristics which we might look for in the artist-type of the age most susceptible to the influence of Wagner. Both Baudelaire and Swinburne were dandies, both early believers in *l'art pour l'art*. Both turned away from careers expected of them by their families, both experimented with excessive indulgence in drugs and drink. Both lived first as art critics. Both maintained aristocratic façades and appeared "irritatingly unreal to their friends". Both were partially impotent, involved in failed love-affairs, and ambiguous in their attitude towards women. Of course, not all early Wagnerian artists were of this type, nor were all young artists of this type conscientious Wagnerians. Still, it is the type of the Wagnerian aesthete parodied in *À rebours*, mythologized in "Lohengrin, fils de Parsifal", derided in *The Case of Wagner*, and satirized in

Mann's early novels. It is generally the type of Englishman who was to adhere
to something like the Wagnerian aesthetic in the last decades of the century.
And, as he was the first to appear, Swinburne might well be seen as a model of
the type.

17. Hueffer's review appeared in *The Academy*. It is reprinted in *Swinburne: The
Critical Heritage*, p. 142.
18. See R. L. Peters, *The Crowns of Apollo: A Study in Victorian Criticism and Aesthetics*
(1965) pp. 103-4. Gosse in "Swinburne and Music", *Spectator* (1917), also
claimed that Swinburne was "remarkably devoid of ear".
19. See Peters, *The Crowns of Apollo*, p. 151; also Thomas Connolly, *Swinburne's
Theory of Poetry* (New York, 1964) p. 73.
20. See Gosse's introduction to the privately printed edition of *Letters to Mallarmé*
(1913) p. 8.
21. Peters, *The Crowns of Apollo*, p. 107.
22. Swinburne, "Notes on the Text of Shelley", *Fortnightly Review*, (1869).
23. *Swinburne: The Critical Heritage*, pp. 144-5.
24. Elliott Zuckerman, *First Hundred Years of "Tristan"* (1964) p. 184.
25. Shelley, *Literary and Philosophical Criticism*, John Shawcross (1909) pp. 121-2.
The image of the Aeolian harp is of course best identified with Coleridge, who,
of early English Romantics, was most steeped in German Romantic philosophy and responsible for introducing German ideas into English aesthetics. As
Swinburne took ideas from Shelley, and Shelley from Coleridge, and
Coleridge in turn from the Germans, Swinburne's aesthetic – like much
English aesthetic theory of the *fin-de-siècle* – had roots in the soil from which
Wagner's theories also grew. Wilde was to note this English debt to the
German *Aufklärung*, as we shall see in the next chapter.
26. For Shelley on the Greeks see ibid., pp. 133-5; see also Peters, *Crowns of Apollo*,
p. 151.
27. "Nocturne" is included in *Letters to Mallarmé*, pp. 17-23.
28. *P*, ii, p. 553.
29. *The Swinburne Letters*, i, p. xxxi.
30. For discussion of the Tristan legend in English see Sturge Moore's article in
The Criterion (1923).
31. *Tristram of Lyonesse* can be found in *P*, ii, pp. 5-151.
32. The phrase is Chamberlain's in *The Wagnerian Drama* (1923) p. 48.
33. Zuckerman, *First Hundred Years of "Tristan"*, p. 183.
34. From the Swinburne chapter in *Modern Studies* (1907), reprinted in *Swinburne:
The Critical Heritage*, pp. 223-4.
35. *P*, ii, pp. 549-52.

NOTES TO CHAPTER THREE: WILDE

1. *The Complete Works of Oscar Wilde* (1966) p. 720. Further references to *W* plus
page number.
2. *The Letters of Oscar Wilde*, ed. Rupert Hart-Davis (1962) p. 821. Further
references to *L* plus page number.
3. Wilde also mentions Morris in "The Garden of Eros". Three stanzas after the
one on Swinburne we find this allusion to the mythic interests Morris shared
with Wagner:

> We know them all, Gudrun the strong men's bride,
> Aslaug and Olafson we know them all,
> How giant Grettir fought and Sigurd died,
> And what enchantment held the king in thrall
> When lonely Brynhild wrestled with the powers
> That war against all passion, ah! . . . (*W*, 721)

4. *The Picture of Dorian Gray*, ed. Isobel Murray (1974) p. 14. Further references to *D* plus page number.

5. "I should like to write a novel certainly," Lord Henry says; "a novel that would be as lovely as a Persian carpet and as unreal" (*D*, 42).

6. For discussion of possible sources for this book, see the Oxford edition; see also Rodney Shewan, *Oscar Wilde: Art and Egotism* (1977) p. 117.

7. Quoted and translated by Symons in *Baudelaire: A Study*, p. 8.

8. In an interview published at the time of the Lord Chamberlain's refusal to permit performance of the play in England. See Stuart Mason, *Oscar Wilde: A Bibliography* (1967) p. 373.

9. For discussion of other sources and inspirations, see Richard Ellmann's essay on *Salomé* in his *Oscar Wilde: A Collection of Critical Essays* (1969).

10. Perhaps *Trois contes* provided a common inspiration. Flaubert's last book appeared during the period of composition of *Parsifal* and shares themes and types with it – St Julien as the saintly mediaeval knight, Hérodias as the *décadente*. Nietzsche, of course, notes this similarity of the Wagner of *Parsifal* to Flaubert (*Case of Wagner*, p. 72).

11. This was a theme suggested throughout Wagner's work but only overt in the last. It ·was typical of subsequent literary Wagnerians – Laforgue in "Lohengrin, fils de Parsifal" as we have seen, and Mann in his early works, to name two. It was always fascinating to Wilde, who treated it in another excursus into musical dramatic prose as well – that is, in *La Sainte courtisane* (1893).

12. Shaw wrote several articles on *Parsifal* and Bayreuth while attending the festival in 1889, and proclaimed loud objections to the interdiction against the production of *Parsifal* elsewhere – "The whole tendency to make Bayreuth an occidental Mecca ought to be resisted tooth and nail in England" – *London Music in 1888–9 as Heard by Corno di Bassetto* (1937) p. 210. But even Shaw could not prevent the interdiction from being respected in London until 1914.

13. W. J. Lucas discusses the attraction of *Parsifal* to artists of the *fin-de-siècle* in "Wagner and Forster: *Parsifal* and *A Room with a View*" in *Romantic Mythologies*, ed. Ian Fletcher (1967) p. 271.

14. See Peter Quennell, *Baudelaire and the Symbolists* (1954) p. 8.

15. Wagner, *Letters to August Roeckel*, trs. Eleanor C. Sellar (1897) p. 154.

16. Ibid., p. 111.

17. See the letter from Rome quoted at the beginning of this chapter; also a letter Wilde wrote from Berneval-sur-Mer just after his release from prison and emigration (*L*, 596).

NOTES TO CHAPTER FOUR: SYMONS

1. See Roger Lhombréaud, *Arthur Symons, a Critical Biography* (1963); also Frederick Love, *Young Nietzsche and the Wagner Experience* (New York, 1966).

2. Arthur Symons, *Collected Works* (1924) III, p. 173. Further references to *W* plus volume and page number.
3. See Richard Ellmann's introduction to *The Symbolist Movement in Literature* (1957); also Frank Kermode's discussion of the central importance of Symons to future critics in *Romantic Image* (1957).
4. See Annette Lavers, "Aubrey Beardsley, Man of Letters", in *Romantic Mythologies*, ed. Fletcher, p. 249.
5. "Prospectus", *The Savoy* (1896), also "Editorial Note" in issue no. 1. Further references to *S* plus issue and page number.
6. *Romantic Mythologies*, p. 252.
7. See the essay "Aubrey Beardsley" in *Studies in Seven Arts* (*W*, IX).
8. The striking similarity between Nietzsche and Wilde in their paradoxical and aphorisitic modes of expression, their amoral philosophies, their propensities to martyrdom, and their dramatizations of pan-European decadence at the end of the nineteenth century was noted by Mann in his address to the American Library of Congress, "Nietzsche in the Light of Contemporary Events" (1947); also by Norbert Loeser in *Nietzsche und Wilde: en andere essays* (Amsterdam, 1960).
9. Ellis and Symons shared rooms at Fountain Court in the early 1890s. Ellis, like Shaw, had belonged in the 1880s to the Fellowship of the New Life, "which the general atmosphere of Nietzschean individualism permeated" – A. G. Randall, "The Poetic Drama of Arthur Symons". (University of London thesis, 1975) p. 51. Though he must have become aware of Nietzsche earlier, Symons "did not really feel Nietzsche's influence until his adoption of Wagnerism later in the Nineties" (ibid., p. 47). From this time until his breakdown in 1908, Symons's interest in Nietzsche seems to have grown increasingly stronger. In 1902 he wrote an article, "Nietzsche and Tragedy", which he later included in *Plays, Acting, and Music*. Then in 1907, a few months before his breakdown, he contributed an article entitled "Nietzsche's Apostasy in Music" to the *Saturday Review*.
10. See Arthur Symons, *A Study of Oscar Wilde* (1930) p. 40.
11. In the first section there is reference to banishment from a garden, parallel to Eliot's hyacinth garden; also such lines as "water my hours' unwatered barrenness", suggesting Eliot's theme of drought and infertility. In the second section there is talk about astrology and horoscopes, parallel to the occult interests of Eliot's Mme Sosotris. In the third section a Decadent female is described in terms not unlike those of Eliot's "A Game of Chess":

> pale smoke of unaccomplished fires;
> Ah! in those shell-curved, purple eyelids bent
> Towards some most dolorous accomplishment.
>
> (*S*, VIII, 15)

In the fourth section the speaker complains of strange voices and visions haunting his memory in terms suggesting the general narrative atmosphere of *The Waste Land*:

> my own soul haunts me, night and day,
> With voices that I cannot drive away,

And visions that I can scarce see and live.

(*S*, VIII, 16)

Such similarities to Eliot's poem (as well as reminiscences of Baudelaire, Swinburne, Browning and others) continue to appear throughout "Mundi Victima".

12. Randall, "The Poetic Drama of Symons", p. 166.
13. Arthur Symons, "Ballet, Pantomime, and Poetic Drama", *The Dome* (1898) p. 69. Parts of this article were included in revised form in *Studies in Seven Arts*.
14. *The Dome* (1898) p. 71.
15. On discovering the Sufi Hafiz in 1852, Wagner declared him immediately to be "the greatest poet that ever lived"; and he incorporated Sufi imagery and philosophy in his dramas from then on, especially in *Tristan* and *Parsifal*. See "Hafiz", *The Meister, the Journal of the London Wagner Society* (1896); also Chamberlain, *Richard Wagner*, p. 152. Yeats's well-known desire to "write poetry like that of the Sufis" is stated in *Autobiographies* (1955); also discussed by John Munro, in *Arthur Symons* (1969) p. 60.
16. See *Mes souvenirs* (1931) for Symons's recollections of this mysterious woman; also Randall, "The Poetic Drama of Symons", p. 152, on her "Hérodiade-like" disposition.
17. *The Dome* (1898) p. 71.
18. Symons points out the importance of Wagner to almost every French writer discussed. In revised studies, such as the one on Villiers, much of what originally appeared in an article for Wilde's *Women's World* in 1888 is jettisoned and discussion of the "sympathy" with Wagner is now included – "There was but one man among his contemporaries to whom he could give, and from whom he could receive, perfect sympathy. That man was Wagner" (*Symbolist Movement*, p. 32). In new studies, such as the ones on Mallarmé and Maeterlinck, emphasis is given to the influence on Symbolist theory of theatre of the practice of Bayreuth, by which Symons had lately been so moved. Of Mallarmé Symons writes, "Carry out the theories of Mallarmé to a practical conclusion, multiply his powers in a direct ratio, and you have Wagner" (ibid., p. 62). We have already quoted Symons's statement on Maeterlinck and Wagner in Chapter 1.
19. Randall's chapter "Towards a Religious Drama", in "The Poetic Drama of Symons" gives a detailed discussion of Symons's dramatic theory.
20. See *The Dome* (1898) pp. 68–9:
21. Symons paraphrases Mallarmé to this effect in *The Symbolist Movement* (p. 73): "We are now precisely at that moment of seeking, before that breaking up of the large rhythms of literature, and their scattering in articulate, almost instrumental, nervous waves, an art which shall complete the transposition, into the Book, of the symphony, or simply recapture our own; for, it is not in elementary sonorities of brass, strings, wood, unquestionably, but in the intellectual word at its utmost, that, fully and evidently, we should find, drawing to itself all the correspondences of the universe, the supreme Music."
22. See Gabriele D'Annunzio, *The Child of Pleasure* (1898 edn) p. xi.
23. The latter chapter ends with a statement which must represent some zenith of Wagner-rhetoric among men of letters: "Only in Wagner does God speak in his own language."

24. Symons was probably already familiar with Miss Weston's work through her translation of Wolfram von Eschenbach's *Parzival* (1894) and her own act of Bayreuth-devotion, *The Legends of the Wagner Drama* (1896). Of Symons's general preparation, Lhombréaud tells us that he "amassed an important collection of Tristan books" (*A Critical Biography*, p. 209). The particular appeal of the Tristan legend may also have been stimulated by a desire to attach himself to the Celtic movement: under the influence of Yeats, Lhombréaud tells us, Symons had recently "rediscovered" his own Celtic origins in Cornwall.

25. Symons eventually deleted the main scene of Iseult of Brittany and made it over into a one-act play, *Iseult of Brittany*.

26. As Wieland Wagner diagrammatically showed it to be (see the notes to the Pierre Boulez recording of *Parsifal*).

27. Nietzsche, *Case of Wagner*, p. 12.

28. Randall sees a pervasive influence of D'Annunzio, especially his *Francesca da Rimini*, which Symons had translated in 1902 – "The operatic quality of *Francesca*, with its long ardent speeches and reiterated images of violence or sensuality, reappeared in *Tristan and Iseult*, in spite of Symons' doubts about the Wagnerian style in ordinary drama" ("The Poetic Drama of Symons", p. 256). The influence of Maeterlinck, specifically *Pélleas*, is apparent in the use of the Yinold-like child at the end of Act II and in the imagery and atmosphere of suspicion at the beginning of Act III. After Wagner, D'Annunzio and Maeterlinck, the greatest influence on the play, particularly in its last act, may be (as Randall suggests) Eleanora Duse, of whom Symons wrote an admiration included in *Studies in Seven Arts* and for whom he designed the role of Iseult.

29. Even if it had been a more original work, Symons's Symbolist drama and subsequent attempts at the genre – the evocation of the anti-Christ in *Nero*, the development of an idea out of Swinburne in *Caesare Borgia*, and the rest – were probably doomed on the English stage of the day. As Symons himself was to reflect in his *Study of Oscar Wilde*, it was a day in which verse drama was virtually a dead art. Shaw's plays, combining Wildean comedy of manners with "Ibsenism", could succeed; and, as we shall see, a superficial sort of Wagnerism could be found in them, as in works by Shavian disciples such as Granville-Barker (Katherine Worth has pointed out the resonances of *Tristan* in *The Secret Life*, for instance, in which Joan and Strowde go out on the moonlit steps and describe their love in Wagnerian terms). But of works with Symbolist design and Wagnerian musical texture, only *Salomé* - a play Symons thought "insincere" – would enjoy a sort of success; though Sturge Moore's Literary Theatre Club, which produced it first in England in defiance of the censor's ban, folded when it attempted similar types of dramas by others (See Randall, "The Poetic Drama of Symons", pp. 393–4, for description of Moore's club, the literary notables who attended it, and its demise). *Salomé* in any case was a curiosity, written in French not English, and never really successful on stage until transformed into a music drama by Richard Strauss. In Paris, where it had been premiered in 1896, symbolical drama could have some *succès d'estime*, Maeterlinck's plays to wit; or in Dublin, though perhaps more through the force of Yeats's personality than the intrinsic appeal of the genre. In either of those cities Symons might have had better luck with his experiments. And in this respect the characterization of the English as

philistine, in which he had concurred with Beardsley in *Savoy* days and was to
voice now and again through his later years, might be seen as a legitimate
aesthetic grievance. In any case, it is clear that Symons the dramatist was out
of time and place in Edwardian London as it approached the Modernist age.

30. Lhombréaud quotes an unpublished poem which was written around 1940
and confirms that *Tristan and Iseult* was yet another dramatization of Symons'
great lost love (*A Critical Biography*, p. 117):

> Tristan and Iseult were given a love-potion
> That made them mad and set their hearts in motion,
> And on that instant the whole world sunk. . . .
> They are immortal lovers, they attained Infinity,
> Lydia and I, fashioned by God, attained Immortality.

As Lydia might be considered the model for Iseult of Ireland, so Symons's wife,
Rhoda, may have inspired Iseult of Brittany. Some synthesis of the two might
be seen in "Song for Iseult" (1918), though it is probably primarily the fiery
Lydia still once again:

> The heart cries for light
> And the soul for Desire,
> In the midst of the Night
> In the heart of the Fire.
> They cry for all things
> That are and that were.
> Desire along brings
> All the night in her hair
> To me as I sit
> And gaze on the fire.
> Finite and infinite
> Are the Gods of the Fire!

(W, III, 229)

31. Gladys Turquet-Milnes, *The Influence of Baudelaire in France and England* (1913)
p. 249.

32. In the Wagner essay (*W*, IX, 150); also to be found in the Blake study, the
Baudelaire study, *Studies in Strange Souls* (1929), and the article "Algernon
Charles Swinburne" in the *Fortnightly Review* (1917).

33. See Munro's discussion in *Arthur Symons*, pp. 109–11.

34. Arthur Symons, *Confessions, a Study in Pathology* (1930) pp. 7–8.

35. Symons himself refers to *De Profundis* – ibid., p. 36.

36. On Swinburne's and Rossetti's women, see Symons, *Studies in Strange
Souls*.

37. Enid Starkie concludes that Baudelaire probably did not get farther than
Mauritius. See *Baudelaire*, pp. 70–5.

38. *Baudelaire, a Study*, pp. 8–9.

39. Conrad and Symons were friends at this period. Symons wrote a study on
Conrad; and, according to Conrad's wife, Symons's was probably the only
poetry that the novelist ever read. See Munro, *Arthur Symons*, p. 126.

NOTES TO CHAPTER FIVE: SHAW

1. *Letters to Florence Farr from G. B. Shaw and W. B. Yeats* (Dublin, 1946) p. 4.
2. Ibid., p. 27.
3. Ibid., p. 16.
4. But E. B. Adams argues convincingly that in many respects Shaw *was* a typical aesthete of the 1890s. See *Bernard Shaw and the Aesthetes* (Columbus, Ohio, 1971).
5. See Hesketh Pearson, *Bernard Shaw* (1975), the early chapters. Recent research by Michael Holroyd indicates that Lee may have been Shaw's *real* father.
6. Pearson, *Bernard Shaw*, p. 108.
7. Shaw, *London Music in 1888–9 as Heard by Corno di Bassetto* (1937) p. 48.
8. Ibid., pp. 398–9.
9. See Chamberlain, *Richard Wagner*, pp. 137–8.
10. G. B. Shaw, "The Religion of the Pianoforte", *Fortnightly Review* (1894); paraphrased and discussed by Julian Kaye in *Bernard Shaw and the Nineteenth Century Tradition* (Norman, Okla, 1955) p. 169.
11. The novel was first published in Chicago in 1909. For a cameo description of Jack's music and the reaction to it as it relates to Wagner, see p. 170.
12. Pearson, *Bernard Shaw*, p. 22.
13. In an article on Shaw in *The Listener* in 1949, H. S. Brailsford discusses the origin of the Life Force idea in Darwin and Darwinians: Lamarck, Samuel Butler, Bergson. He then comments "But my guess is that the starting-point of this train of thought lay in Shelley." See *Shaw: The Critical Heritage*, ed. T. F. Evans (1976) pp. 379–80.
14. G. B. Shaw, *The Perfect Wagnerite* (New York, 1967 edn) p. 64. Further references to *PW* plus page number.
15. Mosley's article appeared in *The European: The Journal of Opposition*, (1956).
16. Chamberlain calls *Parsifal* an "immediate continuation" of the *Ring*. See *The Wagnerian Drama*, p. 203.
17. Shaw, *Corno di Bassetto*, p. 186.
18. Quoted and discussed by Joseph Campbell in *Creative Mythologies* (1974) p. 72.
19. See G. B. Shaw, *Collected Plays* (1931) p. 64. Further references to *P* plus number.
20. From "An End in Paris" in *A German Musician in Paris*, vol. VII of Wagner's *Prose Works* (1897) pp. 66–7.
21. See *Shaw and the Aesthetes*, pp. 127–8. A possible further importance of Wagner to *The Doctor's Dilemma* is noted by Kaye in *Shaw and the Nineteenth Century Tradition*, p. 170: in his parodistic portraits of the doctors, Kaye suggests, Shaw uses "many of Wagner's arguments against vivisection".
22. In personal correspondence.
23. See *Back to Methuselah* (1931): Temple scene, pp. 187–95; the Ancients, pp. 228–36; Lilith, pp. 253–4.
24. See "Bernard Shaw at Eighty", *Atlantic Monthly* (1938); reprinted in *Shaw: The Critical Heritage*, pp. 351–6.
25. As Shaw's men often take the position of the ponderous Wotan, so his women often take that of the rebellious-yet-essentially-loyal Brünnhilde listening at the feet of her father/god. Consider Cleopatra and Caesar, Eliza and Higgins, and to a lesser degree Ann and Tanner.

26. See Ivor Brown's "The Spirit of the Age in Drama", *Fortnightly Review* (1930); also in *Shaw: The Critical Heritage*, pp. 313–16.
27. See H. V. Nevinson, "Shakespeare's Rival", *Spectator* (1932); also in *Shaw: The Critical Heritage*, pp. 329–31.
28. Pearson, *Bernard Shaw*, p. 233.
29. From *Oper und Drama*, as quoted by Chamberlain in *Richard Wagner*, p. 143.
30. Sidney Oliver, who joined Shaw in the attempt to have the Fabian Society publish these works, contended in an early Fabian article that "Socialism appears as the offspring of Individualism". See *Fabian Essays* (1932) p. 138.
31. See Chamberlain, *Richard Wagner*, pp. 169–71.
32. Ibid. Chamberlain devotes a section of his chapter on Wagner's thought to this doctrine.
33. See Shaw's essay "Transition" in *Fabian Essays*.
34. Pearson, *Bernard Shaw*, p. 232.
35. Chamberlain, *Richard Wagner*, p. 126.
36. In an interview for the *Daily Express* in 1938, Shaw said that Hitler was "terribly handicapped by his anti-Semitism, which is a crazy fad and not a political system". Shaw's opinion of the Jews was, however, not always favourable. In a letter to Archer in the 1890s he criticized Pinero, citing that playwright's race, and using arguments that may have partaken of Wagner's in "Judaism in Music". See *Bernard Shaw: Collected Letters 1894–97*, ed. Dan H. Laurence (1965) p. 501.
37. Pearson, *Bernard Shaw*, p. 461.
38. See *The Fabian News* (June 1911). The review begins "This very notable book should be read by all good Fabians."
39. Having said so much, we must of course add that, unlike Symons, Shaw experienced no certifiable breakdown. He retained his attachment to the events of the "real" world, a hyper-rationalist version of its sanity, and an intellectual balance continually demonstrated by flashes of insight. From the first he prophesied that, however successful in the short run, the dictators would cancel their accomplishments through Lord Acton's principle and their own all-too-human errors of judgement – particularly regarding the Jews. He described dictatorship as an "emergency bullyism" which would end by exhausting the dictator and giving way to "a new constitutionalism". (See the preface to the 1931 reprint of *Fabian Essays*.)
40. Shaw, *Corno di Bassetto*, p. 40.
41. See Kaye, *Shaw and the Nineteenth Century Tradition*, p. 173.
42. Shaw's only major critical works other than *The Perfect Wagnerite* were *The Quintessence of Ibsenism* and the prefaces to the plays.
43. Arland Ussher makes this point in the Shaw chapter of *Three Great Irishmen* (1952).
44. The term "heroic vitalist" is Eric Bentley's. We shall discuss heroic vitalism at greater length in the Lawrence chapter.

NOTES TO CHAPTER SIX: MOORE

1. George Moore, *Flowers of Passion* (1878) p. 68.
2. See among others "Sonnet: Night Perfume" (Ibid., p. 71).
3. William Blisset, "George Moore and Literary Wagnerism", in *The Man of*

Wax: Critical Essays on George Moore, ed. Douglas Hughes (New York, 1971).

4. *Confessions of a Young Man* (1904 edn) p. 85. Moore was obviously fascinated by this Eastern sensuality. He was to mention it, with slight changes, in major references to *Parsifal* in the future – as in *Evelyn Innes*, where Sir Owen Asher rhapsodizes about Wagner's "marvellous evocation of Arabia" in the Magic Garden scene; or in the article "After *Parsifal*" in *The Speaker* (1895) which begins "Wagner reminds me of a Turk lying amid houris.".

5. Blisset, in *Man of Wax*, p. 196.

6. Joseph Hone, *The Life of George Moore* (1936) p. 142.

7. See Moore's articles "The New Gallery", "Claude Monet" and "Exteriority" in *The Speaker* (1895).

8. George Moore, "After *Parsifal*", *The Speaker* (1895) p. 588.

9. George Moore, "Wagner's 'Jesus of Nazareth'", *The Musician* (1897) p. 8.

10. Chamberlain, for instance, whose book *The Wagnerian Drama* (1923) is subtitled "an attempt to inspire a better appreciation of Wagner as a dramatic poet", and puts forth the argument that Wagner was first, foremost, and always a dramatist, and only wrote music the better to serve his dramatic intentions. Chamberlain also makes a comparison between Shakespeare and Wagner, calling them "the two great Germanic dramatists" (*The Wagnerian Drama*, p. 139).

11. Ernest Newman, "The Psychology of the Musician in Fiction", *The Musician* (1897) p. 150.

12. "Mr George Moore on Music and Literature", *The Musician* (1897) pp. 392–4.

13. *Letters from George Moore to Edouard Dujardin*, ed. John Eglinton (1929) p. 40. Moore describes his lifelong friend in the first volume of *Hail and Farewell* (1911); also in *Conversations in Ebury Street* (1924). While Moore was writing *Evelyn Innes*, the two were corresponding about a scenario for a one-act opera. See Hone, *Life of Moore*, p. 211.

14. There is some debate on this point. As we have seen in his article for *The Savoy*, Havelock Ellis regarded Zola as the first.

15. But Hone calls *Evelyn Innes* "as convincing as few musical novels written by non-musicians ever have been". He credits it with an "almost complete absence of slips", owing to Moore's habit of "picking the brains of others" – notably Dolmetsch (*Life of Moore*, p. 131).

16. Blisset, in *Man of Wax*, p. 186. Blisset points out that we are later given a description of the "gnawing creeping sensuality" of *Tristan* being played on a harpsichord!

17. George Moore, *Evelyn Innes* (1898) p. 10. Further references to *E* plus page.

18. Blisset, in *Man of Wax*, p. 190.

19. While encompassing Evelyn's psychological anguish with *Tristan*-like melodrama, this passage also suggests a number of motifs external to the novel yet associated with Wagner's work: (1) Tristan's anxious waiting for Isolde's ship in Act III of the music drama, and Isolde's reminiscence of the *Liebesnacht* duet in her *Liebestod*; (2) Wagner's own melancholy days in Venice while finishing that final act of his drama, and perhaps even his death in Venice years later and the lugubrious tone-poem about the funeral gondola which Liszt wrote on that occasion; (3) D'Annunzio's *Trionfo della Morte*; (4) most intriguingly, the madness which Arthur Symons was to experience a decade

later in that city and describe in similar terms. That Symons might have been influenced by this passage is possible. Moore read *Evelyn Innes* aloud to Symons and Yeats as he wrote it; he dedicated the book to both of them ("Two contemporary writers with whom I am in sympathy"); and he would have serialized it in *The Savoy* had that magazine not come to its untimely end. See *The Savoy*, III, "Editorial Note".

20. Hone credits Yeats as the model (*Life of Moore*; p. 234), as does Randall in his Symons thesis ("The Poetic Drama of Symons"). Hone adds that AE might have inspired certain revisions in the character for the 1901 edition.

21. Moore, *Hail and Farewell*, ed. Richard Cave (1976) pp. 346–7. Moore's knowledge of Nietzsche was probably greater than his comments lead one to believe. Hone says this on the subject: "Moore, as John Eglinton recalls for me, caught a good deal from the German 'impressionist' philosopher of whom he had heard much earlier [than 1904] from Dujardin. I myself remember his admiration for his friend, Daniel Halévy's, *Vie de Nietzsche*. . . . Two of his most successful paraphrases resulted from his acquaintance, the one at the close of 'Resurgam' (*Memories of My Dead Life*) from Nietzsche's poem of the Eternal Return, the other in *Evelyn Innes*, where Ulick Dean bids farewell to the opera singer . . . from Nietzsche's page on 'Stellar Friendship' " (*Life of Moore*, pp. 257–8). Nietzsche's famous lines of farewell were, of course, inspired by the break with Wagner.

22. Moore, *Hail and Farewell*, p. 175.

23. Ibid., p. 159. For discussion of this identification, see Blisset, in *Man of Wax*, p. 204.

24. Throughout *Hail and Farewell* Moore evidences the view that sex is an integral part of the whole of life to be embraced openly, without the intriguings of a Kundry or the recoilings of a Parsifal. See his blithe discussion of Dujardin's affairs (pp. 88–9); his teasing of the puritanical Martyn (pp. 158–61); his admiration for the girls on the strand (p. 335); his speculations on the great loves of Wagner's and Yeats's lives (pp. 542–5); and so forth. In the epoch of Wilde's perversity, Shaw's puritanism, Symons's *Angst*, and Yeats's diffidence, Moore's open and easy attitude towards sex seems almost incongruous. With its occasional propensity for the vulgar, the attitude has more in common with that of the author of *Ulysses*.

25. George Moore, *Sister Teresa* (1901) pp. 193–4.

26. Moore, *Letters to Dujardin*, p. 38.

27. In a letter to Lord Howard de Walden which Hone quotes (*Life of Moore*, pp. 258–9), Moore wrote "[In] Mathilde's letters to the poor afflicted soul, afflicted in the first instance by nerves, and in the second by the world's adversity, a sudden light was thrown on the intimacy and mystery of woman's love of man, a thing in itself and quite different from man's love of woman – not always but in Mathilde's case yes. She was one of the great – a word is wanting – lovers of the world, different from Heloise, St Teresa and the Portuguese nun. I hope to finish *The Lake* by the first of August."

28. See George Moore, "The Nineness in the Oneness", *Century Magazine* (1919) p. 66; quoted by Blisset, in *Man of Wax*, p. 214.

29. See Baudelaire, *Wagner et "Tannhäuser" à Paris*, pp. 10–16.

30. George Moore, *Confessions of a Young Man* (1888 edn) p. 269; quoted by Blisset, in *Man of Wax*, p. 195.

31. See Cave's *A Study of the Novels of George Moore* (1978).

32. Hone, *Life of Moore*, p. 261.
33. A favourable view of Moore's later style is offered by Desmond Shaw-Taylor in "The Achievement of George Moore", which Hone includes as chapter 12 of his biography. "He now began to develop the conception of what he called 'the melodic line'," Shaw-Taylor says; "narrative not only shaped from the beginning towards an inevitable end but allowing on the way none of the personal intervention of the author that has always been the bane of English fiction, nor the abrupt transitions from description to dialogue or thought-stream whose avoidance is a continual problem of the novelist's art" (ibid., p. 469). But Moore's experimental style of later years was increasingly neglected by younger writers in favour of that of Stein, Joyce, Proust or Lawrence (ibid., p. 469).
34. Quoted ibid., p. 333.
35. Ibid.
36. Ibid., pp. 325–7.
37. Ibid., p. 332. Moore's affinity with Schopenhauer dates from the early period in Paris, and Hone makes this comment about the Moore of *Confessions of a Young Man*: "[He] certainly shared and continued to share the Frankfurt philosopher's aversion from Judaism and belief in the superior wisdom of India. Years later the Jesus at the end of *The Brook Kerith* was to be conceived as a sort of Buddhist sage to whom all desire, even desire of God, is evil" (*Life of Moore*, p. 142).
38. Ibid., p. 328.
39. Moore, *Hail and Farewell*, p. 24.
40. Ibid., p. 34.
41. See Wilson's *Axel's Castle* (1931) p. 156, for discussion of how Joyce successfully wed the two traditions.
42. James Joyce, *A Portrait of the Artist as a Young Man* (New York 1964 edn) p. 237.
43. Ibid., pp. 252–3.
44. Moore, *Hail and Farewell*, p. 609.
45. Ibid., p. 335.
46. See Shaw-Taylor's discussion (Hone, *Life of Moore*, p. 470).
47. This point is made by Blisset, in *Man of Wax*, p. 203; also by Magee in *Aspects of Wagner*, p. 82.

NOTES TO CHAPTER SEVEN: YEATS

1. See Alfred Loewenberg, *Annals of Opera* (Geneva, 1955).
2. See the *Dublin Review* (1898, 1900). This journal also offers an interesting contemporary view of Theosophy in the hostile article "Theosophy and its Evidence" (1892).
3. On the "musical" quality of Yeats's work, see *Yeats: The Critical Heritage*, ed. Norman Jeffares (1977) pp. 191–2, 201, 223, and elsewhere.
4. See Moore, *Hail and Farewell*, p. 87; also Gerard Fay, *The Abbey Theatre* (1958) p. 70.
5. In personal correspondence.
6. For discussion of Yeats's association with this and other mystical organizations, see G. M. Harper, *Yeats' Golden Dawn* (1974).
7. W. B. Yeats, *Ideas of Good and Evil* (1903 edn) pp. 120–1. Further references to *I* plus page number.

8. See Ussher, *Three Great Irishmen*, p. 107.

9. See Joseph Campbell, *The Masks of God : Creative Mythologies* (1974) pp. 40–2 on the role of art *versus* authority in the love epic; pp. 145–61 on Gnosticism; pp. 262–6 on alchemy and the "left-hand way". See also *Yeats' Golden Dawn*, p. 120, where, in discussing the relationship of Yeats to William Morris, Harper says that Yeats regarded himself in a "brotherhood" with others who had been "striving to achieve the reconciliation of Paganism and Christianity".

10. See Campbell, *Masks of God*, esp. pp. 128–33.

11. See Ronald Gray, *The German Tradition in Literature: 1871–1945* (Cambridge, 1965) p. 248. Gray takes his terms from R. C. Zaehner, *Mysticism Sacred and Profane* (Oxford, 1957).

12. See Vernon Venable's *"Death in Venice"* in *The Stature of Thomas Mann* (New York, 1947) p. 130. Venable quotes Mann to this effect: "The really fruitful, the productive, and hence the artistic principle is that which we call reserve. In the sphere of music we love it as the prolonged note, the teasing melancholy of the not-yet, the inward hesitation of the soul, which bears within itself fulfillment, resolution, and harmony, but denies it for a space, withholds and delays, scruples exquisitely yet a little longer to make the final surrender. In the intellectual sphere we love it as irony: that irony which glances at both sides, which plays slyly and irresponsibly, – and yet not without benevolence – among opposites, and is in no great haste to take sides and come to decisions; guided as it is by the surmise that in great matters, in matters of humanity, every decision may prove premature, that the great goal to reach is not decision, but may lie at infinity; yet that playful reserve called irony carries it within itself as the sustained note carries the resolution."

13. Gray, *The German Tradition*, p. 337.

14. *The Letters of W. B. Yeats*, ed. Allan Wade (1954) p. 371.

15. Katharine Worth, *The Irish Drama of Europe from Yeats to Beckett* (1978) p. 3.

16. See Yeats's introduction to *Certain Noble Plays of Japan, Chosen and Finished by Ezra Pound from the Manuscripts of Ernest Fenollosa* (Dublin, 1916) vol. III.

17. For Moore's description of Yeats's speech, see Moore, *Hail and Farewell*, pp. 550–4.

18. Friedrich Nietzsche *Human, All-too-Human* (Levy edn), I, p. 157.

19. Moore tells of a journey on which AE took him to find out this legendary cave and its secrets (*Hail and Farewell*, pp. 289–300).

20. W. B. Yeats, "Symbol as Revelation" in *The Modern Tradition: Backgrounds in Modern Literature*, ed. Richard Ellmann and Charles Fiedelson (1965) p. 65.

21. Mann, *Freud, Goethe, Wagner*, p. 107.

22. Ussher, *Three Great Irishmen*, p. 93.

23. See Campbell, *Masks of God*, p. 127.

24. Moore, *Hail and Farewell*, p. 313.

25. The play was published in *Dublin Magazine* in 1951; also by De Paul University Press (Chicago, 1974).

26. Moore, *Hail and Farewell*, p. 314.

27. *Letters of Yeats*, p. 458.

28. Ibid., pp. 459–60.

29. Worth, *Irish Drama of Europe*, p. 20.

30. See Campbell, *Masks of God*, pp. 228–31.

31. Worth, *Irish Drama of Europe*, p. 20.

32. W. B. Yeats, *Plays in Prose and Verse* (1922) pp. 185–6.

33. As Ussher says: "Yeats' nostalgia was not for death but for life" (*Three Great Irishmen*, p. 101).
34. Moore, *Hail and Farewell*, pp. 187–8.
35. Worth, *Irish Drama of Europe*, p. 17.
36. The distancing grew increasingly apparent through the rest of his career, and *The Herne's Egg* from his last period has been called a parody of *The Shadowy Waters* and its type of mysticism (in *The Times Literary Supplement*, 1938; see *Yeats, The Critical Heritage*, pp. 394–6).
37. John Eglinton, *Irish Literary Portraits* (Dublin, 1935) p. 30.
38. See Hone, W. B. *Yeats, 1865–1939* (1942) p. 187.
39. Moore, *Hail and Farewell*, p. 246.
40. Ibid., pp. 542–5.
41. Yeats, *Noble Plays of Japan*, xix.
42. Ibid., iii–iv. See also Yeats "Music for Plays" in *Plays in Prose and Verse*, p. 433: "No singer of my words must ever cease to be a man and become an instrument."
43. See Moore, *Hail and Farewell*, pp. 205, 244, and chapters 9–11 of *Ave* in general for Moore's picture of Yeats at Coole.
44. See Yeats, "The Tragic Generation" in *Autobiographies*, p. 287.
45. See Richard Ellmann, *Yeats: The Man and the Masks* (1969) pp. 280–1.
46. Yeats, *Autobiographies*, pp. 207–8. Yeats gives an account of the conflicting tastes of an old Gaelic scholar for Irish songs and of Young Ireland for Wagner. These we might take to represent the antipodes of such musical tastes as Yeats might have had as a young man.

NOTES TO CHAPTER EIGHT: JOYCE

1. *The Letters of James Joyce*, ed. Stuart Gilbert and Richard Ellmann (1957, 1966) ii, p. 25.
2. See Ellmann, *James Joyce*, p. 75.
3. William Blisset, "James Joyce in the Smithy of His Soul" in *James Joyce Today*, ed. Thomas Staley (Bloomington, Ind., 1966) p. 103.
4. "La ci darem" first appears in conjunction with "Love's Old Sweet Song" in "Calypso" – *Ulysses* (New York, 1961 edn) p. 63 (further references to *U* plus page number). References to other operas and arias are frequent: to *Martha* in "Sirens", for instance; to Ferrando's aria from *Trovatore* (*U*, 39); to *La Gioconda* (*U*, 69); and so forth.
5. Ellmann, *James Joyce*, p. 116. However "ninetyish" he found him on first meeting, Joyce was still corresponding with Symons as late as 1932. See Letters from Arthur Symons to James Joyce, 1904–32, *James Joyce Quarterly*, iv (1967–8).
6. *Letters of Joyce*, ii, pp. 217–18.
7. Ellmann, *James Joyce*, p. 278.
8. Blisset, in *James Joyce Today*, p. 104. Blisset suggests that this remark may have been "teasing".
9. Blisset describes both men as having lived "lives of allegory" and also gives a list of similarities (ibid., p. 133).
10. Ellmann, *James Joyce*, p. 473.
11. *Letters of Joyce*, iii, pp. 191–2.

12. Dujardin, *Le Monologue intérieur* (1931) p. 19.
13. Blisset, in *James Joyce Today*, p. 106. Blisset's contention that "Joyce's opinion of Wagner seems to follow the Parisian curve" does not seem entirely accurate.
14. In Helmut Bonheim's *A Lexicon of the German in Finnegans Wake* (1967), I find the following variations on *Götterdämmerung* and *Valhalla*:

    rutterdamrotter (p. 17, l. 15)   Warhorror (p. 91, l. 30)
    gttrdmmrng (p. 258, l. 2)   Welhell (p. 552, l. 16)
    doomering (p. 316, l. 17)   hallaw vall (p. 553, l. 22)
    guttergloomering (p. 565, l. 2)   Wallhall (p. 609, l. 18)

    Also to be found are variations on *Alberich, Nibelung, Nothung* and *Wagner*.
15. *Chamber Music* (1907). Further references to *CM* plus page number.
16. For discussion of the seminal importance of these two epics to Western literature in general and Joyce in particular, see Campbell, *Masks of God*, chapters 2 and 8.
17. " . . . an army charging on the land" might suggest the army of strange knights Parsifal observes charging across the waste land where he lives as a youth (it also anticipates Eliot's "hooded Hordes swarming/over endless plains, stumbling in cracked earth"). " . . . an anvil" suggests the anvil on which Siegfried forges Nothung and anticipates the "smithy of my soul" motif in *Portrait*. "They come out of the sea and run shouting" might suggest the arrival of King Marke and his men at Tristan's castle as he lies hallucinating from his love-wound, an incident not present in Wagner's version of the tale but prominent in Symons's among others; and the last lines of the poem might suggest the attitude of a Tristan despairing that his Isolde's ship will never come – indeed, of the type of the troubadour/lover in general in a moment of solitary despair.
18. Compare the account of Stephen's Sandymount vision in *A Portrait of the Artist as a Young Man* (New York, 1964 edn) pp. 169–73 (further references to *P* plus page number) with the Gospel accounts of the Baptism of Jesus: Matthew 3:16, "And, lo, the heavens were opened unto him, and he saw the Spirit of God descending like a dove, and lighting upon him"; Luke 3:22, "And the Holy Ghost descended in a bodily shape like a dove"; Mark 1:10, "And straightway coming up out of the water, he saw the heavens opened, and the Spirit like a dove descending upon him."
19. *P*, 252–3.
20. *U*, 583. Other motifs from the *Ring* also appear in "Circe": Stephen "chants the air of the blood oath in *The Dusk of the Gods*" (p. 560); Dublin begins to burn in a *Götterdämmerung*-inspired finale (p. 598).
21. *U*, 210: "Fabulous artificer, the hawklike man. You flew. Whereto? Newhaven – Dieppe, steerage passenger. Paris and back. Lapwing. Icarus. *Pater, ait*. Seadabbled, fallen, weltering. Lapwing you are."
22. James Joyce, *Exiles* (1972 edn) p. 80. Further references to *E* plus page number.
23. Compare this imagery to that of poem xxxv in *Chamber Music*.
24. The association of Tristan with Amfortas in Wagner's mind, which tended to metamorphose mythic identities in a way that was only to become common in literature through Joyce and Pound and Eliot, was very close indeed. "What a devilish business!" Wagner wrote to Mathilde Wesendonck as he worked on

the last act of *Tristan* in 1859; "It has become hideously clear to me: Amfortas is my Tristan of Act III in a state of inconceivable intensification." (For further discussion see Campbell, *Masks of God*, p. 506.)

25. I have noted the following motifs in connection with the Parsifal tale:

Saviours/Parsifal: pp. 117, 118, 133.
Racial orders/Grail Order: pp. 131, 142–3.
Mountaintop declamations/Gurnemanz, Klingsor: pp. 140–3.
Boys' shrill voices/"voix des enfants dans la coupole": pp. 128, 129, 144, 146.
Woman's sin-bringing/Kundry: pp. 132, 134 (in connection with the opera-singer, Mme Bloom) p. 138 (in connection with the dangerous kiss) p. 150.
Monks/Grail Knights, Gurnemanz: pp. 121, 122.
Screeching laughter/Kundry, Flower Maidens: pp. 123, 138.
Mountain peaks, whirlwinds/Castle Merveil (Eschenbach): p. 125.
A pillar/Klingsor's magic mirror (Eschenbach): p. 147.

26. Campbell, *Masks of God*, pp. 486–7.
27. See Chamberlain, *The Wagnerian Drama*, chapter on *Die Meistersinger*.
28. Blisset, in *James Joyce Today*, pp. 128–9.
29. See Campbell, *Masks of God*, p. 127.
30. As Blisset points out (in *James Joyce Today*, p. 132). Bloom, who imagines his limp penis as "father of thousands" (*U*, 86), is also a sort of *All-Vater*.
31. In the *James Joyce Quarterly*, II (1965), 156.
32. Nietzsche, *The Dawn of Day* (Levy edn) p. 54. Further references to *DD* plus page number.
33. Blisset, in *James Joyce Today*, p. 131.
34. The last lines of Goethe's *Faust*.
35. See David Hayman, *Joyce et Mallarmé* (1959).
36. Ellmann, *James Joyce*, p. 725.
37. Ibid., p. 536.
38. Ibid., pp. 61–2.
39. This particular observation ironically echoes philosophical profundities of Nietzsche, Kant, Buddha and especially Schopenhauer. In *Masks of God*, pp. 333–48, Campbell discusses the theory common to Kant, Apollo – Vishnu and Schopenhauer that "There is a hidden power, to which all those accidents of the dream conform, which is actually directing and coordinating its incidents." A similar theory stands behind the principle of coincidence governing *Ulysses*, and also behind the concept of *Finnegans Wake*. As Campbell says, Schopenhauer's idea that "The Will to Life itself . . . is a vast dream, dreamed by a single being; but in such a way that all the dream characters dream too" is a perfect expression of the inspiration for *Finnegan*. This applicability of Schopenhauer's metaphysics to his works is yet another respect in which Joyce's art resembles Wagner's.
40. A good discussion of the Wagnerian leitmotiv is offered by Robert Gutman in his *Richard Wagner: the Man, his Mind, and his Music*, chapter entitled "*Leitmotiv* and Wagner's Musical Architecture".
41. Water is linked to the feminine at significant moments throughout Joyce's works: the image of the girl at the edge of the sea in the Sandymount vision in *Portrait*; the association of Stephen's thoughts of his mother with the sea in the "Proteus" chapter of *Ulysses*; most notably, the identification of Anna Livia

Plurabelle with the River Liffey in *Finnegans Wake*.
42. Mann, *Buddenbrooks* (New York, 1952 edn) pp. 586–8.
43. Lawrence Levin in "The Sirens Episode as Music", *James Joyce Quarterly*, II (1964–5) 14, calls the first sixty-eight lines of "Sirens" a combination of a Bach prelude and fugue and a Wagnerian prelude.
44. Nietzsche, *Case of Wagner*, p. xxxi.
45. Mann, *Freud, Goethe, Wagner*, p. 110.
46. Bryan Magee devotes a chapter of *Aspects of Wagner* to an insightful discussion of Wagner's anti-Semitism.
47. Mann, *Freud, Goethe, Wagner*, p. 107.
48. J. P. Stern in "Nietzsche's Aesthetics", *Journal of European Studies*, V (1975) 222, links Joyce to Nietzsche, citing their common aesthetic principle as summed up by this phrase of Stephen Dedalus's. Stern further discussed the points of contact between Nietzsche's and Joyce's aesthetics in a lecture to the English Association (London, 18 Nov 1975): Nietzsche's image of art as a spider-web of metaphor, Stern said, is parallel to Joyce's image of art as a Dedalian maze and finds its most extensive demonstration in *Finnegans Wake*. Beyond Stern's comments I have in mind in this paragraph several statements from *The Dawn of Day*: Nietzsche's comparison of artists to Brahmin priests (*DD*, 94); his observations on music, art, and night (*DD*, 242); his association of artists with sorcerers and madmen (*DD*, 269). On the matter of concealing props, compare the painstaking attention to Naturalist detail in the *Ring* as it was originally produced by Wagner and in *Ulysses*. Both Wagner and Joyce only turned to their great Symbolist works after having explored the extremes of Naturalism.
49. Eric Bentley's terms. See *Cult of the Superman* (1947) p. 119.
50. References to *JW* plus page number.
51. For Stephen and birds, see *Portrait*, pp. 224–6.
52. One example is Baudelaire's "Les Plaintes d'un Icare" in *Les Fleurs du mal*.
53. For the Nietzschean Icarus, see "In the Horizon of the Infinite" (*JW*, 167).
54. See *Masks of God*, pp. 540–1, for Campbell's discussion of the anagogical similarities between *Parzival* and the *Divine Comedy*.
55. See also *Human, All-too-Human*, I, pp. 157–8: "The Art of the Ugly Soul".
56. See also ibid., II, pp. 80–1: "Music and Disease", in which Ithaca is counterpoised against Wagnerian music. Nietzsche not only anticipated Joyce in seeing Homer as the ideal artist and Ulysses as the ideal hero, but also saw them as standing in specific contrast to Wagner and his "Northern" art.
57. Bentley, *Cult of the Superman*, p. 119.
58. Shem and Shaun, the "equals in opposite", are the obvious case of Joyce's dialectical patterning. Dedalus and Bloom, representing among other things the Greek *versus* the Hebrew traditions in Western culture, also suggest a dialectical antithesis – one which is perhaps synthesized in the all-embracing cycle of Molly Bloom's final thoughts.

NOTES TO CHAPTER NINE: LAWRENCE

1. See Rosenthal, *Opera at Covent Garden*, pp. 59–107.
2. See Magee's *Aspects of Wagner*, pp. 82–3; also Blisset on Moore in *Man of Wax*, pp. 185–6.

3. Virginia Woolf also wrote an article on Wagner, *Parsifal* and Bayreuth. Entitled "Impressions of Bayreuth"; it appeared in *The Times* in 1909.
4. See W. J. Lucas, "Wagner and Forster: *Parsifal* and *A Room with a View*" in *Romantic Mythologies*, pp. 271–97.
5. In *Wisconsin Studies in Contemporary Literature* (Madison, Wis., 1966).
6. See Marie Rose Burwell's "A Catalogue of D. H. Lawrence's Reading", *D. H. Lawrence Review* (1970); also R. L. Drain's thesis "Formative Influences on the Work of D. H. Lawrence" (Cambridge, 1962).
7. Quoted by Edward Nehls in *D. H. Lawrence: A Composite Biography* (Madison, Wis., 1957) I, p. 152. Frank Kermode however, in his *Lawrence* (1973), asserts that Ford may have been exhibiting his "usual impressionism".
8. Both reprinted in Armin Arnold's *D. H. Lawrence and German Literature* (Montreal, 1963).
9. See Noel Stock, *Ezra Pound* (1971), p. 77.
10. See Bentley, *The Cult of the Superman*, pp. 210–30.
11. In Arnold, *Lawrence and German Literature*; also *Phoenix: The Posthumous Papers of D. H: Lawrence* (1936) pp. 308–13.
12. Nietzsche, *Case of Wagner*, p. 72.
13. "You can hear the death-rattle in their throats", Lawrence would say of the authors of these works (*Phoenix*, p. 517).
14. On Chamberlain as a possible source for Lawrence's racial and historical ideas see Kermode's *Lawrence*, pp. 57–8.
15. D. H. Lawrence, *Movements in European History* (1921) pp. 59–72.
16. "[Germany is] alien to my psychology and very tissue," Lawrence would write (see *The Letters of D. H. Lawrence*, ed. Aldous Huxley (1932) p. 120). Also, Hans Galinsky in "Deutschland in der Sicht von D. H. Lawrence and T. S. Eliot", *Akademe der Wissenschaften und der Literatur* (1926) p. 25, reports that in 1929 Lawrence said "My health . . . went down . . . in Germany."
17. Lawrence, *Phoenix*, pp. 108–10.
18. See D. H. Lawrence, *Apocalypse* (1932) pp. 56–7; also Kermode's *Lawrence*, pp. 57–8, 70–1.
19. See Lawrence's "New Mexico" (1928) in *Phoenix*, pp. 141–7.
20. See *Lawrence in Love: Letters to Louie Burrows*, ed. J. T. Bolton (Nottingham, 1968) p. 44.
21. *Letters of Lawrence*, p. 22.
22. Lawrence, *Phoenix*, p. 174.
23. Lawrence, *Apocalypse*, p. 49.
24. *Götterdämmerung* may also have appealed to Lawrence for its focus on the issue of male dominance, which preoccupied him throughout his career, especially in the later phase (see Kermode's *Lawrence* for discussion). At the beginning of Wagner's drama Brünnhilde gives up her power to Siegfried; but then in Act II, betrayed, she struggles to destroy him. Siegfried warns Gunther, to whom Brünnhilde is to be married, to learn to control his wife. Brünnhilde wins a pyrrhic victory over Siegfried in Act III; but in the next and last of his dramas Wagner takes up the Lawrentian position that woman must surrender to male dominance – Kundry, once a destroyer of male power, submits to that power in Act III of *Parsifal*, uttering the words of penitence, "Dienen . . . Dienen!"
25. Blisset, in *Wisconsin Studies*, p. 24.
26. Galinsky, for instance, in *Akademe der Wissenschaften* (1926) p. 20.

27. *Letters of Lawrence,* p. 3.
28. Ibid., p. 15.
29. Ibid., p. 20.
30. According to Blisset, in *Wisconsin Studies,* p. 33.
31. D. H. Lawrence, *The Rainbow* (1915) p. 463.
32. The parallels to Wagner's characters are so marked that Stephen Spender in his essay on Lawrence and the war mistakenly refers to Gerald as Gunther. See *D. H. Lawrence: Novelist, Poet, Prophet* (1973).
33. See F. R. Leavis, *D. H. Lawrence, Novelist* (1955) p. 176.
34. For discussion of this vision see Eugene Goodheart, *The Utopian Vision of D. H. Lawrence* (Chicago, 1963) esp. pp. 112–3.
35. See Lawrence, *Apocalypse,* p. 59.
36. For discussion of Lawrence's impassioned Wagnerian style see Blisset, in *Wisconsin Studies,* pp. 44–6; also Saul Cohn, *Naturalisme et mysticisme chez D. H. Lawrence* (1932) p. 129.
37. D. H. Lawrence, *The Plumed Serpent* (1926) p. 383.
38. See Hugh Kenner, *The Pound Era* (1972) pp. 133–8: "Pound omits, omits, but knows what he is omitting and can restore on demand, but behind Eliot's resonances there is frequently nothing to restore."
39. T. S. Eliot, *Collected Poems 1909–62* (1974) p. 189.
40. *The Complete Plays of D. H. Lawrence* (1965) p. 486. Further references to *P* plus page number.
41. *The Ring of the Nibelung,* trs. Stewart Robb (New York, 1960) p. 335.
42. The relationship of David to Saul parallels that of Siegmund to Wotan. David's killing of Goliath parallels Siegfried's of Fafner. Samuel's prediction to David that "to flee away is thy portion" (*P*, 143) parallels the curse of wandering that afflicts Siegmund and the Dutchman. And so forth.
43. Samuel's prayer in scene II might suggest *I Lombardi* or *Nabucco.* The Elders' summoning of the men in scene II might suggest the summoning of the vassals in *Götterdämmerung,* or of the monks in *La Forza del destino.* Michal's expression of intent to win David (*P*, 92) might suggest Kundry or Salomé, while her anxiety for his arrival and the chorus of maidens at the beginning of Scene V might suggest the beginning of the second act of the *Dutchman* or *Parsifal;* likewise, her fear for David's life and attempts to convince him to flee in scene XIV suggests Sieglinde in Act II of *Die Walküre.*
44. The Levy edition of Nietzsche's *Complete Works* was published between 1909 and 1911. *Zarathustra, Beyond Good and Evil* and *The Will to Power* were the first volumes to appear; and Lawrence probably read these and the others as they were acquired by the Croydon library. (See Drain, "Formative Influences".)
45. See D. H. Lawrence, *Women in Love* (1920) pp. 96–9, Hermione's mad will; pp. 102–4, Gerald and his horse; pp. 213–25, Gerald as industrial magnate; pp. 226–36, Gudrun's fascination for the animal will of the rabbit; pp. 283–8, Hermione's theory of the will. For further discussion of Nietzsche and the theory of will in Lawrence, see Leavis, *D. H. Lawrence,* pp. 186, 191; also Gray's *German Tradition,* p. 345.
46. Ibid., pp. 340–54.
47. Ibid., p. 342. Lawrence's own word is "polarity". See also Kermode's *Lawrence* on Lawrence's "trinitarian" patterning.
48. See *Naturalisme et mysticisme chez D. H. Lawrence;* also Ernest Seillière, *D. H.*

Lawrence et les récentes idéologies allemandes (1936) p. vii.

49. The particular importance of the horse in helping the human to come to full realization of the heroic is common to all three. In Lawrence we see this throughout *St Mawr*, in Wagner in the significance attached to Brünnhilde's gift of Grane to Siegfried as he departs for the world. In Nietzsche we find the mystical potency, energy, and clarity that derives from the experience of an exceptional horse summed up in the passage "A Noble Culture" in *Dawn of Day* (p. 204), where he praises "a horseman who takes pleasure in making his proud and fiery animal trot in the Spanish fashion" and "the rider who feels his horse dart away with him like the elemental forces, to such a degree that both horse and rider come near to losing their heads, but, owing to the enjoyment of the delight, do keep very clear heads".

50. For discussion, see Goodheart, *The Utopian Vision*, p. 141; also Seillière, *Lawrence et les récentes idéologies allemandes*, section entitled "Le Dieu chthonique".

51. See Nietzsche, *The Joyful Wisdom*, pp. 293-4.

52. Ibid., p. 68.

53. Lawrence, *The Plumed Serpent*, p. 379.

54. Nietzsche, *The Joyful Wisdom*, p. 351.

55. Nietzsche, *Case of Wagner*, pp. 21-2.

56. Gray's argument is that, since German art strives to be organic, it cannot allow the stray detail. This may be true. Still, Wagner, the most organic of German artists, did it – in *Parsifal* for instance, where he wrote magnificent music to attend Gurnemanz's description of the life of the swan, which music appears nowhere else in the drama.

57. Many of Lawrence's favourite symbols are also prominent in *Zarathustra*. These include, besides the phoenix, the eagle and snake, which combined make "the plumed serpent". The phoenix and Lawrence's earlier emblem of the peacock are also prominent in the symbolism of the Grail legend, being identified in Eschenbach's *Parzival* with the wounded fisher-king, Anfortas (see Campbell, *Masks of God*, p. 501).

58. Nietzsche, *Case of Wagner*, pp. 5-8.

59. From *Zarathustra*, as quoted and discussed by Campbell. See *Masks of God*, p. 41.

60. Peter Viereck in his *Metapolitics* (1941) arraigns Lawrence, "the English semi-fascist" (p. 128). He also, less overtly, arraigns Yeats and Joyce (p. 175, n. 19) and a number of others, including the French Decadents.

61. Lawrence, *Movements in European History*, p. 347.

62. Bentley, *Cult of the Superman*, p. 234.

63. Viereck, *Metapolitics*, pp. 315-16.

64. Ibid., pp. 4-5.

65. For D'Annunzio's relationship to Mussolini, see Blisset, in *Wisconsin Studies*.

66. For Dionys's political theory see "*The Ladybird*", "*The Fox*", "*The Captain's Doll*" (1923), esp. pp. 60-8. Further, Lawrence may be echoing motifs from Wagner in the song which Dionys sings before going to bed, by which he seduces Daphne: "It began with a rather dreary slow, horrible sound, like death. And then suddenly came a real call. . . ." (p. 74). The subject of the song is

a woman who was a swan, and who loved a hunter by a marsh. So she became a woman and married him and had three children. Then in the night one night the king of swans called to her to come back, or else he would die. So slowly she turned into a swan again, and slowly opened her wide, wide wings and left. . . .   (p. 75)

NOTES TO CHAPTER TEN: "THE WASTE LAND"

1. Kenner, *The Pound Era*, p. 559.
2. In T. S. Eliot, *Selected Essays* (New York, 1950) p. 54.
3. See Igor Stravinsky, "Memories of T. S. Eliot", *Esquire* (Aug 1965) p. 92.
4. See T. S. Eliot, "Thomas Hardy" in *After Strange Gods* (1934) p. 55.
5. See Hugh Kenner, *The Invisible Poet* (1960) pp. 146–7.
6. See Stephen Spender, "In Eliot's Cave", *New York Review of Books* (Sep 1974).
7. Herbert Knust, *Wagner, the King, and "The Waste Land"*, Pennsylvania State University Studies no. 22 (University Park, Penn., 1967). Further references to *K* plus page number.
8. See Lyndall Gordon, *Eliot's Early Years* (1977) p. 139.
9. See *The Waste Land*, facsimile manuscript ed. Valerie Eliot (1971) p. 1.
10. See Eliot's essay "Ulysses, Order and Myth" in *Selected Prose*, ed. Frank Kermode (1975), for Eliot's reaction to Joyce's method.
11. Gordon describes Pound's *Hugh Selwyn Mauberley* as a covert dialogue with Eliot about their poetic styles (*Eliot's Early Years*, p. 106).
12. Gordon says that Eliot was so affected by this book, particularly the chapter on Laforgue, that he immediately went out and ordered the three volumes of Laforgue's *Oeuvres complètes* (ibid., pp. 28–9).
13. In "The Critic as Artist" (*Complete Works of Oscar Wilde*, p. 976).
14. See Charles Baudelaire, *Intimate Journals* (1930) p. 22.
15. In his introduction to *Baudelaire and the Symbolists*, Peter Quennell relates how the book was suggested by Eliot as a replacement for Symons's *Symbolist Movement*, "which, despite its merits as a pioneer essay, was written very much from the point of view of a contemporary of Oscar Wilde and Ernest Dowson".
16. See *K*, 18.
17. See Nicolson's *Paul Verlaine*, p. 152.
18. See Laforgue's *En Allemagne* (1930), chapter entitled "L'Imperatrice".
19. The phrase is Leo Weinstein's. See his "Laforgue and his Time" in *Jules Laforgue: Essays on a Poet's Life and Work* (1969) p. 58.
20. Ibid., p. xx.
21. For further discussion of the influence of the French, see Francis Scarfe, "Eliot and Nineteenth-Century French Poetry" in *Eliot in Perspective*, ed. Graham Martin (1970).
22. In his essay on Philip Massinger in *The Sacred Wood* Eliot compares Baudelaire to the seventeenth-century poets. In *Baudelaire and the Symbolists* (p. 47). Quennell states that Baudelaire "is a type anticipated in the plays of the Elizabethan dramatists". In "Laforgue among the Symbolists" (*Laforgue: Essays*, p. 41), with an eye to their influence on Eliot, Henri Peyre states that Laforgue and Corbière had much in common with the Elizabethans and post-Elizabethans.
23. See Eliot's "The Perfect Critic, I" and "Swinburne as Critic" in *The Sacred Wood*.

24. Wilde, *Dorian Gray*, p. 179.
25. Moore, *Evelyn Innes*, p. 385.
26. Moore, *Flowers of Passion*, p. 68.
27. Ibid., p. 51.
28. Eliot uses this word in *The Sacred Wood*.
29. Symons, *Collected Works*, III, p. 59.
30. Ibid., I, pp. 322–3.
31. Ibid., II, pp. 304–6.
32. For an account of Quinn's relationship to *The Waste Land*, see Daniel Woodward's "Notes on the Publishing History and Text of *The Waste Land*", in *The Waste Land: A Casebook*, ed. C. B. Cox and A. P. Hinchliffe (1968) p. 71.
33. Ezra Pound, *The Pisan Cantos* (1949) p. 102.
34. Ibid., p. 83.
35. See Campbell, *Masks of God*, p. 561.
36. See Gordon, *Eliot's Early Years*, pp. 56–64.
37. In conversation at University College, London, 1974.
38. See Gordon, *Eliot's Early Years*, p. 43.
39. The phrase is Viereck's. See his *Metapolitics*, chapter entitled "Greenwich Village Warriors", esp. p. 153.
40. The journal ran several pieces on Nietzsche in 1916–17 when Eliot was associated with it. See "Nietzsche and the War" by William Salter, the review of *Philosophy and War* by Emile Bertroux, *et cetera*.
41. According to T. S. Matthews in *Great Tom* (1974), Eliot was rejected as physically unfit: he was underweight and suffering from hernia.
42. Nietzsche, *The Joyful Wisdom*, pp. 281, 284.
43. Lawrence, "The Novel", *Phoenix*, II, p. 421.
44. See Eliot, *After Strange Gods*, pp. 58–61.
45. See Blisset on Lawrence (in *Wisconsin Studies*, p. 37).
46. See Gordon, *Eliot's Early Years*, p. 57.
47. See *The Waste Land: A Casebook*, p. 68.
48. Seillière, *Lawrence et les récentes idéologies allemandes*, p. 38.
49. From "Critique d'art" as paraphrased by Woolley (see *Wagner et le symbolisme français*, p. 124).
50. *Blast!* I, (1914) pp. 153–4.
51. Symons, *Collected Works*, III, p. 253.
52. Eliot, *Collected Poems, 1909–1962*, p. 39. For discussion of Eliot's anti-Semitism see Graham Martin's introduction to *Eliot in Perspective*, pp. 24–5; also Gabriel Pearson's "Eliot: An American Use of Symbolism" in the same volume, pp. 87–9, for this anti-Semitism as specifically evidenced in "Gerontion".
53. Eliot, *Collected Poems, 1909–1962*, p. 43.
54. See *The Waste Land*, facsimile, p. 119.
55. In conversation.
56. Ezra Pound, *Selected Cantos* (1967) p. 67.
57. Daniel Woodward quotes Pound to this effect: "Rightly or wrongly some of us consider Eliot's employment in a bank the worst waste in contemporary literature" – *The Waste Land: A Casebook*, pp. 72–3.
58. See Matthews, *Great Tom*, pp. 63–4.
59. Gordon, *Eliot's Early Years*, p. 81.
60. Ibid., p. 79.

61. On Eliot's interest in Maurras's programme see Adrian Cunningham's "Continuity and Coherence in Eliot's Religious Thought" in *Eliot in Perspective*.

62. See "Shorter Notices", *The Criterion*, VII (1928).

63. In *Principles of Literary Criticism* (1924) Richards wrote, "The poem is concerned with many aspects of the one fact of sex. . . . There are those who think . . . he confesses his impotence" (see *The Waste Land: A Casebook*, p. 53). In *Axel's Castle* (p. 90) Wilson wrote, "We recognize . . . the peculiar conflicts of the puritan turned artist; the horror of vulgarity and the shy sympathy with common life, the ascetic shrinking from sexual experience, and the distress at the drying up of the springs of sexual emotion, with the straining after a religious emotion which may be made to take its place."

64. In "An Anatomy of Melancholy" (see *A Reviewer's ABC* (1961) pp. 171–97), Conrad Aiken suggests that some passages of the poem contain parodies or echoes "in the Straussian manner"; and in his Eliot (1975) p. 107, Spender likens the beginning of "A Game of Chess" to the music of *Salomé*. Comparison of *The Waste Land* and *Le Sacre du printemps* in both technique and subject has often been made. In *Great Tom* (p. 31) Matthews says that Eliot was "profoundly impressed with *Sacre*"; but, in *A Student's Guide to the Selected Poetry of T. S. Eliot* (1968) p. 70, B. C. Southam reports Eliot as commenting that from the point of view of a vegetation rite the ballet seemed superficial.

65. See Weston, *From Ritual to Romance*, p. v.

66. There are further allusions to Tennyson in the sections of the poem Pound cut, notably to his "Ulysses" in "Death by Water" (see facsimile, pp. 128–9).

67. Scarfe indiciates that Eliot did not share Pound's familiarity with Provençal (see *Eliot in Perspective*, p. 45).

68. See Eliot's introduction to *The Literary Essays of Ezra Pound* (1960) p. 9.

69. Ezra Pound, *The Spirit of Romance* (1910) p. 82.

70. *Romantic Mythologies*, p. 279.

71. The French of the *fin-de-siècle* were fond of referring to Wagner as "Old Klingsor" (see Cornell, *Symbolist Movement*, p. 132), as was Nietzsche (see *Case of Wagner*, p. 40 and elsewhere).

72. Morris's article is included in *The Waste Land: A Casebook*, pp. 165–8.

73. See Southam, *A Student's Guide*, p. 21. Southam goes on to assume that Eliot read *My Past*, but, though he may have recalled and used details in the poem, intended no thorough-going parallels. "*My Past* is irrelevant to the meaning of *The Waste Land* for all that it supplies considerable details; it is an accidental source, whereas 'The Old Vicarage, Grantchester' [Rupert Brooke] is a parallel we are required to keep in sight." Knust obviously disagrees with this assessment, and no doubt with good sense.

74. In his essay on Eliot and the French, Scarfe suggests this comparison. See *Eliot in Perspective*, p. 49.

75. The phrase is D. E. S. Maxwell's in *The Poetry of T. S. Eliot* (1952) p. 101. Maxwell goes on to point out that this motif later accompanies Isolde's words "Degenerate race, unworthy of your fathers", thus combining the themes of love and decay also predominant in *The Waste Land*.

76. Nietzsche, *Case of Wagner*, p. 14.

77. Kenner's phrase in *The Invisible Poet*, p. 132.

78. Chamberlain's phrase. See his *The Wagnerian Drama*, chapter on *Parsifal*.

Index